HISTORY OF EDUCATION

HISTORY OF EDUCATION

By

LEVI SEELEY, Ph.D.

REVISED EDITION

GYAN

Published by

Gyan Publishing House
5, Ansari Road
Daryaganj, New Delhi-110002
Phone: 011-47034999, 9811692060
E-mail: books@gyanbooks.com

Distribution Network
gyanbooks.com
India, USA, Canada, UK, Australia, France

ISBN : 978-81-212-6480-8 (PB)
First Published, 1904

2nd Impression 2022

Printed at: Gyan Press, Delhi.

HISTORY OF EDUCATION
Author: LEVI SEELEY

HISTORY

OF

EDUCATION

BY

LEVI SEELEY, PH.D.
PROFESSOR OF PEDAGOGY IN THE NEW JERSEY
STATE NORMAL SCHOOL

REVISED EDITION

1904

PREFACE

THE importance of a knowledge of the history of education was never so fully recognized as at the present time. Normal schools and teachers' colleges give this subject a prominent place in their professional courses, superintendents require candidates for certificates to pass examination in it, and familiarity with it is an essential part of the equipment of every well-informed teacher. The history of education portrays the theories and methods of the past, warns of error and indicates established truth, shows difficulties surmounted, and encourages the teacher of to-day by examples of heroism and consecration on the part of educators whose labors for their fellow-men we discuss. To the teacher this study is a constant help in the schoolroom, the trials of which are met with the added strength and inspiration from contact with great teachers of the past.

No text-book can be said to contain the last word upon any subject. Least of all can such a claim be made for a history of education, which aims to trace the intellectual development of the human race and to indicate the means and processes of that evolution. Any individuals or factors materially contributing thereto deserve a place in educational history. As to which of these factors is the most important, that is a question of choice, upon which, doubtless, many will differ with the author. Some educators, whose claims to consideration are unquestioned, have been reluctantly omitted on account of the limitations of this work.

On the other hand, many teachers lack time for exhaustive study of such a subject. This book is designed to furnish all the material that can be reasonably demanded for any state, county, or city teacher's certificate. It also provides sufficient subject-matter for classes in normal schools and colleges and for reading circles. The material offered can be mastered in a half-year's class work, but, by using the references, a full year can be well employed. For those who desire to make a more extended study of particular topics, the author gives such authorities as years of careful research have shown to be most valuable. Every investigator knows the labor involved in finding suitable material. To spare the reader something of that labor, the literature is given at the beginning of each chapter. By following the collateral readings thus suggested, this book will be found suitable for the most advanced classes.

The plan of references embraces three features: (1) literature at the beginning of each chapter; (2) foot references to special citations; and (3) a general bibliography in the Appendix. In the first two, titles are sometimes abbreviated because of their frequent repetition. In case of doubt the reader should refer to the general bibliography, in which all the authorities cited are arranged alphabetically, with full titles.

It is generally conceded that the plan of an historical work should be based upon the evolution of civilization. In common with other recent writers on educational history, the author accepts the general plan of Karl Schmidt in his "Geschichte der Pädagogik," the most comprehensive work on this subject that has yet appeared. But the specific plan, which involves the most important and vital characteristics of this book, is the author's own. The details of this specific plan embrace a study of the *history* and *environment*, of the *internal*, *social*, *political*, and *religious* conditions of the people, without which there can be no accurate conception of their education.

Our civilization had its inception in that of ancient Egypt, and thence its logical development must be traced. If desirable the teacher can omit the chapters on China, India, Persia, and Israel. It will be found, however, that the lessons taught by these countries, though negative in character, are intensely interesting to students, and most instructive and impressive. These countries are also admirably illustrative of the plan employed in the book, and thereby prepare the way for later work. That plan is more fully set forth in the Introduction, a careful study of which is recommended to both teacher and student.

The author wishes to acknowledge his appreciation of the valuable assistance in the preparation of this volume rendered by Dr. Elias F. Carr of the New Jersey Normal School, and Professor W. J. Morrison of the Brooklyn Training School for Teachers.

LEVI SEELEY.

STATE NORMAL SCHOOL,
TRENTON, N. J.

REVISED EDITION

I HAVE taken advantage of the necessary reprinting of the book to make certain changes and additions, and to correct a few errors which were found to exist. An attempt has been made to note the recent changes that have taken place, especially in the French and English school systems.

L. S.

TABLE OF CONTENTS

CHAPTER VI

CHAPTER VII

CHAPTER VIII

CHAPTER IX

CHAPTER X

CHAPTER XI

CHAPTER XII

CHAPTER XIII

CHAPTER XIV

CHAPTER XV

CHAPTER XVI

CHAPTER XVII

CHAPTER XVIII

CHAPTER XIX

CHAPTER XX

CHAPTER XXVII

CHAPTER XXVIII

CHAPTER XXIX

CHAPTER XXX

CHAPTER XXXI

CHAPTER XXXII

CHAPTER XXXIII

CHAPTER XXXIV

CHAPTER XXXV

CHAPTER XXXVI

CHAPTER XXXVII

CHAPTER XXXVIII

HISTORY OF EDUCATION

CHAPTER I

INTRODUCTION

The history of education begins with the childhood of the race, and traces its intellectual development step by step to the present time. As such history is academic in character, and furnishes information concerning the educational systems, methods, theories, and practices of the past, it should be placed early in the professional pedagogical course, to serve as the foundation for an improved educational science which profits by the experience of mankind. The history of education presents many of the great problems that have interested thoughtful men, shows how some of these have been solved, and points the way to the solution of others. It studies educational systems, selecting the good, and rejecting the bad, and introducing the student directly to the pedagogical questions that have influenced the world. For these reasons, the study of education should begin with its history.

Karl Schmidt says: "The history of the world is the history of the development of the human soul. The manner of this development is the same in the race as in the individual; the same law, because the same divine thought, rules in the individual, in a people, and in humanity. Humanity has, as the individual, its stages of progress, and it unfolds itself in them. The individual as a child is not a rational being; he becomes rational. The child has not yet the mastery over himself, but his environment is his master; he belongs not to himself, but to his surroundings. *The oriental peoples are the child of humanity. . . . Classical antiquity represents the period of youth in the history of the world. . . . Christ is the type of perfected manhood.* The history of the individual reflects and repeats the history of humanity, just as the history of humanity is a reflection of the history of the Cosmos, and the history of the Cosmos is an image of the life of God; all history, be it that of humanity or of the individual, of the starry heavens, or of the earth, is development of life toward God." "Where there is development, there is progress. Progress in history is only the more visible, audible, perceptible embodiment of God in humanity."[1]

In the study of the education of a people it is necessary first to become acquainted with their social, political, and religious life. To this end a knowledge of the geography and history of their country is often essential, because of the influence of climate, occupation, and environment, in shaping the character of a people. Examples of this influence are not wanting. The peculiar position of the Persians, surrounded on all sides by enemies, required a martial education as a preparation for defensive and offensive measures. Physical education was dominant among the Spartans, because of serfdom which involved the absolute control of the many by the few. No less striking are the effects of physical conditions upon all peoples in stimulating mental activity and in developing moral life, both of which processes are essential to true education. The intellectual product of the temperate zone differs from that

[1] "Geschichte der Pädagogik," Vol. I, pp. 1, 2.

of the torrid zone, the product of the country from that of the large city. For these reasons stress is here laid upon the geographical and historical conditions of the peoples considered.

For the same purpose we must study the home and the family, the foundations upon which the educational structure is built. The ancient Jew looked upon children as the gift of God, thereby teaching the great lesson of the divine mission of children and of the parents' responsibility for their welfare. This race has never neglected the home education, even when it became necessary to establish the school. The family was the nursery of education, and only when diversified duties made it no longer possible to train the children properly in the home was the school established. Even then the purpose of the school was but to give expression to demands which the home created. The spirit and purpose of the education of a people can be understood only when the discipline, the ideals, and the religion of the home are understood.

When we have learned the environment of a people, we are ready to study their elementary education. This takes us into the schoolroom, introduces us to the place where the school is held, indicates the course of study pursued, the discipline, methods of instruction, spirit and training of the teacher, as well as the results obtained. After this we are ready to consider the higher education, which completes the system and measures its efficiency.

Another task demanded of the student is to draw lessons from the educational systems studied, to note what can be applied to modern conditions, and to avoid the errors of the past. The product of a method, as shown in the character of the people pursuing it, is of great interest in estimating the value of a scheme of education.

Great movements have often been the outcome of the teachings of some individual who, inspired by a new idea, has consecrated his life to it. Through such men the world receives new and mighty impulses toward its enlightenment, civilization takes vast strides in its development, and man approaches nearer his final emancipation. Confucius, Socrates, Augustine, Charlemagne, Luther, Bacon, Comenius, Pestalozzi, Froebel, are names that suggest the uplifting of humanity and the betterment of the world. The study of the lives of these men, of their victories and their defeats, cannot fail to be an encouragement and a suggestive lesson to teachers of all lands and all times. The history of education must therefore consider the biographies of such men as well as their theories and their teachings.

Finally, modern systems of education are the outgrowth of the experiences of the past. They represent the results attained and indicate present educational conditions. Nothing can better summarize the total development reached, or better suggest lines of future progress than a comparative discussion of the leading school systems of the world. The last chapters of this book, therefore, are devoted to a study of the school systems of Germany, France, England, and America. These are typical, each being suggestive of certain phases of education, while one of them has largely influenced the education of several other countries. Each furnishes lessons valuable to the student of history. Although many practices in other countries may not be applicable to our conditions, the broad-minded, genuine patriot will not refuse to accept sound principles and good methods from whatever source derived.

General Outline

- Pre-Christian Education
  - Oriental.
    - China.
    - India.
    - Persia.
    - Israel.
    - Egypt.
  - Classical.
    - Greece
      - Athens.
      - Sparta.
    - Rome.
- Earlier Christian Education
  - The Great Teacher.
  - Monasticism.
  - Scholasticism.
  - Charlemagne.
  - The Crusades.
  - The Universities.
- Modern Education
  - The Renaissance.
  - The Reformation.
  - The Jesuits.
  - The Sixteenth Century.
  - The Seventeenth Century.
  - The Eighteenth and Nineteenth Centuries.
  - Present School Systems.

CHAPTER II

CHINA

Literature.—*Martin*, The Chinese; *Clarke*, Ten Great Religions; *Houghton*, Women of the Orient; *Doolittle*, Social Life of the Chinese; *Johonnot*, Geographical Reader; *Lord*, Beacon Lights of History; *Ballou*, Due West and Footprints of Travel; *Ploetz*, Epitome of Universal History; *Barnes*, Studies in Education; *Stoddard's* Lectures; *Pierre Leroy-Beaulieu*, The Awakening of the East; *McClure's Magazine*, December, 1900, A Character Study of the Chinaman.

THE civilization of the "Celestial Empire" has certainly contributed but little to the advancement of the world. Were it not that this nation furnishes a most striking illustration of the evils of false methods, the study of Chinese education might be omitted without loss. But a system of education that produces intellectual stagnation, that fails to stimulate national and individual progress, that fosters narrow egotism, suggests negative lessons which the student of education will do well to heed. The result in China furnishes the best argument against a method of instruction that appeals solely to the memory. This alone is a sufficient reason for a study of Chinese education, aside from its strange and unique characteristics which never fail to interest the reader.

Geography and History.—The Chinese Empire occupies a position on the eastern side of the Asiatic continent within about the same parallels of latitude as the United States, extending from twenty degrees latitude on the south to fifty-three degrees on the north. Its area is about four and a quarter million square miles, being somewhat larger than that of the United States. Its population is estimated at about six times that of our country. It has an abundance of rivers, intersected by numerous canals, which greatly facilitate internal commerce. Many parts of the country are densely populated. The people are largely engaged in agriculture. Tea and silk are the chief articles of export, while rice and millet form the principal food.

The Chinese belong to the Mongolian or yellow race. They are an industrious, frugal, and temperate people, though the opium habit is very general and is disastrous in its effects. Doubtless the overcrowded population, which has driven many to live in boats and in crowded apartments, has had much to do in molding the Chinese character. They are slow to admit modern improvements, being content with their lot and conservative in the maintenance of their customs, religion, education, and social practices. Consequently they have for many centuries made but little progress. Their authentic history covers, according to extant records, a period of nearly four thousand years. The government is an absolute monarchy; the emperor is regarded as the father of all his people and has complete power over the lives of his subjects.

The Chinese language contains no alphabet; each symbol represents a different word; the substantives are indeclinable, and the verbs are without inflection. It thus becomes necessary in mastering the language to learn by rote a vast number of signs and characters, — a prodigious feat for the memory.

The religion most widespread among the Chinese is Buddhism (which was imported from India), though ancestor worship is still universal. Women are the principal worshipers, yet the Chinese believe that women have no souls. The belief in transmigration of souls is implicit, and this is used to keep woman in a most degraded condition. If a woman is obedient to her husband and his relatives, and is the mother of sons, she may hope to return to this world, in the future, as a man, and thus have a chance ultimately to reach Buddha's heaven. The belief in the transmigration of souls explains the vegetarian diet of the Buddhist. No zealous Buddhist will touch meat or even eggs, neither will he kill the smallest insect, lest he should thus inadvertently murder a relative.[1] The men care but little for any religion beyond a veneration for their ancestors.

Polygamy is very generally practiced, the limit to the number of wives being determined by the ability to support them. Women usually become more religious as they advance in years, and they spend much time in worshiping in the temples. It is they who preserve the national religion and make most difficult the work of missionaries.[2]

The Home.—The wife exists only for the comfort of her husband. It is her duty to serve and obey him. If she abuses her husband, she receives one hundred stripes; but abuse from him is not a punishable offense. Instruction, at home as well as at school, is confined to boys. The birth of a boy is indicated by hanging a bow and arrow over the door; that of a girl, by a spindle and yarn. In naming the number of his children, the father counts only the boys. Boys are clothed in the finest material the family can afford; girls, in rags. Parents may destroy their children, but only girls are ever sacrificed. The

[1] Mrs. E. E. Baldwin, Foochow, China.

[2] Houghton, "Women of the Orient," p. 14.

mother can seldom read and write, her chief duty being to instill into her children the two cardinal Chinese virtues —*politeness* and *obedience*. The relation of parents and children is the highest and purest representation of the relation between the Creator and the creature, and to venerate the parents is the first and holiest of all duties, higher than the love of wife to husband, higher than the reverence for the emperor; therefore the emperor's father cannot be his subject.

To the Chinaman all other duties are included in filial duties. The bringing up of the children is left almost entirely to the mother. The training begins very early, and greatest stress from the first is laid upon obedience. Disobedience is a crime punishable by the father with death.

There are no illustrated children's books, no nursery rhymes to inspire the imagination, none of the bright and useful things so necessary to a happy childhood. The child grows up with but few playthings calculated to stimulate the powers of the mind.

The Elementary School.—At about six or seven years of age the child enters school. Sometimes a few parents unite to employ a teacher for their children. The government has no concern for the qualifications of the teacher; no license to teach is required, there is no governmental inspection or control, nor does the State assume any part of the expense of the school. Attendance is not compulsory, and yet male education is so universal that scarcely a boy can be found who does not enjoy opportunities for education. Charity schools are furnished by the wealthy for those who cannot afford to contribute toward the maintenance of a school.

There are no public schoolhouses. The school is sometimes held in the temple, sometimes in the home of the schoolmaster, and sometimes in the home of a wealthy patron. The furniture of the schoolroom consists of an altar consecrated to Confucius and the god of knowledge, a desk and a chair for the teacher, and the pupils' desks and stools, provided by the children themselves. No effort is made to render the room attractive.

The child is admitted the first time with much ceremony in order that the day may be one of pleasant memories. He also receives a new name, the name of his babyhood being dropped. Indeed, a change of name accompanies each new epoch of his life, as the time he takes a new degree, the day of his marriage, etc. Thus the boy enters upon his new work. The first years of study are devoted to reading, writing, and the elements of arithmetic, which studies complete the education of the majority of the pupils. No effort is made to interest the child; he is simply required to memorize and write as many as possible of the fifty thousand characters. Not until after the names of the characters have been learned by rote is there any effort to teach the meaning of the words which they represent. The child's writing, too, is mechanical, for the expression of thought is but a secondary consideration. Thought awakening is not encouraged in the Chinese course of education. Fear, not interest, is the motive which drives the child to study. Memory is the chief faculty to be cultivated, and each child vies with the others to make the most noise in study.

The teacher is greatly revered, only less so than the father. His discipline is rigid, the rod not being spared. There are no new methods to learn; the practice to-day is the same as that of hundreds of years ago; it consists simply in hearing what the children have learned by heart.

The second stage of study consists of translations from text-books and lessons in composition. This work brings some pleasure to the child, as it is a little less mechanical. The third stage consists of belles-lettres and essay writing. Only a few ever reach this stage, and the purpose of this advanced work is not intellectual development, or even the accumulation of knowledge, but to prepare for a position under the government, which can be reached by no other means. Even in these last two stages of study memory is the principal faculty brought into play. Without great exercise of this power the vast amount of material can never be mastered.

Higher Education.—There are no high schools, but men who have taken degrees gather about them young students, who are to devote themselves to study, and give them instruction in the Chinese classics and prepare them for the State examinations for degrees. Great attention is paid to style, and in order to cultivate a good style, students are required to commit to memory many of the productions of their classical authors. They write a great many essays and verses, which are criticised by their teachers. The attention is confined solely to the Chinese classics. The educated Chinaman is usually ignorant of any field of knowledge not embraced in his own literature.

There is in the royal library at Pekin a catalogue consisting of one hundred and twelve octavo volumes of three hundred pages each, containing the titles of twelve thousand works, with short extracts of their contents. These works treat of science, medicine, astronomy, and philosophy, while history has an especially rich literature. The Chinese knew how to observe the heavens four thousand years ago, and yet were unable to construct a calendar without the help of the Europeans. They invented gunpowder, the mariner's compass, porcelain, bells, playing cards, and the art of printing long before they were used in Europe, yet they lacked the ability to use these inventions as instruments to their advancement.

China is divided into provinces which are subdivided into districts. Candidates must pass three examinations in their own district and those who are successful receive the lowest degree, that of "Budding Intellect." Many thousands enter for this degree, but only about one per cent succeed in attaining it. The possession of this degree does not yet entitle the holder to a public office, but most of those who have secured it become teachers, physicians, lawyers, etc. Once in three years there is another examination for the second degree, called "Deserving of Promotion," conducted by an examiner sent from Pekin. A third examination is also held once every three years, in Pekin, and success in this is rewarded by the title "Fit for Office." Holders of the last two degrees are entitled to an appointment to some office, the highest aim of a Chinaman. All of these examinations are conducted with great strictness and fairness, no one being excluded. Thus every Chinese child of ability has the opportunity to reach the highest positions in the country.

There is a still higher degree called the "Forest of Pencils," which is open only to members of the Royal Academy, the *Hanlin*. The acquirement of this degree is the greatest honor to be attained; its possessor is highly esteemed, and may hold the highest offices in the country.

During the last few years, military, polytechnic, and other high schools have been founded in China, and teachers from France, Germany, England, and America have been placed in charge of them.

Criticism of Chinese Education. — 1. It is not under government control.

2. It has no interest beyond the boundaries of China, and regards no literature save the Chinese classics.

3. It is non-progressive, having made practically no improvement for many centuries.

4. It cultivates memory to the neglect of the other powers of the mind, and places more emphasis on the acquirement of knowledge than on the development of the human faculties.

5. It obtains its results through fear, not by awakening interest in or love for study.

6. Women are not embraced in the scheme of education.

7. It produces a conservative, dishonest, untruthful, cunning, and cowardly people.

8. It reaches practically all of the male sex, and there is opportunity for all to rise to the highest positions of honor, but its methods are so unnatural as to awaken little desire for education on the part of the young.

9. Its motive is debasing to the character.

CONFUCIUS (B.C. 550–478)

The name of Confucius is the one most revered among the Chinese. To him and his disciples are due not only the native religion, now supplanted by Buddhism, but also the language and literature. He began to teach in a private school at the age of twenty-two. He rejected no pupil of ability and ambition, but accepted none without these qualities. He said, "When I have presented one corner of a subject, and the pupil cannot make out the other three, I do not repeat the lesson." The following are extracts from the analects of Confucius: —

1. What you do not like when done to yourself, do not to others.

2. Learning without thought is labor lost; thought without learning is perilous.

3. To see what is right and not do it is want of courage.

4. Worship as if the Deity were present.

5. Three friendships are advantageous: friendship with the upright, friendship with the sincere, and friendship with the man of observation. Three are injurious: friendship with a man of spurious airs, friendship with the insinuatingly soft, and friendship with the glib-tongued.

6. Shall I tell you what knowledge is? When you know a thing, to hold that you know it; and when you do not know a thing, to confess your ignorance.

CHAPTER III

INDIA

Literature. — *Marshman*, History of India; *Ragozin*, Vedic India; *Spofford*, Library of Historical Characters; *Butler*, Land of the Veda; *Houghton*, Women of the Orient; *Clarke*, Ten Great Religions; *Johonnot*, Geographical Reader; *Macaulay*, Essays; *Ballou*, Footprints of Travel; *Stoddard's* Lectures; Encyclopaedia Britannica; *Arnold*, Light of Asia; *Chamberlain*, Education in India.

Geography and History. — India lies between the sixth and thirty-sixth parallels of north latitude. It is bordered on the north by the Himalayas and on the south by the Indian ocean. The climate in general is hot, which makes the natives indolent and accounts for their lack of enterprise. The country is very rich, the chief products being wheat, cotton, rice, opium, and tea. The area is about one and a half million square miles, and the population two hundred millions.

The early history of India is obscure, as the Brahmans, from religious scruples, have ever been opposed to historical records. It is certain that there was an aboriginal race which occupied the country from an unknown period, and that a branch of the Aryan [1] or Indo-Germanic race came

[1] The Aryans are supposed to have originally occupied the country east of the Caspian Sea, though some authorities locate them north of it. The branches of this race are the Hindus, Persians, Greeks, Romans, Celts, Teutons, and Slavs. These branches are related in language and color, and the peoples that find their common origin in the Aryans represent a large part of the world's enterprise and progress.

to India and struggled for supremacy. The Aryans succeeded in reducing the natives to subjection or in driving them into the mountains. The comparatively pure descendants of these races are about equal in number in India, their mixed progeny composing the great mass of the Hindu population. The Sanskrit was their classic language, and the Veda their Bible.

The Caste System. — There are four great castes in India: —

1. The *Brahmans*, or highest caste, who are the priests, scholars, lawyers, physicians, teachers, etc. This order is highly reverenced by the lower castes, and its members are dignified, abstemious, and sedate. Their highest ideal is to bring their desires and appetites under complete control. They exercise great influence in the land.[1]

2. The *warriors*, who comprise the army and the office holders.

3. The *merchants*, *mechanics*, and *farmers*, who constitute the bone and sinew of India.

4. The *servants*, who receive no education excepting in matters of politeness and other things connected with their station in life.

Each caste must pay respect to the higher castes, and association with persons of a lower caste is considered a degradation. The English government of India does not interfere with the caste system, but it is gradually breaking down.

Besides the above-mentioned castes, there are tradesmen's castes which have grown up as new occupations have been introduced. Thus there is a potters' caste, a weavers' caste, a carpenters' caste, etc., each son following his father's trade. This accounts for the marvelous skill

[1] See article in Johonnot's "Geographical Reader," p. 197.

of the craftsmen of India in weaving carpets and fine muslins, in metal work, and other arts, — workmanship not equaled anywhere else in the world.

Brahmanism and Mohammedanism are the chief religions. Buddhism overran the country in the fifth and sixth centuries B.C., but it did not seem to be suited to the Hindus, and now it is found in its purity only in Ceylon. Unlike the Chinese, the Hindus are a very religious people. The Shastas[1] declare that "when in the presence of her husband, a woman must keep her eyes upon her master, and be ready to receive his commands. When he speaks, she must be quiet and listen to nothing besides. When he calls, she must leave everything else and attend upon him alone. A woman's husband is her god, her priest, and her religion. The most excellent work that she can perform is to gratify him with the strictest obedience."[2] The system of sale of girls at birth, for wives, of early betrothal and marriage, of perpetual widowhood under most degrading circumstances,[3] and the practice of polygamy make the condition of woman in India still worse than in China.

The English now rule the country with such wisdom and justice that the people are generally contented and loyal. Reforms have been introduced, commerce has been established, improvements have been made, and new life has been awakened. They have also established schools and universities; but as the purpose here is to give a pic-

[1] A commentary on the sacred book, the Veda of the Hindus.

[2] Houghton, "Women of the Orient," p. 34.

[3] A betrothed girl becomes a widow upon the death of her promised husband even though she be only two or three years old and may never have seen him. She must always remain a widow, and as such is constantly humiliated.

ture of the *caste* education, the English system will not be described.

The Home. — Woman has no educational advantages in India, and she is regarded more as the servant than as the equal of her husband. She may never appear uninvited in the presence of any man except her husband. This has worked great hardships for her, especially in cases of sickness, as she can have no medical attendance unless a female medical missionary can be reached. This fact has opened a fertile field for missionary enterprise which has been a great blessing to Hindu women.

A member of a caste may marry in his own or in a lower caste; thus the Brahman may have four wives, the warrior three, the farmer two, and the servant one.

Parents love their children, and expect of them unquestioning obedience. Children are taught to love and honor their teachers even more than their parents. They are taught to reverence and respect older persons under all circumstances. Contrary to the Chinese idea of education, which is to prepare for this life, the Hindu idea is to prepare for the future life, and children in the home, from their earliest years, are trained with reference to this idea.

The Elementary School. — All teachers belong to the Brahman caste. They receive no salary, depending upon gifts for their support. They are mild in discipline, and generally humane in their treatment of their pupils. The instruction is given under trees in the open air on pleasant days, and in a tent or shed when the weather is bad. Instruction is given in reading, writing, and arithmetic, though religion constitutes the principal theme. Memorizing the holy sayings of Brahma occupies a large portion of the time. While the Chinaman worships nature and his ancestors, the Hindu worships Brahma. The cultivation of the memory is considered important, but by no means so essential as in the Chinese system.

The reading lessons are from the Veda. In writing, the child begins by forming characters in sand with his finger or a stick, then he writes upon leaves, and finally upon paper, with ink. The work in arithmetic is very elementary, being only such as will fit the learners for practical life. Servants and girls are excluded from even this limited education.

M. Ida Dean says: "How amused you would be if you could take a peep at a school in India taught by a native teacher. The school is often held in an open shed, and no pains whatever is taken to keep it clean. Often the rafters are festooned with cobwebs and dirt. Of furniture, save the teacher's low desk, there is none. The teacher uses a grass mat, while the boys sit cross-legged on the earthen floor. The teacher, in a singsong voice, reads a sentence which the boys shout after him. Then another sentence is read, which the pupils likewise shout in a singsong voice, while their bodies sway to and fro. This goes on until sentence after sentence is memorized. No one knows nor cares what he is saying. The teacher never explains. Neither teacher nor pupil is ever bothered by that troublesome and inquisitive little word *why*."

The castes are taught separately, and especial attention is given to such instruction as will fit them for their station in life. The highest virtues to be cultivated are politeness, patience, modesty, and truthfulness. Morning, noon, and evening there are impressive religious ceremonies in the school, and the pupils must throw themselves at the feet of their teacher with reverential respect. There is no theory of education among the Hindus, each teacher instructing as he pleases, according to historic custom. This precludes any considerable improvement in method or advance in the art of education. There is no authority to decide upon qualifications of teachers, the only essential requisite being that they shall belong to the Brahman caste.

Higher Education. — The Brahmans are the only educated class, although warriors attend their schools for the purpose of such study as is necessary in connection with their calling. The farmer caste, too, may attend the Brahman schools to learn the studies pertaining to their caste. They pursue in their schools the study of grammar, mathematics, astronomy, philosophy, medicine, law, literature, and religion. Many of them still speak their classic language, the Sanskrit. As their religion is based on philosophy, this study takes precedence over all others.

"The Hindus are believed to have originated the decimal system of arithmetical notation which has been transmitted to us through Arabian channels."[1]

The end of Hindu wisdom is to rise above all human suffering through knowledge. Wuttke says, "Christians pray, 'Thy Kingdom come'; the Chinese, 'Thy Kingdom remain'; the Hindus, 'Let whatever thou hast created pass away.'"

Criticism of Hindu Education. — 1. It is not universal, a large part of the people being excluded from its benefits.

2. It is based on castes and the promulgation of the caste system, which is baneful.

3. It depends too much upon the cultivation of the memory.

4. It has no philosophy of education, and, therefore, is non-progressive.

[1] Williams, "History of Modern Education."

5. It does not properly honor woman, and excludes her from its advantages.

6. It produces a dreamy, self-satisfied, indolent, selfish, and non-progressive people.

7. It makes the people self-reflective, which doubtless accounts for their profound philosophical and mathematical discoveries.

BUDDHA[1]

Buddha lived in the first half of the sixth century B.C. He sought to overthrow Brahmanism and taught that all men are brothers, that they should show friendship, kindness, pity, and love toward their fellow-men. His religion and his spirit approach nearer to Christianity than any other oriental faith, and doubtless his influence was great for the uplifting of the race, though it cannot be classed as technically educational. "Self-denial, virtuous life, suppression of all self-seeking, love for fellow-men," said he, "are cardinal virtues which bring blessedness to mankind." T. W. Rhys Davids says, "Buddha did not abolish castes, as no castes existed at his time." Had the spirit of his teaching prevailed, India would never have been cursed by this baneful system. Buddhism is a religion based on moral acts. In a corrupted form it has many millions of adherents in China, Tibet, Japan, and other countries; but it is found in its purity only in Ceylon.

[1] See North American Review, Vol. 171, p. 517.

CHAPTER IV

PERSIA

Literature. — *Benjamin*, Story of Persia; *Ragozin*, The Story of Media, Babylon, and Persia; *Rawlinson*, The Seventh Great Oriental Monarchy; *Myers*, Ancient History; *Clarke*, Ten Great Religions; *Lord*, Beacon Lights of History; *Fergusson*, History of Architecture.

Geography and History. — Persia lies in the pathway of the great caravans which formerly carried on trade between Europe and India. It consists largely of a high plateau, surrounded by mountains. Large parts of the country are sandy and dry from lack of sufficient rain, and therefore are unproductive. The people are a branch of the Aryan race. They doubtless lived a nomadic life, and were obliged to be ever ready to defend themselves. Success in defense against the frequent assaults of their surrounding enemies stimulated them to become a nation of warriors. This fact had much to do in shaping their education. Cyrus the Great conquered Media and brought Persia to the summit of her greatness. The Persians boasted that they had become great by the sword, hence they cared but little for agriculture or manufactures. They levied tribute upon the nations they had subdued. Home production was therefore unnecessary, and they could devote all of their time to the art of war. About one fourth of the population are still classed as wandering tribes, and the nation is an aggregation rather than a unity of peoples.

The early Persians worshiped fire, and holy fires which only the Magi, or priests, were allowed to approach, were kept perpetually burning upon the mountain tops. The sun also was worshiped, the Persian kneeling with his face toward the east at sunrise in beatific joy. This worship may have been borrowed from the Egyptians, who were conquered by the Persians, and with whom they stood in close relations. In later times the religion of Zoroaster became the religion of the people.

The Home. — Wife and children were required to show the father great respect. Each morning the wife was expected to ask her husband nine times, "What do you wish me to do?" The teacher stood next to the father in the child's esteem. The child was kept at home under the care of the mother until seven years of age. An astrologer gave him a name and outlined his future destiny by reference to the stars. It was forbidden to tell him the difference between right and wrong before his fifth year. No corporal punishment was administered before his seventh year. The mother was greatly beloved by her children, though women were excluded from education. The position of woman was much higher than in either China or India. The chief training of children in the home was physical. Throwing, running, archery, riding, etc., were the principal employments of children. Absolute truthfulness and justice were early inculcated. A quick eye, a steady hand, accurate power of observation, and unwavering courage were qualities sought for in every child, and all of the training in the home, as well as in the later education, had for its aim the acquirement of these powers. Thus children were early taught to be self-reliant and fearless.

The State Education. — 1. Persian education was national in character. After the seventh year the boy was taken from home and educated entirely by and for the State.

His training in the use of arms, in riding, and in other athletic exercises was continued. There were large public institutions in which the boys were quartered, and simplest food and clothing were given them. Besides the training for war, they were taught religious proverbs and prayers, and were led to practice truth and justice. This education continued until their fifteenth year. The teachers were men who had passed their fiftieth year, and who were chosen for virtue as well as knowledge, that they might serve as models to their pupils.

2. The second period of education consisted of a military training, which occupied the ten years between the age of fifteen and twenty-five.

3. The final period was that of the soldier, which continued till the fiftieth year, when the Persian could retire from the army with honor. The most competent were retained as teachers.

Reading and writing were taught to a limited degree, but the chief end of education was to prepare the citizen for war. The Magi were educated in astronomy, astrology, and alchemy, and many of the dervishes have ever been renowned for their acuteness, sense of justice, great powers of observation, and good judgment.

Criticism of the Persian Education. — 1. The State robs the family of its inherent right to educate the children.

2. It neglects intellectual education, giving undue prominence to the physical and moral; and demands too great a part of the active life of man.

3. It makes the highest aim of education to prepare for war, and therefore does not cultivate the arts of peace.

4. It excludes woman from the benefits of education.

ZOROASTER[1]

Zoroaster, the founder of the Persian religion, was a great teacher. The exact date of his birth is unknown, but it is generally placed at about B.C. 600. The testimony of ancient classic literature confirms the belief that he was an historical person. A tablet unearthed in Greece contains an account of his life and his doctrines. Pliny says that he laughed on the day of his birth and that for thirty years he lived in the wilderness on cheese. He was the founder of the Magi priesthood, but did not teach the worship of fire.

His philosophy is *dualistic.* There are two spirits or principles that rule the universe. These are Ormuzd, the principle of light, and Ahriman, the principle of darkness. These two opposing principles are in constant conflict, each striving for the mastery. Man is the center of the conflict, but Ormuzd as his creator has the greater power over him. All influences are summoned to bring about the success of the good, and in the end it will surely prevail. No remission of sin is taught, but judgment is represented as a bridge over which those whose good deeds outweigh their evil deeds are allowed to pass to paradise: in case the evil deeds outweigh the good, the person is cast off forever; in case of a balance of good and evil deeds, there is another period of probation.

This dualism shows itself in nature as well as in the spiritual world. Order is opposed to lawlessness, truth to falsehood, life to death, good to evil. It is a religion in which the ideas of guilt and merit are carried out to the extreme. Zoroaster believed that he was the prophet chosen to promulgate these doctrines, and his influence as a teacher upon the Persian nation was unquestionably great. Persia is now a Mohammedan country.

[1] North American Review, Vol. 172, p. 132.

CHAPTER V

THE JEWS

Literature. — *Hosmer*, Story of the Jews; *Clarke*, Ten Great Religions; *Durrell*, New Life in Education; *Myers*, Ancient History; *Stoddard's* Lectures; *Lord*, Beacon Lights of History; *Josephus*, Antiquities of the Jews; *Morrison*, The Jews under Roman Rule; *Larned*, History for Ready Reference; *Hegel*, Philosophy of History; Report of the United States Commissioner of Education, 1895; *Peters*, Justice to the Jew.

Geography and History. — The Jews were the ancient people of God, the "chosen people," whose history is recorded in the Old Testament Scriptures. They reached their greatest power and glory during the reigns of David and Solomon, and they occupied Palestine, with Jerusalem as their capital city. Within this small territory, some six thousand square miles in extent, have occurred some of the most important events of history, and the Jewish race has been the representative of God's purposes toward man. The Almighty communicated directly with his people, who were thus made acquainted with the divine will. The early Jews were nomadic in their habits, living in tents, and tending their flocks. The patriarch, who was at the head of a family or tribe, made laws for the people under him and governed them according to the command of God, whose representative he was. Because God directly or through the patriarch led and instructed the people, their education, like their government, is called *theocratic*.

The Jews lost their independence B.C. 63 in becoming subject to the Romans, and in A.D. 70 Jerusalem was destroyed and the Jews were dispersed. Since that time they have been wanderers on the face of the earth, and there is no part of the world where they are not to be found. They have maintained their racial characteristics with remarkable purity; but their early agricultural instinct has changed, and they have become a commercial people. This is doubtless owing to the persecutions which have almost universally followed them, making the acquirement of fixed property unsafe.

The Home. — The Jewish family was the purest of antiquity. In general, monogamy was practiced, and the wife was regarded as the companion and equal of the husband. Children being accepted as the gift of God, the father stood in the same relation to his children as Jehovah stood to man. Therefore the father's highest aim was to bring up his children in the knowledge and service of the Lord. We have here the highest and best type of family training to be found in history, a characteristic that still holds in Jewish families wherever they exist, and that has contributed largely to the maintenance of the strong racial peculiarities of the Jews. The father taught his boys reading and writing, and the mother taught the girls household duties; but the latter were not entirely excluded from intellectual training.

Great attention was given to the rites and ceremonies of the tabernacle and the Jewish law. History was also taught as a means of stimulating patriotism. The Jewish child was early made acquainted with the Scriptures, and history, law, and prophecy became familiar to every Jew. As there were no schools, this was all done in the home by the parents. Religion was the central thought of all education, and preparation for the service of the tabernacle and the worship of God was early given to every child. Thus in an atmosphere of love and piety the Jew discharged his sacred duty with care and faithfulness. Obedience to the commands of parents, veneration for the aged, wholesome respect for their ancestors, and familiarity with the Jewish law were instilled into the minds of all children. Music and dancing were taught in every household, not for pleasure, but as a means of religious expression. By prayer and holy living, by precept and example, by word and deed, the father discharged the duty committed to him by God, leading his children by careful watchfulness toward the ideal manhood which was revealed to him by the teachings of Holy Writ.

There were no castes among the Hebrews, and the same kind of training was given to the children of rich and poor, high and low, alike. No other race of people has given such careful home training to its children, from earliest times to the present.

The Jewish School. — There were no Jewish schools until after the destruction of the nation and the loss of their civil liberty. After the defeat at Jena the Prussians turned to education as the sole means of retrieving their national greatness; the same was true of the Austrians after the defeat of Sadowa, and of the French after the fall of the empire at Sedan. But the Jewish people had set this example eighteen centuries before. Dittes says, "If ever a people has demonstrated the power of education, it is the people of Israel."

The rabbis required, A.D. 64, that every community should support a school, and that attendance should be compulsory. This is the first instance of compulsory education on record. If a town was divided by a stream without a connecting bridge, a school was supported in each part. Not more than twenty-five pupils could be assigned to one teacher, and where the number was greater an assistant was employed. If there were forty pupils, there were two teachers. It will thus be seen that the Jews put into practice eighteen centuries ago a condition of things which, owing to the complexity of our civilization, is with us to-day largely an unrealized ideal.

Teachers were respected even more than parents, for it was held that parents prepared their children for the present, but teachers for the future. None but mature married men were employed as teachers. It was said that "he who learns of a young master is like a man who eats green grapes, and drinks wine fresh from the press; but he who has a master of mature years is like a man who eats ripe and delicious grapes, and drinks old wine."

The child entered school at six. Previous to that age physical exercise and bodily growth were to be the ends sought. "When he enters school," says the Talmud, "load him like an ox." Other authorities, however, encouraged giving him tasks according to his strength. The subjects taught were reading, writing, natural history, arithmetic, geometry, and astronomy. The Scriptures were taught to all the children, and all were versed in religious rites.

The methods were good and attractive, great effort being made to lead the children to understand, even though it might be necessary to repeat four hundred times. The discipline was humane. According to the Talmud, "children should be punished with one hand and caressed with two." Corporal punishment was administered only to children over eleven years of age.

The Schools of the Rabbis. — Karl Schmidt says: "Culture in a people begins with the creation of a literature and the use of writing." The oldest monument of writing among the Israelites is found in the tables of stone containing the Ten Commandments. Moses, David, Solomon, and Isaiah, and the other prophets were the founders of the Hebrew literature.

Among the instrumentalities of higher education were the Schools of the Prophets, which taught philosophy, medicine, poetry, history, and law to the sons of prophets and priests, and of leading families. These schools were influential in stimulating the production of the historical, poetical, and prophetic books of the Old Testament.

But more important as direct means of higher education were the Schools of the Rabbis. These sprang up in Alexandria, Babylon, and Jerusalem in the early centuries of the Christian era. They were private institutions founded by celebrated teachers. Doubtless it was in such a school as this that St. Paul was brought up at the feet of Gamaliel. The principal subjects studied were theology and law,—politics, history, mathematics and science being excluded. The collection of the sayings and discussions was begun in the second century A.D. and afterward took form in the Talmud.

Criticism of Jewish Education. — 1. It exalted the home and insisted on the control of children by their parents.

2. It gave to woman an honored place in the home.

3. It gave an intelligent interpretation of the school and its functions. In regard to school attendance, the number of pupils under one teacher, the respect due to teachers, the course of study, and many other matters, it showed practical wisdom.

4. It taught obedience, patriotism, and religion.

5. It provided only for Jewish children.

6. It was mild and generally wise in discipline, though mistaken in forbidding corporal punishment before the eleventh year, while admitting its use after that.

7. It developed an honest, intelligent, progressive, God-fearing people.

8. It produced some of the greatest poets and historians of the world.

THE TALMUD[1]

This book, as we have seen, is the outgrowth of the discussions of the rabbis, whose sayings, collected from the second to the sixth century A.D., are herein contained. It proclaims with great minuteness rules of life which the faithful Jew still rigidly observes. It has aided in perpetuating Jewish laws, ceremonies, customs, and religion, and has been the most potent means of preserving the national and racial characteristics of the Jews for nearly two thousand years. Driven from one country to another, they have always carried the Talmud with them and have been guided and kept united by its teachings. During the last quarter of the nineteenth century the study of the Talmud has been revived, not only among the Jews, but also among Christians and students of all classes.

EXTRACTS FROM THE TALMUD

1. Even if the gates of heaven are shut to prayer, they are open to tears.

2. Teach thy tongue to say, "I do not know."

3. If a word spoken in its time is worth one piece of money, silence is worth two.

4. Not the place honors the man, but the man the place.

5. The world is saved by the breath of school children.

[1] See Peters, "Justice to the Jew."

CHAPTER VI

EGYPT

Literature.—*Maspero*, Egyptian Archaeology; *Wilkinson*, The Ancient Egyptians; *Stoddard's* Lectures; *Myers*, Ancient History; *Routledge*, The Modern Wonders of the World; *Johonnot*, Geographical Reader; *Edwards*, A Thousand Miles up the Nile; *Knox*, Egypt and the Holy Land; *Ballou*, Due West; *Clarke*, Ten Great Religions; *Ebers*, Uarda; and Egyptian Princess; *Curtis*, Nile Notes of a Howadji.

Geography and History. — Egypt consists of a narrow strip of land about six hundred miles long, lying in the northeastern part of Africa. Its geographical importance is due to the river Nile, which flows through it, and which, by its annual overflow, enriches the soil, and makes one of the most productive portions of the globe. For many centuries reservoirs for the storage of water in time of the overflow, and irrigation canals for its later distribution, have secured the country against drought, and thus abundant harvests were always assured "independent of the seasons and the skies." This, with the mild climate and exceedingly rich soil, made food attainable with slight labor, furnishing an abundance, not only for its own population, but making Egypt the granary of the Mediterranean countries. We learn from the Scriptures, of the visits of the sons of Jacob to Egypt to buy corn of Joseph when famine existed in their own land. These conditions, which made living so cheap, were doubtless the main causes of the early settlement of the valley of the Nile, and the rapid increase in its population. In confirmation of the foregoing we have the testimony of Diodorus Siculus, a Greek writer, who visited Egypt nearly two thousand years ago. He tells us that the entire cost to bring up a child to manhood was not more than twenty drachmas (less than four dollars of our money).[1]

Of the antiquity of Egyptian history we have abundant evidence. Swinton says, "Egypt is the country in which we first find a government and political institutions established. Egypt itself may not have been the oldest *nation*, but Egyptian history is certainly the oldest *history*. Its monuments, records, and literature surpass in antiquity those of Chaldea and India, the two next oldest nations."[2] The records of the history of Egypt are found in abundance carved on her monuments, tombs, buildings, implements, etc. They were written in hieroglyphics, the meaning of which was unknown until the discovery of the "Rosetta stone," which furnished the key to their interpretation.

The ancient Egyptians excelled in mechanics and arts. It is doubtful whether to-day we know as much of certain sciences as they did four thousand years ago. Their applications of mechanics, engineering, dyeing, and embalming still remain to us "lost arts." The wisdom of the Egyptians was proverbial, and the great scholars of other countries made pilgrimages to Egypt to study philosophy, literature, law, and science.

The Caste System.—The caste system existed also in Egypt, but in no such strict sense as in India. The first and highest caste consisted of the priests, who represented the learning and wealth of the country. They owned

[1] The student should bear in mind the fact that the purchasing power of a sum equivalent to four dollars was much greater in those days than now.

[2] "Outlines of the World's History," p. 12.

one third of the land, upon which they paid no tax. They held all the offices, were the surveyors, engineers, teachers, —indeed, their caste alone furnished all the higher professions. They ruled the land with an iron hand. Concerning their influence, Swinton says, "The priests were the richest, most powerful, and most influential order. It must not be supposed, however, that the modern word 'priest' gives the true idea of this caste. Its members were not limited to religious offices; they formed an order *comprising many occupations and professions.* They were distributed all over the country, possessing exclusively the means of reading and writing, and the whole stock of medical and scientific knowledge. Their ascendency, both direct and indirect, over the minds of the people was immense, for they prescribed that minute religious ritual under which the life of every Egyptian, not excepting the king himself, was passed."[1]

The second caste consisted of the military class, who also belonged to the nobles. There was freer intercourse between the two higher castes than was possible in the Hindu system. It was not uncommon to find brothers belonging to different castes. Ampère found an inscription on a monument mentioning one son as a priest, another as governor of a province, and a third as superintendent of buildings. To each member of this caste was assigned a parcel of land (six and one half acres), which also was free from taxation. These two higher castes were especially privileged, and the gulf between them and the lower castes was very wide.

The third, or *unprivileged* caste was subdivided into three orders: (1) the farmers and boatmen; (2) the mechanics and tradespeople; and (3) the common

[1] "Outlines of History," p. 20.

laborers. Between these, also, there were bonds of common interest, though a decided difference between the orders was recognized.

The caste system may be outlined as follows: —

Egyptian Castes.

- I. *Priests*, who represented the learning and wealth and ruled the land.
- II. *Soldiers*, who, though lower in caste than the priests, yet associated with them.
- III.
  1. *Farmers* and *boatmen*, who stood the highest in rank of this caste.
  2. *Mechanics* and *tradespeople*, who ranked next.
  3. The common laborers.

The slaves were lower than the common laborers, and were not classified among the castes. They were generally captives taken in war. Respect and reverence for the higher castes were by no means so marked as in India, and outbreaks between the various classes were common.

The Home. — Woman occupied a much higher plane in Egypt than in China or India, though polygamy was practiced by all classes except the priests. She was the recognized mistress of the home, possessed some education, and largely directed the education of the children. Children of wives of different castes had equal rights before the law to inheritance. Great attention was paid to religious ceremonies, and the children were taught piety and obedience in their early youth. They were highly regarded in the Egyptian home, and were brought up in an atmosphere of love and filial respect. The day of a child's birth was regarded as determining its destiny. The child was brought up on the simplest food, and furnished with scanty clothing, in order that its body might be strong and supple.

The Education. — The education, like that of India, was suited to the different castes. Priests were the only teachers. While chief attention was given to the education of boys, girls also received some instruction. The principal subjects taught in the lowest caste were writing and mathematics. The papyrus plant, found along the Nile, furnished a material on which writing was practiced. In arithmetic we find an anticipation of modern principles in the concrete methods employed. Religious instruction was also given. Bodily exercise was severe, running being a favorite pastime. The expense of schooling was very small. The boy usually followed the trade of his father, though this was not an inflexible rule. The occupation he was to follow had some influence in shaping his education.

The higher castes received an extensive education, including a knowledge of higher mathematics, astronomy, language, natural science, medicine, music, engineering, and religion. The annual overflow of the Nile necessitated the construction of reservoirs and irrigation canals, and caused frequent changes of boundary lines. For all this a knowledge of mathematics was necessary, and this study was therefore greatly encouraged. Institutions of higher learning for the training of priests and soldiers were found at Thebes, Memphis, and Heliopolis. The Museum of Alexandria, which reached its highest prosperity about the middle of the third century B.C., and which made Alexandria the center of the learning of the world at that period, attracted philosophers and investigators from Athens and Rome. In connection with the Museum was the celebrated Alexandrian library, which was fostered by the Ptolemies, and which contained a vast collection of books, variously estimated at from four hundred thousand to seven hundred thousand volumes.[1]

[1] It must be observed that the ancient volume, or roll, contained much less matter than the modern book.

Criticism of Egyptian Education. — 1. It was dominated by the priests under the caste system, and did not recognize equality of man.

2. It encouraged greater respect for woman than other oriental systems, but took little account of her intellectual training.

3. It made use of concrete methods, at least in writing and arithmetic, for the first time in history.

4. It was non-progressive in its elementary education, the father generally expecting his son to follow his calling.

5. In higher education it was justly noted, as it attracted wise men from Greece and Rome to study its science and philosophy.

GENERAL SUMMARY OF ORIENTAL EDUCATION

With the discussion of Egyptian education, the consideration of oriental systems ceases. Concerning the education of the Phoenicians, Babylonians, and other oriental nations we know but little. To the Phoenicians the invention of the alphabet, glass making, and purple dyeing is generally credited, and the knowledge of these things was communicated to the Mediterranean nations with whom they engaged in trade. The classical countries were materially influenced by Egyptian culture, and the way was prepared for a broader and more enlightened interpretation of the purpose of education, and for a more successful evolution of civilization on soil better suited to that end. We may briefly summarize the lessons of oriental education, as follows: —

1. The Oriental systems fostered class distinctions by furnishing but little enlightenment to the lower classes, and affording superior advantages to the privileged few.

2. They were non-progressive, for centuries witnessed no improvement in methods of instruction, reached no higher ideals, and marked no advance in civilization.

3. They did not feel the need of trained teachers.

4. The importance of the individual was not appreciated, and man was regarded as belonging to the State.

5. The end sought was good conduct, which was to be attained through memorizing moral precepts. This gave undue importance to the memory.

6. Little encouragement was given to free investigation; authority of teachers and ancestral traditions were the principal factors employed. There was therefore no stimulus toward progress or intellectual growth.

7. In general, woman had no part in education, being regarded as incapable of any considerable intellectual development.

8. In China the motive of education was to prepare for success in this life; in India, for the future life; in Persia, to support the State; in Israel, to rehabilitate the nation; and in Egypt, to maintain the supremacy of the priests.

9. In no case was the conception reached that the aim of education should be to emancipate all the powers of man, — physical, intellectual, moral, spiritual.

10. Finally, we may sum up the conditions that prepared the way for classical education in the words of Karl Schmidt: "In Greece at last the idea of human individuality as the principal end, and not as a means to that end, was grasped. Conformable to this truth, all human, social, and political conditions were shaped and education given its form. This idea of the emancipation of the individual became established in Greece with a brilliancy which attracts attention to that land until the present time."

CHAPTER VII

GREECE

Literature. — *Davidson*, Education of the Greek People; *Felton*, Ancient and Modern Greece; *Grote*, History of Greece; *Curtius*, History of Greece; *Morris*, Historical Tales (Greek); *Mahaffy*, Old Greek Education; Social Life in Greece; The Greek World under Roman Sway; *Clarke*, Ten Great Religions; *Guhl* and *Koner*, Life of Greeks and Romans; *Timayenis*, History of Greece; *Wilkins*, National Education in Greece; *Lord*, Beacon Lights; *Monroe*, Source Book of the History of Education.

Geography and History. — Greece lies in the center of the ancient world. The numerous islands between it and the mainland of Asia made stepping-stones for the hardy mariners who, filled with the spirit of adventure, pushed out farther and farther from the Asiatic shores until they reached Greece — the first European country to be settled. Here we find another branch of the great Aryan race.

The coast is broken up by many indentations which afford fine harbors and invite seafaring life. The surface is mountainous, the ranges cutting the country up into many sections or states. The climate is varying, depending upon proximity to the sea, and upon the elevation. The scenery is beautiful, and the soil in the valleys is fertile. The productions are fruit, grain, and silk. As might be expected from the nature of the country, the people show much commercial enterprise. The area is about twenty-five thousand square miles, and the population about 2,200,000.

The Greeks were a brave and ambitious people, and their history is full of heroic deeds and stirring events. The many small states were often hostile to one another. Athens and Sparta were the two most important cities. Around them centered two diverse forms of civilization, and in them were developed two very different standards of education. It will be necessary, therefore, to discuss separately the education of these two cities. When the Grecian states were united in defense, no outside power was able to conquer them; but, unfortunately, jealousies often arose which brought them into conflict with one another, and which finally caused the overthrow of all. In art and literature Greece reached the summit of her glory in Athens in the age of Pericles, the fifth century B.C. The work accomplished by Athens has been the inspiration of the world for nearly twenty-four hundred years.

In government, in manners, and in customs the Greeks were very different from the oriental nations. The spirit of political freedom prevailed here for the first time in the history of the world. Doubtless the small size of the states, which were separated from each other by natural boundaries, was an important factor in stimulating the people to secure and maintain this independence. "Man's character is formed by the surroundings of his home." The beautiful valleys and mountains, the varying climate, the sea with its many islands and harbors, the soil, in the main yielding its fruit only by hard labor, were elements well calculated to produce a hardy race, — a race with lofty ideals, loving beauty both of mind and body.

The Olympian Games. — Because of their national popularity and their direct influence on the education of the people, a description of the Olympian games is not out of place in a history of education. At first they were religious in character. They were celebrated in honor of Zeus, at Olympia, in Elis, which became the Holy Land of Greece. They took place once in four years, and this period, called an Olympiad, furnished the basis of computing time. The first Olympiad begins with B.C. 776. All of the states took part in these contests, and when at war, hostilities were suspended during the games, that visitors might attend them unmolested. Thus once in four years the various states of Greece were united in friendly contest and joyous festivity.

At first there was only the foot race, but afterward wrestling, jumping, and throwing the spear were added. Still later, chariot and horse races, and contests in painting, sculpture, and literature, were included. Only Greek citizens of good moral character could enter the contests. The prize, though but a simple wreath of laurel or olive, was most highly esteemed. At first spectators were attracted from the different parts of Greece only; but afterward the games became great fairs for the exchange of commodities, as well as contests which attracted people from all parts of Europe.

The Olympian games tended to unite the people and cultivate the arts of peace. They encouraged the development of perfect bodies, the training being designed to produce superior athletes. They inculcated broader views, bringing together people from different parts of their own land and from other lands. They incited intellectual ambition by adding in later times literary productions. They created a manly spirit and stimulated a national patriotism.

CHAPTER VIII

ATHENS

Literature. — (See general literature for Greece.) *Harrison*, Story of Greece; *Macaulay*, Essays; *Curtius*, History of Greece; *Davidson*, Education of the Greeks; *Wilkins*, National Education in Greece; *Freeman*, Historical Essays.

History. — The ideals of Athens — educational, political, and moral — were in direct contrast to those of Sparta. At Athens, love of liberty, love of knowledge, and love of beauty went hand in hand. Though the body was not neglected, as is proved by the beautiful types of manhood preserved for us in Athenian art, the Athenians believed that the truest beauty was to be reached only by the development of the mind.

Hence Athens brought forth great men like Pericles, Socrates, Plato, and Aristotle, she created a literature that has influenced the world, she developed art to its highest excellence, and gained for herself a permanent and high place in the world's history. Sparta did none of these things, therefore her ruin was sure and speedy; while the decline of Athens was slow and her influence still lives.

The spirit of Athens was liberty, while that of Sparta was tyranny. It is true that Athens had slaves; indeed, only one fourth of the inhabitants were free; but even the slaves had a large share of freedom, and enjoyed some means of education. We learn that children of the wealthy were committed to trusted slaves, called *pedagogues*, who escorted them to school, instructed them in many things, and had a right to punish them for disobedience. This could not have been allowed by parents with such high ideals had the slaves been debased as were those of Sparta.

In Athens we find for the first time the democratic idea of government; this was by no means so completely realized as it is in modern times, especially in the western world. The "Age of Pericles" (B.C. 480–430) forms the most brilliant period of Athens, a period hardly surpassed in some respects by any other in the world's history. Solon (B.C. 638) was the great lawgiver of Athens. His wise laws had much influence on the prosperity and intellectual development of the people.

The Home. — In Athens the child was left with the mother until the sixth or seventh year. The toys were greater in variety than with any other people of antiquity. They were much the same in character as those of modern times, and their purpose was to amuse the children rather than to furnish a definite preparation for life, as in Persia and Sparta. Play, therefore, was recognized as an important factor in the child's life, and the toys in use stimulated and encouraged the joyous element in the child's nature. That toys are a potent influence toward healthful mental and physical growth is an educational truth that has been fully recognized by us only within recent years. And yet the Athenians appreciated it in the home, twenty-five centuries ago.

The training was intellectual and humane, though strict obedience was enforced. Great attention was paid to the works of the poets, selections being taught to all the children. The father interested himself chiefly in the education of the boys, and when he was unable to discharge this duty an elderly male relative was selected as mentor, who devoted his leisure hours to such training. Little attention was paid to the mental training of the girls.

Women were not held in so high esteem as in Sparta, nor were they as worthy of respect. The husband exercised over his wife the same authority as over his children. Neither by social position nor by intellectual attainment was she his equal. "Her own chamber was the world of the Athenian woman; her maids were her companions; household duties and the preparation of clothing for her family were her employment."

Education. — The father was free to choose for his children their school and the character of their education. The State furnished gymnasia in which schools could be held, fixed the qualifications of teachers, the school hours, and the number of pupils to a teacher. Once a year public examinations were held, the expense of which the State defrayed. The schools were private institutions, supported by private means, though under State inspection. The teachers were philosophers or wise men, thoroughly competent to discharge the duties of their office.

At six or seven years of age, the boy was sent to school in charge of a pedagogue, or leader of the young, — usually an old and trusted slave. While not intrusted with the actual teaching of his charge, he was responsible for his morals and manners, and was allowed, as we have seen, to administer punishment. The pedagogue was the constant attendant of the boy. The character of the school chosen depended upon the means of the parents.

The first two years were devoted chiefly to gymnastics. The two subjects of the elementary course were *gymnastics* and *music*, the latter term including reading and writing. But little arithmetic was taught, as the Athenians believed that the object of the study of arithmetic was simply utility, and but little arithmetic was needed for practical use. "Calculating boards" made the reckoning for all business needs a purely mechanical process. The idea of education was the development of the *beautiful*, and they held that arithmetic contributed but little to this end. The works of the poets were given prominence throughout the Athenian education, and pupils were required to commit to memory many selections. Later, under the Sophists, the study of grammar was begun.

Children of the poorer classes were kept in school until their fourteenth or fifteenth year, when they learned a trade. Those of the rich remained in school until their twentieth year. The course of study of the latter included music, rhetoric, grammar, and philosophy. At twenty the youth's education was regarded as completed, and the young man became a citizen. Teachers were paid fees and not fixed salaries.

It was the atmosphere of Athens, more than the discipline of the school, that fostered culture and inspired learning. The aim of education was the *beautiful*, and the ideal was the aesthetic in mind and body.

Criticism of Athenian Education. — 1. It sought to educate the entire man, giving him beauty of form, keenness of intellect, and nobleness of heart.

2. It acknowledged the right of parents to direct and determine the education of their children.

3. It recognized the importance of the individual as no other people had before.

4. Strict, but not blind, obedience was required of the children.

5. It produced great men, with high moral and intellectual ideals, but these ideals were centered in Athenian culture.

6. It excluded women and slaves from its benefits, and was by no means universal.

7. It recognized the value of play as an educational force, thereby anticipating the kindergarten.

8. The State exercised a certain control over the school by furnishing places where it might be held, by defraying the expense of examinations, by determining the number of pupils to a teacher, by fixing the limit of school hours, and by deciding upon the qualifications of teachers. And yet the choice of education was free, and its aim was the good of the individual and not the glory of the State.

CHAPTER IX

ATHENIAN EDUCATORS

Literature. — *Bulkley*, Plato's Best Thoughts; *Schwegler*, History of Philosophy; *Morris*, Historical Tales; *Curtius*, History of Greece; *Lord*, Beacon Lights; *Spofford*, Library of Historical Characters; *Jowett*, The Republic of Plato; *Vogel*, Geschichte der Pädagogik; *Emerson*, Representative Men; *De Quincey*, Plato's Republic; *Hegel*, Philosophy of History.

SOCRATES (B.C. 470–399)

SOCRATES was the son of a sculptor of Athens. Though he learned his father's trade and followed it in early manhood, he relinquished it to devote himself to the study of philosophy, for which he had a natural bent. In person he was far from fulfilling the Athenian ideal of beauty, being short of stature, corpulent, with protruding eyes, upturned nose, large mouth, and thick lips. His domestic life was not happy, his wife, Xantippe, being a noted shrew. His failure to provide for the material welfare of his family, though quite natural in a man to whom all material things seemed unessential, must have sorely tried her patience. But Socrates bore her scolding with resignation. Indeed, he seemed to regard it as furnishing an opportunity to practice the philosophic patience that he preached.

Socrates believed that he had a divine call to "convince men of ignorance mistaking itself for knowledge, and by so doing to promote their intellectual and moral development." Like many other philosophers, he spent his time in the streets, markets, and other public places, arguing with any one who would stop to listen or converse. This manner of teaching was common in Athens, and he never lacked hearers. The whole atmosphere of the classic city was charged with the spirit of intellectual activity and philosophic discussion. Socrates did not teach positive doctrines, but assumed ignorance himself in order to convince others of ignorance. By a series of suggestive questions he would lead his pupils or opponents into admissions which finally established the truth that Socrates saw at the outset. This is known as the "Socratic Method," or the dialectical method, and this form of inductive teaching was an important contribution to education.

Although Socrates left no writings, his great pupils, Xenophon and Plato, have given the world a full account of his teachings. Plato speaks in highest terms of his moral character, declaring that "he was not of this world." Xenophon also adds his testimony in the following words: "No one ever knew of his doing or saying anything profane or unholy." Socrates believed in one Supreme Being, the intelligent Creator of the universe. He also believed in the immortality of the soul. These doctrines were altogether contrary to Greek polytheism, the prevailing religion of Athens, and they prove him to have been far in advance of the age in which he lived. While he established no school, Socrates nevertheless must ever rank as one of the world's greatest teachers and thinkers.

In his death he fully exemplified the truth of his own philosophy. He was accused of corrupting the youth and denying the deities, and was condemned to die by drinking a cup of hemlock. He calmly submitted to his fate, refusing to avail himself of an opportunity to escape. According to the account given in Plato's "Phaedo," he spent his last hours discussing with the friends who attended him the question of the immortality of the soul.

PLATO (B.C. 429-347)

Plato was a disciple of Socrates, and to him we are chiefly indebted for an account of the teachings of his great master. For twenty years he sat at the feet of the philosopher, and drank from the fountain of knowledge possessed by that wonderful man. He also traveled in other lands, particularly Egypt and Italy, in pursuit of knowledge. He became one of the most remarkable scholars and philosophers, not only of antiquity, but of all time. When forty years of age he founded a school at Athens, though it is not as a teacher that he is chiefly known, but as a writer and sage. "Plato among the Greeks, like Bacon among the moderns, was the first who conceived a method of knowledge." His great work is his "Republic," in which he pictures the ideal State and outlines his scheme of education, which is built on ideals of both Spartan and Athenian citizenship. From Sparta comes the thought of an education which shall be controlled by the State from birth; while Athens adds the aesthetical aspects to those purely physical.

In his scheme he divided the people into the following classes: —

1. The *common people.* They should be allowed to rise, but no education is provided for them in his scheme.

2. The *guardians* or *citizens,* who shall study music and gymnastics. Music includes literature, that is, human culture as distinguished from scientific knowledge. Writ-

ing and arithmetic are also included under music, the latter not being studied for practical purposes, but to develop the reason.

3. The *rulers*, who, in addition to the preceding subjects, shall study geometry, astronomy, rhetoric, and philosophy.

The State is to have absolute control of every citizen; it shall arrange marriages, destroy weak and unpromising children, and remove the healthy babes at birth to public nurseries, where mothers may care for the children in common, but will not recognize or take special interest in their own children. Boys and girls are to be educated alike. Great care is to be taken that nothing mean or vile shall be shown to children; their environments shall be beautiful and ennobling, though simple.

From birth to seven years of age the child is to have plenty of physical exercise. He shall hear fairy tales and selections from the poets, but careful censorship must be placed on everything presented to him. Suitable playthings are to be provided, precaution taken against fear of darkness, and by gentleness combined with firmness a manly spirit is to be produced. Beauty of mind and body are to be harmoniously united.

From seven to thirteen intellectual as well as physical activity is required.

The special education begins at twenty by the selection of the most promising youths. At thirty another selection of those able to continue their education five years more is made.

Higher mathematics, astronomy, harmony, and science constitute the work of the first ten years, and philosophical study that of the last five. Fifteen years then are to be given to the service of the State, after which, at fifty, the student may return to the study of philosophy for the remainder of his life.

Education is to be compulsory, as the child belongs to the State and not to the parent.

Plato gave predominance to intellectual rather than to physical culture, as he said, "If the mind be educated it will take care of the body, for the good soul improves the body, and not the good body the soul."

He taught that it is the aim of education to bring all of the powers of man into harmonious coöperation.

It will thus be seen that Plato's scheme of education centers around the oriental idea that man belongs to the State, and the main purpose of education is to fit him to serve the State. And Plato clearly set forth how the education which he demanded should be attained, and therefore he is to be remembered as originating the *first systematic scheme of education in history.*

ARISTOTLE (B.C. 384-322)[1]

Aristotle was born in Stagira in Macedonia, and from this fact he is called the Stagirite. For twenty years he was a pupil of Plato, as Plato had been of Socrates. Aristotle was not only one of the greatest philosophers that ever lived, but he enjoyed the distinction of being the teacher and chosen counselor of Alexander the Great. Much of the greatness of the man who conquered the world and "wept because there were no more worlds to conquer" was due to his wise teacher. Alexander loved and revered Aristotle as much as his father, declaring "that he was indebted to the one for *living*, and to the other for living *well*." He assisted Aristotle in founding a school at his native place, Stagira.

[1] Brother Azarias, "Essays Philosophical."

It is not simply as the teacher of Alexander the Great that Aristotle is to be remembered in the history of education, though that would entitle him to lasting fame. After the education of Alexander was finished, Aristotle went to Athens, where he founded the Lyceum. Here he lectured for many years, in the morning to his riper pupils on philosophical subjects, and in the evening to the masses on such topics as were within their comprehension and as would tend to elevate them.

His *pedagogy* may be briefly outlined as follows: —

1. Education is a lifelong task, beginning at birth and continuing till death. The first seven years are to be spent in the home under the fostering care of the parents. During this period the child is to have no severe tasks, but chief attention is to be given to physical development. He must learn obedience, as the first step to an ethical life. His food and clothing are to be simple, and his toys and games of a character to stimulate wholesome activity. At the age of seven he is to enter upon the direct intellectual training, and nothing must interfere with this during the next seven years. From fourteen to twenty-one the education is to include such exercises as directly prepare for life. The diet is to be simple, the physical training severe, for the double purpose of counteracting the tendencies of the adolescent period, and of preparing for war.

2. Education includes the development of the body, the character, and the intellect. Courage, endurance, self-denial, temperance, truthfulness, and justice are essential characteristics to be sought. The purpose of instruction is to develop the imperfect, untrained child into the well-rounded, intelligent, and patriotic citizen.

3. The course of study, which begins seriously after

the seventh year, includes music, gymnastics, drawing, grammar, rhetoric, and mathematics. Later, dialectics, philosophy, and political science are to be added.

4. Woman is to have part in education that she may properly train her children, and may, by an intelligent understanding of the laws, uphold the State.

5. Aristotle considered education as the most important and most difficult of all problems. He based his pedagogy upon a knowledge of the individual.

6. His method was the analytical. He began with things and advanced from the concrete to the abstract.

The foregoing will show that Aristotle began the study of problems that still occupy the minds of educational thinkers, after more than twenty-two centuries of search for the truth. Some of the problems he discussed have found their solution, and the seed sown by the great thinker has come to fruitage. Karl Schmidt says, "Aristotle is the intellectual Alexander. Rich in experience and profound in speculation, he penetrates all parts of the universe and seeks to reduce all realities to concepts. He is the most profound and comprehensive thinker of the pre-Christian world,—the Hegel of classical antiquity,—because, like Hegel, he seeks to unify all knowledge, brings together the scattered materials of the present into one system, constructs in a wonderful intellectual temple the psychical and physical Cosmos, the universe and God, proclaims the destruction of an earlier culture epoch, and sets in motion waves in the ocean of history that are destined to influence the intellectual life of all centuries to come. . . . Aristotle stands for the highest intellectual summit of antiquity,—the bridge which binds the Grecian to the modern world,—the philosophical mouthpiece and the intellectual master of twenty centuries."

CHAPTER X

SPARTA

Literature. — (See general literature for Greece.) *Sankey,* Spartan and Theban Supremacies; *Smith,* History of Greece; *Plutarch's* Lives; *Mombert,* Great Lives; *Spofford,* Library of Historical Characters.

History. — Sparta was the capital of Laconia, the southern province of Greece. Its inhabitants consisted of: —

1. *Citizens,* composed of nine thousand families of nobles, who ruled the other classes.

2. *Perioeci,*[1] composed of thirty thousand families of freemen who lived in the territory surrounding Sparta, but who were subject to the nobles.

3. *Helots,*[2] about three hundred thousand in number, who were slaves.

The Perioeci and the helots, with the love of freedom characteristic among the Greeks, chafed under their yoke of subjugation, and eagerly watched for opportunities for revolt. Only by an exercise of superior force could the nobles maintain their supremacy, and they were obliged to

[1] The Perioeci (dwellers around) were the older population of the land, who inhabited the mountains and hillsides about Sparta. They were farmers, and they also worked the mines and quarries, manufactured articles for the Spartan market, and carried on the commerce. Though freemen, they were allowed no part in the government, could not bear arms, and had to pay tribute to Sparta.

[2] The Helots were probably peasants who occupied the land about Helos, and, defeated in war, became Spartan subjects. They could not be sold or given away, but belonged to the inventory of the farm.

seek by martial training the strength they lacked in numbers. Hence the education of the Spartan youth was of necessity military, and every citizen was trained to become a warrior.

The Spartans were dignified, austere, and of few words, "laconic" in speech. The young were expected to be silent in the presence of their elders except when addressed. They were taught to give way to their seniors, especially to old men, whenever they met upon the street or in a public place.

The Home. — The child was left in charge of the mother until six or seven years of age. Toys inciting to warlike sports were provided, and childhood was made happy. The father usually superintended the child's training, but sometimes an aged relative assumed the responsibility. The treatment was humane and intelligent. From the first the child was taught implicit obedience and modesty.

The *Iliad* and the *Odyssey* have been called the Bible of the Greeks, and children early learned extracts from the works of the great poet, Homer. The Spartan mother was highly respected by her husband and her children, and she was noted for her chastity and nobility of character. She entered fully into the Spartan idea, and cheerfully gave her sons to her country, while she often inspired them to deeds of bravery and patriotism. The lofty and self-sacrificing patriotism of the Spartan mother is illustrated by her words upon sending her son to battle, — "Return either with your shield or on it!"

It is said that weak and unpromising children were either killed as soon as they were born, or abandoned to the wild beasts upon the mountains. This was because the State would assume the training only of strong children, such as were likely to make good soldiers. It is probable that many of these abandoned children were rescued and reared by the lower classes, which would partially account for the fierce resistance so often offered by these classes to those who deprived them of liberty. If such an inhuman practice had been encouraged by other nations of the world, many of the greatest benefactors of the race would have been consigned to an untimely death, for some of the noblest men that have ever lived were weak in infancy.

Education.—At six or seven the boy was taken from the home, and the State had entire jurisdiction over his education. The boys were placed in groups in charge of young men who were responsible for their education, which was almost wholly physical. They lived on very simple food, and were often obliged to appease hunger by theft. They were taught that crime did not lie in the commission of the offense, but in its detection. Their dress from seven to twelve consisted of a long coat of very coarse material, the same for summer and winter. They were taught to bear blows without a murmur, and instances are related of boys being whipped to death without crying out.

Children sat at table with older men and listened to their conversation, but they were never allowed to speak except in answer to questions. Thus they absorbed wisdom and were incited to deeds of bravery by the stories of heroism related by their seniors.

The State furnished barracks poorly provided with the comforts of life, in which the boys slept in severe weather; at other times they slept in the open air. They were wholly separated from their homes, and completely under control of the State. The purpose was to secure strong, beautiful, and supple bodies, inured to hardship, as a preparation for the life of the soldier. The only intellectual education was music, which consisted in playing the lyre as an accompaniment to the dance. Reading and writing were despised as being fit only for slaves.

At the age of twelve the boy exchanged the long coat for the mantle, thereby entering upon manhood. From this time until the age of thirty, much the same form of training was continued, though it became more definitely military. At thirty the Spartan youth became a citizen and was expected to marry. Girls also received gymnastic training, in many cases with the boys. The purpose of this was to develop strong and beautiful wives and mothers. The effect of this coeducation of the sexes was in the highest degree salutary, impurity among women being unknown in Sparta. We have already noted the patriotism of the Spartan mother. Woman was highly esteemed in the home. Her praises and her reproofs were alike respected, and all her opinions bore much weight.

Criticism of Spartan Education. — 1. It produced men and women of beautiful physique.

2. It inculcated obedience, politeness, modesty, sobriety, respect for the aged, courage, and patriotism.

3. It checked luxury and extravagance.

4. On the other hand, it gave little attention to intellectual training, hence it produced few men of lasting fame.

5. Its aim was martial supremacy, and this attained, the State fell into a hasty decline because of the instability of such a foundation.

6. It excluded a large part of the inhabitants from its benefits, only the nobles being included.

7. It was selfish because it trained for Sparta and not for Greece, or for humanity.

8. It taught the duty of man to the State, and not the duty of man to man.

9. It took boys at an early age away from the influences of home, thus robbing the parents of the sacred prerogative of directing the education of their offspring.

10. It produced men cruel in battle and revengeful in victory, men incapable of cultivating the arts of peace.

LYCURGUS

There is so much that is mythical and uncertain concerning Lycurgus that many have doubted whether he ever lived. Curtius, however, says, "There really lived in the ninth century B.C. a legislator of the name of Lycurgus." Lycurgus formed the constitution which gave Sparta its peculiar institutions, and which established its place in history. His laws were intended to check luxury and to inculcate the simplest habits. Some of his important laws led to the introduction of the following customs:—

1. All the men ate at common tables, fifteen at a table.

2. Children sat at these tables, but were required to maintain silence save when addressed. They were not allowed to ask for food. The object was to teach them good manners, to inculcate implicit obedience, and to impart to them the wisdom of the Spartan fathers.

3. The food was of the simplest kind.

4. Sparta was divided into nine thousand parts, a part for each of the nine thousand citizens, or noble families. The provinces under Spartan rule were divided into thirty thousand parts, a part for each Perioeci family.

5. Iron was made the only money, so that the people could not become rich; for its great weight rendered burdensome the possession of a considerable amount.

6. All children belonged to the State, to which only

soldiers were valuable, therefore weak or deformed children were cast out. Marriage was also controlled by the State.

Lycurgus exerted a great influence upon Sparta, and his laws were responsible for her peculiar political system and her resulting greatness.

PYTHAGORAS

Pythagoras, though not a Spartan, is associated with southern Greece. Little is known of his early life. He was born on the island of Samos, about B.C. 582. He was familiar with the Ionic philosophy, and probably visited Egypt for study, a custom common among scholars of that time. Such a visit would in part explain his knowledge of mathematics, as the Egyptians had long been masters in that science. One of his teachers was Thales, the father of philosophy. The fundamental thought of the Pythagorean philosophy was the idea of proportion and harmony. "Through number alone, the quantitative relations of things, extension, magnitude, figure (triangular, quadrangular, cubic), combination, distance, etc., obtain their peculiar character; the forms and proportions of things can all be reduced to number. Therefore, it was concluded, since without form and proportion nothing can exist, number must be the principle of things themselves, as well as the order in which they manifest themselves in the world." (Schwegler's "History of Philosophy.")

While mathematics was the central idea of his system, medicine, physics, and philosophy were also taught in his school. He did the world great service in the discovery of the so-called Pythagorean theorem in geometry, that the square of the hypotenuse of a right-angled triangle is equal to the sum of the squares of the other two sides.

CHAPTER XI

ROME

Literature. — *Bryce*, The Holy Roman Empire; *Bury*, The Roman Empire; *Church*, Pictures from Roman Life and Story; *Clarke*, Ten Great Religions; *Gibbon*, Decline and Fall of Roman Empire; *Lord*, Beacon Lights; *Capes*, Roman Empire; *Merivale*, History of the Romans; *Shumway*, A Day in Ancient Rome; *Mommsen*, History of Rome; *Liddell*, History of Rome; *Ploetz*, Epitome of Universal History; *Gilman*, Story of Rome; *Collins*, Ancient Classics; *Monroe*, Source Book of the History of Education.

The Age of Augustus. — The history of Rome covers a period of a thousand years. From the little village on the Palatine Hill Rome grew to be the mightiest empire of the world. The "Age of Augustus" represents not only the summit of military glory, but also the highest civilization, and the noblest ideals of the Roman people. It was the age of Vergil, Horace, Ovid, Livy, and Seneca. Rome was at peace with the world, and therefore had time to devote to art, literature, and other intellectual pursuits. It was during this period that Christ was born.

Like Sparta, Rome for a long time maintained her supremacy by force of arms, and therefore encouraged physical education. But when she became mistress of the world, and came in contact with the culture of the Greeks, she began to feel the need of an intellectual and aesthetic development. Accordingly it became the fashion to study Greek, to bring teachers from Athens to Rome, and to send young men to Athens to study. The Roman Empire was therefore the medium through which Grecian culture was transmitted to the western world, and during the Augustan Age the center of learning was transferred from Athens to Rome.

Gibbon says, "The first seven centuries were filled with a rapid succession of triumphs; but it was reserved for Augustus to relinquish the ambitious design of subduing the whole earth, and to introduce a spirit of moderation into the public councils."[1] The Augustan Age shows Rome at her best, and a study of the educational system at that time will be most fruitful for the student of pedagogy.

Geography and History. — We have seen that Rome began with a small territory in the center of Italy, and that province after province was added, until in the time of Augustus she ruled the world. Italy, the center of the empire, has a diversified surface, a mild climate, and a fertile soil. In the time of Augustus, the Roman Empire embraced all of the border of the Mediterranean, extended as far north as the North Sea, as far east as the Euphrates, as far south as the Sahara, and west to the Atlantic. With the great Mediterranean entirely under its control, including the seas, bays, and rivers tributary to it; with its rich territories; and with its vast population, which represented most of the enterprise and civilization of the world, — this great empire possessed wonderful advantages for the spread of Christianity, for the dissemination of intelligence, and for the improvement of the human race.

The government of the Romans was generally some form of republic, the people always being jealous of their rights. Their religion took on gross forms of idolatry, for they readily adopted and worshiped the gods of the Grecians, Egyptians, and other conquered peoples. Tem-

[1] "Decline and Fall of the Roman Empire," Vol. I, p. 2.

ples to Faith, Hope, Concord, and other virtues were erected and maintained. The Romans were very superstitious. These facts have a bearing upon Christian education, and will explain some of the chief difficulties which it had to encounter.

The Home. — While in Athens the father had charge of the education of the boy in his early years, in Rome that duty devolved almost entirely upon the mother. In early Roman history the matron was celebrated for her virtues — fidelity to her husband, love for her children, and queenly guardianship of the sacred precincts of the home. The name of the Roman matron became a synonym of all that is noble, wifely, and motherly in the home. Without doubt the character had sadly deteriorated at the period of which we write, but there still remained with many the lofty ideals which had been fostered in earlier times.

The husband was the head of the house, but to the wife was committed the care of the children and their instruction for the first six or seven years of their lives. She taught them strict obedience and politeness, and instructed them in the "Twelve Tables of Roman Law."[1]

The mother also took great pains to teach her children correct pronunciation. She taught them their letters, —

[1] The "Twelve Tables" were formulated about B.C. 450. They constituted the code of written law, and were written or engraved on tables of wood. They settled usages long in practice, but never before written, defining the rights of *plebeians* and *patricians*. They were agreed to only after ten years of dispute and mutual concession. They resembled Solon's laws, owing, doubtless, to the commission which was sent to Greece to study the laws of that country. These tables were destroyed when the Gauls sacked Rome (B.C. 390), but their contents had been widely committed to memory, and were handed down from generation to generation. The mothers saw to it that these laws were early taught to their children, who thus came to venerate them and to have respect for authority.

first the name and then the form, a practice which is pedagogically false, as Quintilian pointed out. She also taught them poems from the great masters. In taking pains with pronunciation she prepared the way for later training in oratory, which was the most important study in Roman education.

Only when Rome had begun to decay did mothers commit the training of their children to nurses and slaves. When Rome was at her best, the child grew up in an atmosphere of love under direct care of the mother, who shaped his morals and guided his religious life as well as his early mental development. Around the mother centered all that was ennobling and elevating in the first seven years of the child's life. The father had but little to do with this period, and did not interfere with the mother's work. His duty lay in public life; hers lay within the home, and well did she meet her responsibilities until the time of her debasement with all the other elements of Roman society.

Elementary Education.—At six or seven years of age the child was sent to school in charge of a slave, who carried his books and protected him from harm. This was in imitation of the practice in Athens, where the pedagogue performed a like office. But the duties of the Roman slave do not seem to have been as responsible as those of the Athenian pedagogue. As we have seen, in Rome the mothers looked after the morals of their children with great care, and the attendant of the child to school was regarded as but little else than a servant. In some of the wealthier and more aristocratic families, however, in addition to the slave who performed the menial duties mentioned, there was also a pedagogue who attended the youth to school and to the theater, superintended his games, and, in short, accompanied him wherever he went. This pedagogue was intrusted with full power to discipline and to direct the morals of his charge. In some cases several boys were placed in the care of the same pedagogue. On the other hand, it often happened that a boy had a whole retinue of slaves, each having his special duty to perform.

The schools were in charge of *literators*, usually men of little culture and no social standing. These institutions were public, though supported by private means. The discipline was severe, strict obedience being exacted by the teacher, who made use of the rod when he thought it necessary. The subjects taught were reading, writing, and arithmetic. Great care was taken with pronunciation, just as had been done in the early years under the mother's instruction. In writing, the characters were traced with the stylus on waxed tablets. Arithmetic was learned for its utility. Indeed, the whole purpose of the schools was to prepare the children for practical life. The easier poets were read, explained, and committed to memory, not so much for their content as to fit youth for public speaking. Obedience, politeness, modesty, cleanliness, and respect for teachers were virtues insisted upon. These schools, which covered the instruction of children from five to twelve years of age, did not, as already intimated, reach the very highest classes, who preferred to employ private tutors.

Secondary Education. — At twelve the boy entered a school taught by an educated man, called *literatus*. Many of the teachers of this class were Greeks. Here, in addition to the studies of the elementary school, the pupils were taught the Greek and Latin languages; and the poets, history, oratory, philosophy, and criticism were also studied. The school of the *literatus* was much better than that of the *literator*, but it reached only a limited number of the Roman youth.

Higher Education. — Upon entering his sixteenth year, the boy was inducted with ceremony into the dignity of manhood, and was clothed with the *toga virilis*, the dress of men. He now chose his calling and began definite preparation for it. Five vocations were open to him, — namely, oratory, politics, arms, law, and agriculture. Those without talent or inclination for any of the others devoted themselves to agriculture. They were taken to the farms, where they received definite instruction in the principles and practices of this occupation. To those who chose oratory, politics, or law, were assigned persons experienced in their respective fields, and the boys were taken to the forum, the senate, and other places where they could hear renowned orators and become familiar with public life. They had also definite instruction in their chosen branch. Those who entered the army were placed in charge of military officers, who taught them military tactics and the practical duties of life in camp. These learners also gave attention to oratory and other intellectual studies.

It will thus appear that in their schools, as in life, the Romans were thoroughly practical. Each boy was carefully prepared for the life which he had chosen, by being inducted into it during his school course. Cicero asked the question, "What have we to learn?" and answered it, "To honor and strengthen the State, in order that we may become the rulers of the world." Roman parents demanded that their children should be trained in the practical duties of life, in order that they might know how to become rich. Therefore all training for children was in this direction.

While this in general was the purpose of education, the Romans had their ideal of what an educated man should be, and that ideal found its expression in the name of *orator*. He who was the best orator was the best educated man. The schools, however, were for boys, little account being taken of the education of girls except in household duties. Still, women were more respected, and had wider privileges than they had before enjoyed. Most of the wealthy citizens employed Greek tutors for their sons, and sought to ape Grecian manners and culture. Education was completed by study in Athens and by travel — advantages within reach only of the very wealthy.

Criticism of Roman Education. — 1. It took great care to instill respect for law and obedience to parental and civil authority.

2. It honored the home and taught respect for the mother. In this, Rome took a great step in advance over many nations of antiquity.

3. It was not a State institution, and therefore could not offer equal advantages to all.

4. Its end was to prepare the youth for practical life and to fit him for the acquirement of wealth, rather than for the development of all the human powers.

5. It was superficial, and sought to apply Greek culture to Roman conditions and character.

6. It did not take a strong hold upon the Roman people so as to shape the course of the nation.

7. It ignored the claims of the masses, including women, to equal education and equal rights.

CHAPTER XII

ROMAN EDUCATORS

Literature. — (See Literature, Chapter XI.) *Forsyth*, Life of Cicero; *Spofford*, Library of Historical Characters; *Watson*, Quintilian's Institutes (Pedagogy, in Bks. I & II).

CICERO[1] (B.C. 106–43)

CICERO was born B.C. 106, of noble parents. As a boy he had the advantage of the best schools and teachers that Rome could furnish. Later he studied at Athens, under the greatest Greek masters, and became proficient in the Greek language. According to the common practice among the better classes in Rome, he spent some time in travel to complete his education, visiting Egypt, Asia Minor, and other parts of the known world. But Cicero's education can hardly be said to have been "completed" as long as he lived, for he remained a student even in the midst of his most exacting duties of State, and often employed teachers, especially in oratory. Forsyth says of him, "Philosophy and oratory seem to have been the two chief objects of his study; but if of any man before Bacon appeared that might be said which the great master of modern philosophy claimed for himself, that he 'had taken all knowledge for his province,' it might be truly declared of the youthful Cicero. His appetite for knowledge was insatiable, and his desire for distinction boundless."[2]

[1] Forsyth, "Life of Cicero." This is a very complete, just, and discriminating treatment of Cicero and his relation to the times in which he lived.

[2] "Life of Cicero," Vol. I, p. 30.

Becoming an advocate in Rome, he devoted himself chiefly to the defense of men high in position, often those who were charged with bribery, extortion, or other abuse of political trust. Some of his finest orations were delivered on these occasions. In the meantime he lost no opportunity to advance his own political interests. He was elected to one office after another until he reached the height of his political ambition, — the consulship of Rome, the loftiest position attainable by the Roman citizen. As consul he devoted himself with such zeal, integrity, and success as to win the title "Father of his Country." While he held this office he exposed the conspiracy of Catiline and saved Rome from civil war. He conducted the office with honesty and efficiency. Indeed, at a time of great corruption, Cicero stands out during his entire life of nearly sixty-four years as the purest patriot, the broadest-minded statesman, the noblest man of the age. His honesty in public or private life is unquestioned. Of his intellectual greatness Forsyth says, "The greatness of his intellect dwarfed that of every other man alive."[1]

That he was vain of his accomplishments admits of no doubt. That he also sometimes lacked moral courage and was vacillating seems also true. But he was incorruptible in a corrupt age; above reproach when impure life was the rule; and when treason was common, he remained a firm patriot. His celebrated "Philippics" were delivered against practices which indicated the approaching ruin of the republic. That ruin was complete when the Second Triumvirate was formed, — an event which also sealed the doom of Cicero. Upon learning that he was proscribed, Cicero attempted to escape from Italy, but was overtaken and assassinated. His head and hands

[1] Vol. II, p. 213.

were carried to Rome and presented to Antony, who gave the head to his wife, Fulvia, whose crimes Cicero had often rebuked. Forsyth says, "She took it, and placing it on her lap, addressed it as if it were alive, in words of bitter insult. She dragged out the tongue, whose sarcasms she had so often felt, and with feminine rage pierced it with her bodkin. It was then taken and nailed to the rostra, together with the hands, to molder there in mockery of the triumphs of his eloquence, of which that spot had so often been the scene. A sadder sight was never gazed upon in Rome."[1]

Cicero's Pedagogy.—It is not as a teacher, but as a writer, that Cicero demands a place in educational history. His writings furnish the finest examples of Latin style, and his orations are studied for their classic beauty and rhetorical finish. He wrote many philosophical works, in which are set forth advanced ideas on education. Especially was he in advance of his age in regard to the punishment of children. He held that corporal punishment should be resorted to only when all else has failed; that the child should not be degraded in the mode of punishment; that punishment should never be administered in anger, should be deferred until ample time for reflection has been allowed to both teacher and pupil; and that reasons for it should be given, so that, if possible, the child may be led to see the justice of the punishment inflicted. The teachings of Cicero on this subject are of great pedagogical importance, and they have at last come to be recognized in the school practice of the present day.

While these were Cicero's most important pedagogical teachings, he also taught many other truths valuable in education. Among them are these: that education begins

[1] Vol. II, p. 317.

in childhood, and is a steady growth throughout life; that memory should be cultivated by learning extracts from classic authors; that great care should be taken to make the amusements and environments of the child such as to elevate and refine, as well as properly to develop its powers; that at the suitable time some calling should be chosen for which the youth has evident fitness; that religion is the basis of morals, therefore careful attention should be given to religious instruction.

SENECA (B.C. 3–A.D. 65)

Seneca was one of the most distinguished men that Rome produced. Even as a boy he showed remarkable talent, and his father furnished him the best educational opportunities by placing him under the greatest masters in the city. He also had the benefit of travel in Greece and Egypt, after which he practiced law in Rome. The student of education is interested in Seneca chiefly as the tutor of Nero, who was committed to his charge at the age of eleven. Without doubt the lad had already formed vicious habits, as his teacher had great trouble in managing him; nor did Seneca eradicate those evil tendencies which bore such terrible fruit in Nero's later years.

Nero retained his love for his teacher for a long time, keeping him as a trusted counselor for several years. Seneca drew up all of Nero's state papers, among others one defending the crime of matricide, Nero having put his own mother to death. This brought deserved odium upon Seneca's name. It indicates that he was a time-server, lacking moral independence and firmness. This may explain his failure in the training of his royal pupil. Nero himself wearied of his old teacher and friend, and condemned him to death. Seneca, however, committed suicide, a mode of death quite in accord with his Stoic philosophy.

Seneca was the most eminent writer, rhetorician, and orator of his time. He anticipated many modern ethical teachings, and in some of his writings we find a strong religious sentiment, quite like that of Christianity, leading one to think that he may have been influenced by Christ and his disciples, with whom he was contemporary. On the other hand, some of his teachings are decidedly repulsive to Christianity.

Seneca's Pedagogy. — 1. Like Cicero, he believed that punishment should be mild and reasonable. "Who condemns quickly, condemns willingly; and who punishes too much, punishes improperly."

2. The office of education is to correct the evil tendencies in the child.

3. The character of each child must be studied, and each individual should be developed according to his peculiarities.

4. Do not flatter the child, but teach him truthfulness, modesty, and respect for his elders.

5. Take great care that the environment of the child is elevating, and allow only pure and ennobling examples to be reflected before him.

6. Give the child but few studies, in order that he may be thorough and acquire right habits of learning.

7. The office of teacher is one of the most important of all offices. "What the teacher, who instructs us in the sciences, imparts to us in noble effort and intellectual culture, is worth more than he receives; for, not the matter, but the trouble; not the desert, but only the labor, is paid for. . . . Such a man, who consecrates his

whole being to our good, and who awakens our dormant faculties, is deserving all the esteem that we give a benevolent physician or our most loved and dearest kindred."

QUINTILIAN[1]

No other Roman contributed so much pedagogy to the world as Quintilian. He was born in Spain, but early moved to Rome, in order to be trained in the atmosphere of culture which that city alone afforded. His education was conducted by his father, a celebrated rhetorician, to whom he owed the particular direction of his powers which afterward made him so famous. He chose the law as a profession, because it offered the best opportunity for the exercise of oratory. Not finding the practice of law congenial, he soon abandoned it, and devoted his time to teaching. He founded a school at Rome, and conducted it with great success for twenty years, having for pupils children from the most distinguished patrician families. Among these were the grandnephews of Domitian, possible heirs to the throne. This was the best school in Rome at that time. Vespasian honored Quintilian by creating for him a chair of rhetoric and conferring upon him the title "Professor of Oratory." This is the first instance in history of State endowment of a chair for teaching a specific subject. Royal recognition was not without effect upon the fortunes of Quintilian, as it placed him in the front rank of the teachers of Rome.

[1] Authorities differ as to the dates of Quintilian's birth and death, placing his birth at from A.D. 35 to 42, and his death from A.D. 95 to 120. Drieser, who is perhaps the best authority, places his birth at A.D. 35, but does not fix the date of his death, which, however, was probably much later than A.D. 95 as he lived to a ripe old age.

This, together with his subject, the teaching and mastery of which were considered by the Romans to be the climax of education, enabled him to wrest supremacy from the Greek teachers who so long had enjoyed a monopoly of teaching in the city.

When fifty-three years of age, Quintilian retired from his school, and devoted himself to authorship. In the first two books of his great work, "Institutes of Oratory,"[1] he sets forth his ideas on education. This is the most remarkable treatise on education bequeathed to us by antiquity.

He taught that as oratory was the climax of Roman education, especial attention should be given to it. He was not in sympathy with the prevailing use that was made of oratory. Oratorical contests were frequent, and they excited popular interest. Courts, lawyers, and public speakers resorted to all the tricks of speech to win popular favor, and audiences demanded something startling, dramatic, and unusual. Quintilian tried to stay this tide, and taught that oratory should conceal itself. He met, however, with poor success in reforming the evil.

Quintilian's Pedagogy.—His pedagogical teachings, some of which we present, are of the greatest importance.

1. There should be no corporal punishment, as punishment administered to slaves is not suitable for children who are to be citizens.

2. Nurses must be irreproachable in life and language, so that children be not brought in contact with anything impure.

3. Amusements should be turned to account as a means of education.

4. Teachers should be men of ability and of spotless character.

[1] *Institutio Oratoria.*

5. Children should begin early with a foreign tongue, as their own language will come to them naturally in their intercourse with those about them.

6. Education should begin with the earliest childhood.

7. The forms and names of the letters should be learned simultaneously, playthings being utilized to assist in this.

8. Care should be taken that children do not acquire a distaste for learning.

9. In learning to read, advance very slowly.

10. Writing should begin with tracing, and the copies should consist of moral precepts.

11. The individuality of the child should be studied.

12. Public schools are preferable to other means of education, because they do not subject the child to greater moral danger, while they stimulate him by association, friendship, and example, to nobler endeavor.

13. Under the *literatus*, grammar, composition, music, geometry, astronomy, and literature are to be studied.

14. The climax of education should be *rhetoric*.

CHAPTER XIII

CHRISTIAN EDUCATION

Literature. — *Bryce*, Holy Roman Empire; *Guizot*, History of Civilization; *Lord*, Beacon Lights; *Sheppard*, Fall of Rome; *Draper*, Conflict between Religion and Science; *Clarke*, Ten Great Religions; *Gibbon*, Decline and Fall of Roman Empire; *Laurie*, Rise of Universities; *Stillé*, Studies in Mediaeval History; *Arnold*, Essays in Criticism; *Lecky*, History of European Morals; *Hegel*, Philosophy of History; *Allies*, The Formation of Christendom; *Châteaubriand*, The Genius of Christianity; *Azarias*, Essays Philosophical.

INTRODUCTION

Oriental civilization was based on the theory that the individual belonged to the State, and could have no interest except that which was bound up in the interests of the State. Christianity, on the other hand, taught that while the individual has duties which he owes to the State, and while he must look to the State for his protection, and for the preservation of his material interests, he owes a higher allegiance elsewhere, and no fetters can be placed on the aspirations or wants of his own soul. In a word, Christianity taught the importance and worth of the individual.

The great teachers, Confucius, Buddha, Socrates, Plato, had many glimpses of truth, but Christ is truth itself. He discovered to the world the final principle of the value of the human soul, and brought to fruition the truth that "all men are equal before God." This thought made human development possible; a new principle was introduced upon which civilization could build and advance, and improve to the end of time. Perhaps the highest test of civilization is found in the respect shown to women. Measured by this test, the oriental nations have made but little progress, as the position of woman with them is much the same to-day as it was centuries ago. While this is true of each individual nation, we have found among the nations themselves, as we have traced the growth of civilization, steady improvement in the condition of woman. Thus, in Athens and Rome, where we find the highest types of ancient civilization, there was also the greatest respect for woman. In no country of the East was it equaled. If the Jews are mentioned as an exception, it must be admitted that the Jewish women held the highest place among those of antiquity; but this eminence was given by the Jews only to the women of their own race, and was by no means universally accorded to womankind, as it is by the spirit of Christianity. If we discover a greater respect for woman in Rome or Athens than in China or India, it only shows the movement of civilization toward the west.

The coming of Christ marked a new era both in religion and education. Let us look at some of the lessons which Christianity teaches.

1. *God is the common Father of all men.*—This does not limit the blessings of the world to the Jew and exclude the Gentile. All men of whatever race or color may approach God as their Father, and all are equal in his sight. This gives hope to all, and makes possible an exercise of faith in the present and in the future life. It proclaims a higher citizenship than that of the State, and demands allegiance first of all to God.

2. *The universal brotherhood of man.*—This principle

sweeps away castes, abolishes slavery, destroys class distinctions, and gives equal rights to all men. It stimulates love for fellow-men, checks selfishness, promulgates peace and good will, and implants the spirit of the Golden Rule in the hearts of men.

3. *Marriage is a divine rite and husband and wife are equal.* — Nothing like this teaching had been practiced in the pagan world. Woman was simply the servant, the creature, of man. She was to do his bidding, and might be divorced for trivial cause, or for none. Man was supreme and his will was law. The home in the Christian sense did not exist, because the husband and wife were not one.

4. *Children are the gift of God.* — This was a Jewish as well as a Christian teaching. If children are the gift of God, the power of life and death over them cannot rest with the father, as in China, Persia, or Rome. It is the duty of the father to preserve them, teach them, train them for this life, and prepare them for the life to come. Since the children come from God, the pious parent must consider them as a sacred trust which he does not neglect. Hence he must see to it that they are properly educated.

5. *The central pedagogic truth of Christ's teaching is this: All education is for the individual.* Oriental education had for its end the interests of the State. Christian education has for its end the interests of the individual. The State is the creature of man, and not man the creature of the State. Man will create, and support, and preserve the State for his self-protection and for his own good. The highest ideal of the State is that in which the people rule, that which furnishes the greatest liberty. This is the logic of Christianity, and the logical conclusion of education. It is really for the individual. The world

has been slow to learn this lesson taught by Christ; but now it is mastering it more thoroughly every day, as shown by the more liberal forms of government, the broader interpretation of courses of study, and the greater attention to the needs of the individual child.

All these teachings of Christianity have a direct educational meaning, and suggest lessons for all humanity. For the school is not the only contributor to the education of a people. Every truth that affects mankind, every principle that touches the home or the State, has its influence upon the life and character of the individual, and is, therefore, an element in his education.

The natural consequence of these principles is that education must be universal. Every child must be fitted for the duties of life, both for his own sake and for the sake of the State of which he is a part. As an individual, he must work out his destiny, and to make this possible in the broadest and best sense from the Christian standpoint both mind and heart must be developed. As a member of the State he must assume duties in public affairs which require the possession of superior intelligence. This is particularly true in free governments which are the logical product of the spirit of Christianity. While the idea of universal education had its beginning with the Christian era, we shall see that many centuries elapsed before it reached its fulfillment. There were many serious and almost insurmountable obstacles against which the early Christians had to contend, and these made progress necessarily slow. Let us look at some of these obstacles.

Their Poverty. — The early Christians were almost without exception poor. Christ appealed to the poor and lowly, and chose his disciples from among them. The acknowledged followers of the Nazarene had to face confiscation of property, persecution, death. Homeless and without protection they wandered about, and had neither the opportunity nor the right to acquire property. They, therefore, had little means to apply to the education of their children. They could neither establish schools nor employ teachers; they could give only such instruction as the limitations of their poverty, their misery, and their fear permitted. Consequently, only the most meager training could be secured, and that almost wholly in religious matters.

Their Own Ignorance.—Chosen as they were from the lowly ranks of life, many of the early Christians were ignorant. Most of them were servants and slaves, who had been converted from paganism, and who did not possess even the rudiments of education. They had to be instructed in the rites and ceremonies of the Church, and in the practices and requirements of their new belief. Unlettered as they were themselves, they could scarcely undertake to educate their children. It is marvelous that under these conditions any attempt was made to do it; yet we find that great pains were taken even in the early centuries of the Christian era to perform this duty toward those who were regarded as gifts of God and heirs of salvation.

Their Small Number.—Even when free from persecution and under comparatively happy conditions, they were so scattered and so few in number, as well as so poor, that to maintain schools was almost an impossibility. They would not permit their children to attend the pagan schools, as they feared moral and intellectual contamination. The only safety, especially for the converts from paganism, was in being "separate from the world" about them. So where their numbers were sufficient they established schools of their own. But in many communities they could not do this; hence they could only teach their children at home.

Opposition of the Rulers. — Rome ruled the world, and her highways, her commerce, her military expeditions, and her mighty enterprises furnished excellent means for the spread of Christianity. But while Rome had many religions, adopted from her conquered peoples, Christianity was so different from these that the rulers were readily brought to regard the Christians with suspicion. Humility, returning good for evil, refusal to avenge, were contrary to the Roman spirit. Therefore many persecutions followed, which disturbed the life of the Christians so as to make impossible the work of educating their children.

Lack of Christian Literature. — The early Christian Fathers fully realized the dangers that surrounded their children. To come in contact with pagan schools, or even with pagan literature, they felt to be dangerous. How easy it would be for pagan converts to fall away, or even for others not pagan, attracted by popular influences. For Christianity was not yet popular. Hence the only safety of the converts lay in totally abstaining from the use of pagan literature. Here was introduced a discussion that affected the Church and educational progress for centuries, and caused learned men when converted to abjure their favorite authors who had furnished the material for their education in their early years. Having no literature of their own, and condemning the use of pagan literature, the Christians found it hard to overcome the obstacles which stood in the way of Christian education. As a result, almost the only things taught to children were certain parts of the Bible, and the rites and duties of the Church.

Other Difficulties. — New ideas do not readily take hold of the world. Men naturally cling to the old and tried, and are not easily turned to new thoughts and practices. The teachings of Christ were so radically new that men were slow to adopt them. Their acceptance involved a change of habit, the abandonment of customs not before regarded as evil, the yielding up of social caste, the humbling of the individual. Herein existed a most serious obstacle to the establishment of Christian education.

These are a few of the great difficulties that had to be met, many of which were not overcome for centuries. We shall see, as we trace the development of education, how the new ideas which had their birth with the Christian era struggled for recognition, how they have become established, how they have brought great blessings to mankind, how they have aroused ambition and awakened hope, and how they give promise of still greater advancement in times to come. The boundless field thus opened to mankind, and the knowledge of how to enter and possess it, constitute the world's great inheritance from Christ. But to know how to appreciate and use this inheritance, we must study the slow and painful growth of these new educational ideals from the Christian era till the present time.

CHAPTER XIV

THE GREAT TEACHER

Literature. — The Bible; *Beecher*, Life of Christ; *Hanna*, Our Lord's Life on Earth; *Geikie*, Life of Christ; *Azarias*, Philosophy of Literature; *Fouard*, Life of Christ.

Life and Character. — Christ was born in Bethlehem, spent his early life at Nazareth, entered upon his ministry when thirty years of age, continued it for three years, and was then crucified by the Romans at the instigation of the Jews. These are simple facts of history corroborated by both sacred and profane writings. All agree that his was the most noble character that ever appeared on earth. The most careful study of his life for nineteen centuries, by friends and enemies, by scholars and critics, by philosophers and statesmen, by Christians and unbelievers, only adds to its luster, and sustains the conviction that, though he was a man, he was also more than man. The most critical research, the most careful examination of his life, his motives, his teachings, only compel the testimony that he was "without spot or blemish." The great have studied his sayings and his life, and have bowed in admiration before the sublime teachings of the Son of Man. The simple and unlettered have listened to his words of truth and been comforted. Faith has been awakened, hope inspired, love quickened, and man redeemed by the power of the Christ. Millions have been influenced by the sweetness and purity of his life. The spirit of Christianity has led to the founding of hospitals, asylums, and institutions of mercy everywhere; to the establishment of schools and colleges; to the universal spread of education; to the uplifting of the individual; to the furtherance of human brotherhood; and to the fostering of peace among men and nations.

Christ produced a profound impression alike upon the great and the small. Rousseau says of him, "The life and death of Jesus Christ are those of a god." Napoleon says of Christ, "His birth and the story of his life; the profoundness of his doctrine, which overturns all difficulties, and is their most complete solution; his gospel; the singularity of his mysterious being; his appearance, his empire, his progress through all centuries and kingdoms, — all this is to me a prodigy, an unfathomable mystery. I defy you to cite another life like that of Christ." It has well been said that "Christ is the God who is man, and the man who is God."

Nor was the impression upon the lowly less profound. He called ignorant fishermen to discipleship, and by three years' contact and instruction prepared them to "go into the world and teach all nations." The inspiration of his life and teachings made them able to stand before kings, and to "confound the wisdom of the wise."

His Work as a Teacher. — But the question here is not concerning Christ as the founder of a religion, nor of his divine character or life, but of Christ as a *teacher*. He is justly entitled to be called "The Great Teacher." Karl Schmidt says, "By his doctrines and through his deeds, — in and with his entire life, — is Christ the teacher and educator of humanity." His method is the foundation of all true teaching. Let us note some of the important characteristics of this method.

1. *It was suited to his hearers.* — When Christ taught

the people he used material that they could comprehend. Thus, when he spoke his parable of the sower, while he sat by the seaside, the multitude before him had gathered from the villages and farms of the country round about. They therefore could thoroughly appreciate the lesson. His parable of the vineyard was doubtless suggested by the vine-clad hills of Judea, and the lessons taught were made more forcible by their suitableness. In his conversation with the learned Nicodemus he plunged at once into the most profound doctrines, but when he talked with the ignorant Samaritan woman, his approach to the truth he would teach was most simple and gradual. No one ever failed to understand him, and he is a most remarkable example of the teacher suiting himself to the capacity of his pupils.

2. *It was full of illustrations.*—When he wished to teach the evil of covetousness he told of the rich man and his barns; he encouraged faithfulness by the parable of the talents; he stimulated to fruit bearing by the story of the fig tree; he taught mercy by the account of the Good Samaritan; joy over repentance was illustrated by the story of the ninety and nine. And so we find that by ample and suitable illustration the Savior enforced the sublime truths that he taught.

3. *It was simple and yet logical.*—There was no effort to be philosophical, yet the teachings of Christ are full of philosophy. The language used and the manner of putting the truth were so simple that the ignorant man and the child were never left in doubt as to his meaning. Nevertheless his teaching was not haphazard; it was connected and logical. It contained so much of truth, so systematically put and so much to the point in view, that, while it appealed at once to the understanding of his

hearers, it also furnished material for thought for the most learned of all ages. Whether it was a parable or a story, an admonition or a rebuke, a sermon or a prayer, a word of comfort to the sisters of Bethany or an argument with the chief priests, a familiar conversation with his disciples or a stern rebuke of the scribes and Pharisees, — Christ always expressed himself with simplicity and clearness.

4. *It drew from Nature.* — Christ loved to walk in the fields with his disciples and draw lessons from the plants, the birds, the sowing of the farmer, the gathering of fruit from the vineyard, the ripening harvests, and the whispering breezes. "Consider the lilies of the field how they grow; " "behold the fowls of the air;" "a sower went forth to sow;" "a certain man had a fig tree planted in his vineyard; and he came and sought fruit thereon and found none;" "lift up your eyes and look on the fields; for they are white already to harvest;" "the wind bloweth where it listeth," — these and many other texts show that Christ was familiar with Nature, and loved to call upon her for illustration and example.

5. *It elevated the truth and sought to enforce it.* — Christ gave himself a sacrifice for the truth. He allowed no thought of personal safety or success to overshadow the truth. All his words, his acts, his teachings, aimed at establishing the truth. He overthrew old systems and introduced a new spirit into the world, even the spirit of truth. He was the very essence of truth, declaring to Thomas, "I am the way, the truth, and the life." He thus gave to teachers for all time a noble example and an immortal principle, vital to their success in true teaching. It is the *truth* that must be taught and practiced by every one worthy of the name of teacher.

6. *It was earnest and full of sympathy.* — The earnest-

ness of Christ aroused the populace to shout "Hosanna!" and provoked the bitter hostility of his enemies. It drew multitudes into the wilderness and attracted crowds wherever he went. His sympathy went out to the people as "sheep having no shepherd." It led him to feed the multitude, heal the sick, raise the dead, take little children in his arms and bless them, and weep over Jerusalem. He came close to the lives and hearts of those whom he instructed. This is one of the grandest lessons that the Great Teacher left for teachers of all time.

These are some of the chief characteristics of Christ's spirit and method. He loved little children, and taught his disciples, when he had set a little child in the midst of them, "Whosoever, therefore, shall humble himself as this little child, the same is greatest in the kingdom of heaven." Every one of the principles above stated is essential to the teacher, and these principles contain the sum and substance of all true pedagogy. Well has Karl Schmidt expressed the truth, when he says, "Christ, the perfect teacher, gave by his example and by his own teaching the eternal principles of pedagogy."

CHAPTER XV

GENERAL VIEW OF THE FIRST PERIOD OF CHRISTIAN EDUCATION

Literature. — *Allies*, Peter's Rock in Mohammed's Flood; *Newman*, Historical Essays.

THIS period covered the time from the birth of Christ till the Reformation. It included the early centuries of struggling Christianity, in which old customs had to be combated, and the new ideas, born with the coming of the Savior, and propagated by him and his followers, were slowly and surely to take possession of the world. These fifteen centuries embrace those generally known in history as the "Dark Ages," during which progress was indeed slow. But when we remember the obstacles which, as we have seen, were to be met, the prejudice to be set aside, the great changes inaugurated, and the limited means at command, we marvel at the great results attained. Let us now briefly examine some of the factors that are prominent in Christian education during its first period.

1. *The apostles and Church Fathers were foremost in all educational matters.* — These men were not simply spiritual leaders; they caught the spirit of the Master, and sought to instruct the head as well as the heart. They established schools and themselves became teachers, directed educational movements, formed courses of study, and by fostering education furthered the success and perpetuity of Christianity. Men like Paul, Origen, Chrysostom, Basil the Great, and Augustine did much

good, not only in building up the Church, but also in promoting education, the chief handmaid of the Church. Indeed, all educational progress during the early Christian centuries centers around the names of these men.

2. *The Church was the sponsor of the schools.* — During this long period the State had not yet assumed the obligation of educating her youth, and we find only rare instances of the State taking any part in the training of the young. No attempt at universal education was made, and none could be made, for the Church could not furnish the means to do it; consequently nearly all educational effort was directed to training the priesthood and providing for the perpetuity of the Church. The Church was the mother of the schools, and to her fostering care alone do we owe their establishment and maintenance during this long period. Her authority was supreme, and acknowledged by all temporal powers; hence the subjects studied in the schools and the persons chosen to share the benefits of education were such as would subserve the interests of the Church.

3. *The monasteries rendered valuable service to education.* — They were long the centers of learning, being the only places where schools existed. They were the repositories of valuable manuscripts, which were copied with marvelous diligence and preserved for future generations. The monasteries adopted courses of study which, however incomplete, were efficiently carried out, and formed the basis of future courses. The influence of the monasteries for many centuries was of great value to learning.

4. *The crusades brought new life into education.* — While the crusades were primarily religious movements, they were also educational in their results. They

infused new life into the stagnant conditions of Europe. They aroused the people to physical and mental, as well as religious, activity. They led to the establishment of schools and universities.

5. *The Teutonic peoples became an important instrument of progress.* — Rome began to decline, and the Teutons of the north, whom Rome had never been able to subjugate, became her conquerors. The Latin race had served a noble purpose in the world's history, but now another, perhaps stronger race, joined in the work of civilization. The physical and intellectual vigor of the various branches of the Teutonic family, — the German, the Anglo-Saxon, the Scandinavian, — which has won for them leadership in evangelization, in commerce, in conquest, and in educational enterprise, showed itself unmistakably during the period under discussion. These peoples now joined with the Latin peoples in assuming the ever increasing responsibilities of Christian civilization, and the interests of education were greatly enhanced and furthered through these combined influences.

These are the principal agencies to which were committed the most vital interests of humanity during the first fifteen centuries of the Christian era. We shall see that some grave errors were made, errors that blocked the path of improvement sometimes for centuries; we shall find that narrowness, bigotry, prejudice, and ignorance often hindered the introduction of truth because it did not coincide with tradition; we shall see how the Church assumed prerogatives that did not belong to her, especially in the field of scientific research, and thereby delayed human progress; nevertheless, we shall ever remain thankful to these agencies for the encouragement they gave to education, and for whatever good results they were instrumental in attaining.

CHAPTER XVI

THE FIRST CHRISTIAN SCHOOLS

Literature. — *White*, Eighteen Christian Centuries; *Durrell*, A New Life in Education; *Laurie*, Rise of Universities; *Lecky*, History of European Morals; *Allies*, The Formation of Christendom; *Azarias*, Philosophy of Literature; *Azarias*, Essays Philosophical.

WE have already seen that the early Christians were obliged to endure great hardships and surmount great difficulties in securing education for their children. Indeed, during the first two centuries almost all that was done was to train the converts in the rites and ceremonies of the Christian Church. But as they grew stronger in numbers, and as persecution diminished, they could give greater attention to education. Unwilling to make use of pagan schools, which could not satisfy their chief need — to prepare for the new religion — they gradually established their own.

Catechumen Schools. — The first Christian schools were *catechumen schools*. A *catechumen* was a person who desired instruction in the new faith with a view to baptism and admission into the Church. As many of the converts had been pagans, and as all were ignorant of the requirements of the Church as well as of the new doctrines, such instruction was absolutely necessary. Therefore the converts were divided into classes, at first two, later, four; and instruction was given them in the rudiments of Christianity. In the beginning the catechumen schools were for adults only, but afterward children were admitted, and reading and writing were taught. Previous to this change, if children received any secular instruction at all, it was given at their homes by parents or tutors, or in the pagan schools. At the close of the second century Protogenes established a school at Odessa, in which reading, writing, texts of Scripture, and singing of psalms were taught. This was the first *Christian common school*. Other schools followed rapidly as the persecutions ceased, until Rome became Christianized, and pagan schools gave place to Christian schools throughout the empire. Two great names are closely connected with this movement.

CHRYSOSTOM (347-407)

One of the greatest representatives of the early Christian Church interested in education was Chrysostom.[1] He was born at Antioch in Syria, and educated in the pagan schools, but the influence of his devout Christian mother kept him true to her faith. He was noted for his eloquence, hence the name by which he is known in history, for Chrysostom means *golden-mouthed*. John Malone says of him, "First of the great Christian preachers after the Church came from the caves, he was not less able as a teacher."[2] He became bishop of the Church, and was the greatest pedagogue of his time. Some of his educational principles may be stated as follows:—

1. As Christ lowered himself to man's estate in order to raise man to his estate, so the teacher must lower himself to the capacity of his pupils in order to elevate them.
2. Christ did not reveal everything to his disciples,

[1] Warner's "Library of the World's Best Literature," Vol. VI, 3665. Lord, "Beacon Lights," Vol. I, Lecture on Sacred Eloquence.

[2] Warner's Library, Vol. VI, 3666.

suggesting sometimes truths for them to discover; so the teacher must not do for his pupils what they can do for themselves.

3. The foundation of all true education is the Christian life and example; therefore teachers and parents must walk circumspectly before children.

4. Women, especially mothers, are the natural educators of children.

5. Religious instruction is an essential factor of the school work. It is of the highest importance that children should be brought up "in the nurture and admonition of the Lord."

BASIL THE GREAT (329–379)

Basil the Great was born at Caesarea. He studied at Constantinople and Athens, and sat at the feet of the greatest pagan philosophers and teachers of his time. He was not perverted by their teachings, but told them frankly that, though they possessed all learning, he had found something greater than this, and that was the Christ. Basil was one of the foremost Fathers of the Church, a great writer, and a promoter of education. He was very fond of classic literature, and, in face of the bitter opposition of many of the Church Fathers, urged its proper use in the schools. He was instrumental in founding monasteries, hospitals, orphanages, and refuges for the poor.

Pedagogical Teachings. — 1. Every misdeed should be punished in such a way that the punishment shall be an exercise in self-command and shall tend to correct the fault. For example, if a child has lied, used profane language, or been quarrelsome, give him solitude and fasting. If he is greedy and gluttonous, let him stand by and see others eat while he remains hungry.

2. Orphan children and those that are dependent should be taught in the cloister.

3. The Bible, with its stories, promises, history, and doctrines, should be the chief text-book.

4. Not only monks and priests should be allowed to teach, but also the laity.

5. Children while still young and innocent must be taught good habits and right precepts.

It is worthy of note that Chrysostom and Basil were the first to mark out definite lines of Christian instruction. During this period, also, the first songs of the Christian Church originated in the huts and caves of the poor. Thus in religious instruction and church song the foundations of the Christian common school were laid.

Catechetical Schools. — The principal catechetical school was established at Alexandria A.D. 181, by Pantaenus. Others were located later at Antioch, Odessa, and Nisibis. The Alexandrian school, however, was by far the most important. Alexandria, at the close of the second century, was the seat of philosophy, as Athens had formerly been. It possessed the most important library in the world, and students and sages from all parts of the world flocked to this place of learning. Laurie says, "The great Alexander, in founding Alexandria, connected Europe, Asia, and Africa, not merely by mercantile bonds, but in their intellectual and literary life. Here arose, under the Ptolemies, a complete system of higher instruction, and libraries such as the world had not before seen. The books were lodged in the temple of Serapis, and accumulated to the number of seven hundred thousand. They formed the record of all human thought, until they fell a prey to internal civic and religious dissensions. The Serapeum dates from B.C. 298, and, after recovering from the fire of B.C. 48, it finally disappeared about A.D. 640."

Under the stimulus of these surroundings, and with such an abundance of literary material at command, pagans and Christians vied with each other in their search for truth. But the pagans had better schools and better means of preparing themselves for intellectual combat. Christian teachers were called upon to defend their faith against subtle philosophers and trained thinkers, who had had the advantage of excellent schools. In order to meet this apparent defect and fortify themselves against their skillful opponents, the Christians established the catechetical school at Alexandria, the most celebrated school of its kind at that period. It took the name *catechetical* from the fact that the method of instruction was largely that of catechising, though lectures were also given. Many pagans had been converted to Christianity, and it was necessary that they should be taught the reason of their faith, in order that they might maintain their ground when they came in contact with unbelievers. This was particularly necessary, if Christianity was to hold its own, in a city like Alexandria, where so many learned men had gathered. It was also necessary for the extension of the new faith among men of superior intelligence. Thus the object of the catechetical school was to instruct learned men in the doctrines and usages of the Church, to prepare believers to meet the arguments of the philosophers, and to train teachers.

While it was a sort of theological school, it also taught philosophy, rhetoric, grammar, and geometry. From the nature of things it will be seen that the catechetical school was for adults only, and it may be called a kind of university, whose chief attention was given to the study of the Scriptures and the promulgation of religious doctrine. The catechetical school was much higher than the catechumen school in its course of study, and in the intelligence and learning of its students and professors.

CLEMENT OF ALEXANDRIA (150–220)

Among the most promising of the pupils of Pantaenus was Clement of Alexandria, who was his successor in the direction of the school. Clement was brought up a pagan, but was not satisfied with the heathen religion, and made a careful study of Christianity. He traveled everywhere, and sought out old men who had listened to the apostles, or whose parents had done so; and thus he hoped to learn the truth directly. As a result of his research, he became profoundly impressed with the purity of the morals of the Christians and the truth of their religion. He was a great teacher as well as Father of the Church.

His Pedagogy.— 1. Faith is the cornerstone of knowledge.

2. Mosaic law and heathen philosophy are not opposed to each other, but simply parts of the same truth. Both prepared the way for Christianity. Jewish law and Greek philosophy are steps in the development of the world which prepare the way for revelation. Christianity is the fulfillment of law and philosophy.

3. He brought all the speculations of the Christians and the culture of the Greeks to bear upon Christian truth, and sought to harmonize the two.

The teachings of Clement gain in importance when we remember the bitter strife in the Church over the use of classic literature, which lasted for centuries, and the scholastic movement a thousand years later, which also sought to harmonize philosophy and religion.

ORIGEN (186–253)

Origen was a pupil of Clement in the catechetical school at Alexandria, and became his successor. Besides being brought up in an atmosphere of culture in his native city, and surrounded by influences that stimulated intellectual growth, he was fortunate in having a man of learning for his father. From him he learned Greek, mathematics, grammar, rhetoric, logic, and a knowledge of the Holy Scriptures. He began to teach in the catechetical school when only eighteen years of age, a remarkable fact when one remembers that he had among his students learned pagan philosophers, and that it was very unusual for so young a man to be allowed to teach. He was abstemious in his habits, self-sacrificing, generous, and withal consistent in his life.

Origen's Pedagogy. — 1. Never teach pupils anything that you do not yourself practice.

2. The end of education is to grow into the likeness of God.

3. Pupils must be taught to investigate for themselves.

4. The teacher must seek to correct the bad habits of his pupils, as well as to give them intellectual instruction.

Under Origen, the catechetical school at Alexandria reached its highest prosperity, and its decay began soon after his death. Already in the middle of the fourth century its power and influence were practically gone.

None of the other catechetical schools ever reached the fame of that at Alexandria, and they, too, gradually disappeared. Indeed, as the Roman Empire became Christianized, and as Christians gained in education and intelligence, there was less and less occasion for the existence of schools of this character.

CHAPTER XVII

CONFLICT BETWEEN PAGAN AND CHRISTIAN EDUCATION

Literature.—*Lord*, Beacon Lights; *Spofford*, Library of Historical Characters; *White*, Eighteen Christian Centuries; *Fisher*, Beginnings of Christianity; *Azarias*, Essays Educational; *Allies*, The Formation of Christendom; *Allies*, The Monastic Life; *Maitland*, The Dark Ages.

GENERAL DISCUSSION

As Christianity became more powerful; as the Roman nation privately and officially accepted the new religion; as the bishops of the Church came more and more to be recognized as the vicegerents of Christ and the apostles; as the Church authorities became convinced that tolerance of paganism was dangerous to believers, and irreconcilable with the principles of Christianity,—as these things became apparent, it was seen that nothing would suffice short of the utter destruction of pagan schools. Pagan philosophy and art were tolerated only as they served the Church. Pagan education had an earthly purpose; the new education, a spiritual aim, a preparation for eternal life.

The pagan temples and schools preserved the spirit of paganism long after the Roman Empire had become Christian, and the leaders of Christianity finally became convinced that ultimate success would be reached only when these institutions were destroyed. The conflict between these two parties continued during the fifth century and until 529, when a complete victory was gained by the Christians. After 529 we have therefore only

Christian schools to consider. For the next thousand years education was entirely in the hands of the Church, whose power was not always exercised for the good of humanity, but often for the furtherance of her own ends. Still, it must not be forgotten that all that was done for education was done by her, and therefore the world owes her a debt of gratitude, as later pages will show. She did not undertake the education of the masses, a task that was beyond her power, and perhaps beyond the scope of her vision. Yet great honor is due the Church for what was accomplished in education during the Middle Ages, and to her alone must be given credit for an advancement in civilization by no means small, considering the difficulties to be met and the obstacles to be overcome. During this long period there were many bright spots in the educational firmament, many brilliant leaders of the Church who also were conspicuous educators, and many important movements toward higher civilization. An examination of this period has led recent historians to abandon the term "Dark Ages." A more careful study of some of these leaders and the movements that they inaugurated will be reserved to later pages.

We shall find the spirit of the period best illustrated by a study of two great men who are preëminent in the educational affairs of the time, — namely, Tertullian and St. Augustine.

TERTULLIAN (150–230)[1]

Tertullian was born at Carthage of pagan parents. He was converted to Christianity when forty years of age, and by his talent, his zeal for the new religion, and his faithfulness, he rose rapidly until he became Bishop of

[1] See Draper, "Conflict between Religion and Science," p. 59.

Carthage. He was an orator, a writer, and a teacher. His immoderate zeal led him into the vice of rigorism, quite foreign to the real spirit of the Christian religion. He joined the Montanists, a sect that believed in withdrawal from the world, the unlawfulness of second marriages, and the speedy second advent of the Savior. Having received a thorough training as a jurist at Rome, he became a great controversialist.

He was the founder of Christian Latin literature, being bitterly opposed to everything pagan. He would use nothing manufactured by the pagans, would not dress like them, nor have anything to do with their schools or writings. This of course excluded classic literature, and was in direct opposition to the teachings of the catechetical schools, especially that of Alexandria. Tertullian's attempt to create a literature for the schools which should take the place of classic literature, while it produced discord for centuries, and influenced other great men to follow his example, had no permanent result. Perhaps the downfall of paganism may have removed all danger to the Christians from pagan philosophy and letters; at all events it is certain that in later centuries the Church was most efficient in preserving them. Tertullian held that philosophy of whatever kind is dangerous, claiming that it makes man arrogant, and less inclined to faith.

In the fourth century the Fathers of the Church were opposed to pagan literature. The "Apostolic Constitutions" commanded, "Refrain from all writings of the heathen; for what hast thou to do with strange discourses, laws, or false prophets, which, in truth, turn aside from the faith those who are weak in understanding." It was urged that, "As the offspring of the pagan world, if not, indeed, inspired by demons, they were dangerous to the new faith." This introduced into education a narrow view, which evoked many bitter discussions, and which it took centuries to eradicate.

ST. AUGUSTINE (354-430)

Augustine was born in Numidia, Africa. His father was a pagan, and his mother a devout Christian. Augustine grew up in the faith of neither, and in his early years seems to have had no settled belief. As a student, he was wild and profligate, though attentive to his studies. He became thoroughly versed in Greek and Latin. He studied at Carthage and later at Milan. At the latter place he made the acquaintance of St. Ambrose, Bishop of Milan, who was instrumental in Augustine's conversion. His life was radically changed, and he who had been the wild, careless unbeliever became the greatest of the Church Fathers. Like Tertullian, he condemned the very classic literature to which he was indebted for his intellectual greatness. His greatest literary works are "City of God" and "Confessions."

"Confessions." — In this work are found his chief pedagogical teachings. Karl Schmidt says, "In his 'Confessions' he develops a complete psychology of the human soul, from which the pedagogue can learn more than from many theories of education."

This work shows step by step his own development from childhood to mature manhood, — how a word, a look, an act may awaken passions, and lead to evil desire, or stimulate to noble deed or self-sacrificing consecration. From his own life and experiences he portrays the whole nature of man. Augustine is called the "St. Paul of the fifth century," and he certainly was the greatest man, since Paul, that the Church has produced. In his writings is found the most luminous exposition of the Catholic doctrine, and probably Augustine is the most noted of all Catholic Fathers. In the domain of theology and morals he based all teaching on authority rather than on investigation, yet the excessive application of this principle to subjects of physical science was destined later on to hinder investigators in the fields of scientific research. Draper says, "Augustine antagonized science and Christianity for more than fifteen centuries." This was doubtless due to the application of the principle of authority in fields that Augustine did not contemplate. But we shall have occasion to recur to this subject in later pages.

Augustine's Pedagogy. — 1. All teaching is based on faith and authority.

2. All pagan literature must be excluded from the schools.

3. The chief subject in the school course is history pursued in the narrative form.

4. Make abundant use of observation in instruction.

5. The teacher must be earnest and enthusiastic.

While the Roman Empire became officially Christian in the fourth century under Constantine, it was not until Justinian decreed the abolition of pagan schools and temples, A.D. 529, that paganism, as we have seen, was finally destroyed. Thus the long conflict was ended, and henceforth we have to do only with Christian education. We now enter upon the thousand years of the world's history known as the Middle Ages, the close of which brings us to the Reformation.

CHAPTER XVIII

MONASTIC EDUCATION

Literature.—*Lord*, Beacon Lights; *Lecky*, History of European Morals; *Myers*, Mediaeval and Modern History; *White*, Eighteen Christian Centuries; *Harper*, Book of Facts; *Mrs. Jameson*, Legends of Monastic Orders; *Gasquet*, Henry VIII. and the English Monasteries; *Châteaubriand*, The Genius of Christianity; *Allies*, The Monastic Life; *Taunton*, The English Black Monks of St. Benedict.

Monasteries.—Monasteries were established as early as the third century A.D.; but it was not until the sixth century that they became powerful. The spirit of asceticism, urged by the Church as one of the most important virtues, took a strong hold upon the people, and led many to withdraw from the world. For such the founding of monasteries became a necessity. The monasteries were the result of the ascetic spirit, and their teaching was based upon authority and not upon free investigation or original research. Thus there was introduced into society and education a principle that, wrongly interpreted, impeded progress for a thousand years.

Most of the time during this period the Church held supremacy over the State with authority unquestioned. This authority was carried not only into spiritual matters, but also into social, political, and educational affairs. Everything that conflicted with that authority, or with the decrees of the Church, was condemned. Even scientific discoveries that did not harmonize with preconceived and accepted theories were reluctantly received, if not absolutely rejected. Discoverers in the realm of science were silenced, and sometimes actually punished, for promulgating theories contrary to the teachings of the Church. A notable example is that of Galileo, who taught the Copernican theory of the universe, and for which teaching he was condemned to imprisonment and a ban put upon his work. This exaggerated interpretation of authority worked harm to the Church. It seemed to be forgotten that the Bible is a book of religion and morals and not a text-book of science.

The Benedictines. — The most important monastic order from the standpoint of education was that of the Benedictines. St. Benedict founded the first monastery of the order that bears his name — Monte Cassino, near Naples, — in 529. It will be remembered that this is the date of the abolition of pagan schools by Justinian. On the site of Monte Cassino had stood a pagan school. The monastery which supplanted it remains to the present day.

Benedict's two important principles — to which cloisters hitherto had been unaccustomed — were industry and strict discipline. These principles made the Benedictine the most successful and beneficent of all monastic orders. It grew rapidly, and within one hundred years from its foundation there were more than two hundred and fifty Benedictine monasteries. It is claimed that the order has produced 4600 bishops, 1600 archbishops, 200 cardinals, 40 popes, 50 patriarchs, 4 emperors, 12 empresses, 46 kings, 41 queens, 3600 canonized saints, and 15,700 authors, and that prior to the French Revolution it possessed 37,000 cloisters. There have been times when the wealth of this order in some states comprised more than half of all the property. The Benedictine monks tilled the soil of the country surrounding their monasteries, literally making the "desert blossom as the rose." They were untiring in zeal for the Church and in deeds of mercy. They established cloister schools in Italy, France, Spain, England, Ireland, Germany, and Switzerland. Monte Cassino (529), Italy; Canterbury (586) and Oxford (ninth century), England; St. Gall (613), Switzerland; Fulda (744), Constance, Hamburg, and Cologne (tenth century), Germany; Lyons, Tours, Paris, and Rouen (tenth century), France; Salzburg (696), Austria; and many other schools were founded chiefly by the Benedictines. Among the many great teachers that they produced were Alcuin of England, Boniface of Germany, Thomas Aquinas, Duns Scotus, and Abelard. It thus appears that the Benedictine order took a deep interest in education, and their work deserves a most honorable place among the educational agencies of the period under discussion.

The Seven Liberal Arts. — We have seen that much attention was always given to religious instruction in the Christian schools. The Bible, the doctrines of the Church, and its rites and ceremonies were at first exclusively taught. But later secular branches were introduced. These secular branches were known as the seven liberal arts, which comprised the following subjects: —

The Seven Liberal Arts.
- I. Trivium[1] . . .
  - 1. Grammar. { Reading and Writing.
  - 2. Rhetoric.
  - 3. Logic.
- II. Quadrivium[1] . .
  - 1. Arithmetic.
  - 2. Music.
  - 3. Geometry.
  - 4. Astronomy.

This course required seven years. Latin was the only language used, and consequently the native tongues suf-

[1] Laurie thinks that these names were first appropriately used about the end of the fourth century.

fered. The *trivium* was the most popular course; such knowledge was considered an absolute necessity for any one making claim to culture. After completing the *trivium*, those who wished for higher culture studied the *quadrivium*.

Under the term *grammar* were included reading and writing, as well as the construction and use of language. In *rhetoric* the works of Quintilian and Cicero were studied, and sermons delivered in the churches were made to serve for a practical application of the rules. In *logic* the works of St. Augustine were used in the exercises of constructing syllogisms, of disputation, and of definition. In *arithmetic*, before the introduction of the Arabic notation, numbers were considered to have a mysterious meaning. The hands and fingers were used to indicate numbers. For example, the left hand upon the breast indicated ten thousand; both hands folded, one hundred thousand. For the practical purposes of life the reckoning board was used. This was a board with lines drawn upon it, between which pebbles were placed to indicate the number to be expressed. For example, the number 3146 would be indicated as follows:—

3	1	4	6
///	/	////	//////

Music was designed for the church service. Knowledge of music was held to be positively essential to priest and teacher. Under the term *music* were also sometimes included the fine arts, painting, drawing, architecture, sculpture, etc.

In *geometry* Euclid was used. Lines, angles, surfaces, and solids were studied. With geometry there seems to have been connected a meager study of *geography*. Early maps have been found, one dating from the seventh century, being in possession of St. Gall monastery. *Astronomy* was closely connected with *astrology*. Its practical application was limited to the formation of the Church calendar, fixing the date of Easter, etc.

This celebrated course of study formed the basis of secular instruction in the monasteries, and, indeed, in all schools, for several centuries. Religious instruction always remained a prominent feature of the work. History had no place in the curriculum.

Summary of Benefits conferred upon Civilization by the Monasteries. — 1. They preserved classic literature. Though many of the Church Fathers, as we have seen, were bitterly opposed to pagan literature, the monasteries copied it with great industry and preserved it with care. The archives of these institutions have yielded up some most remarkable and valuable manuscripts that otherwise would have been lost to the world.

2. They kept alive the flickering flame of Christianity. The Middle Ages were indeed dark for Christianity, as unbelief, ignorance, and faithlessness prevailed. But the monasteries were centers of religious interest and zeal.

3. They maintained educational interest during this long, dark period. We have seen that the monasteries contained the only schools. Through them the Church kept up whatever educational interest survived during the Middle Ages, and her work then conserved the energies employed in later educational enterprise.

4. They originated a great course of study by giving to the world the seven liberal arts.

5. They furnished places of refuge for the oppressed.

CHAPTER XIX

SCHOLASTICISM

Literature.—*Fisher*, History of the Reformation; *Lord*, Beacon Lights; *Thalheimer*, Mediaeval and Modern History; *Schwegler*, History of Philosophy; *Seebohm*, Era of the Protestant Revolution; *Hegel*, Philosophy of History; *Azarias*, Philosophy of Literature; *Azarias*, Essays Philosophical; *Schwickerath*, Jesuit Education, its History and Principles.

COMPAYRÉ remarks, "It has been truly said that there were three Renascences: the first, which owed its beginning to Charlemagne, and whose brilliancy did not last; the second, that of the twelfth century, the issue of which was Scholasticism; and the third, the great Renaissance of the sixteenth century, which still lasts, and which the French Revolution has completed."[1]

As scholasticism, in a sense, was the rival of monasticism, and as it covered a large part of the Middle Ages, we shall discuss it at this point. Scholasticism was a movement having for its object the harmonizing of ancient philosophy, especially that of Aristotle, with the doctrines of Christianity. It covered a period reaching from the ninth to the fifteenth century, and displayed its greatest activity between the eleventh and thirteenth centuries. It is called the philosophy of the Middle Ages. The term *scholastic* is also applied generally to forms of reasoning which abound in subtleties. Scholasticism was a dissent from the teachings of St. Augustine and the ascetics. It laid chief stress upon *reason* instead of *authority*,

[1] "History of Pedagogy," p. 71.

thus asserting a vitally different principle, which would tend to change the whole spirit of education.

The first prominent leader of this movement was Erigena, who lived during the ninth century, and was the most interesting writer of the Middle Ages. He was also a great teacher, and was called to give instruction at the court of Charles the Bald, and afterward at Oxford. He opposed the prevailing tendencies of the monasteries to base all teaching on authority, and made its foundation philosophy and reason. Schwegler[1] denominates Anselm (born about 1033) as "the beginner and founder of scholasticism." Thus it was not till the eleventh century "that there was developed anything that might be properly termed a Christian philosophy. This was the so-called scholasticism."[2]

Greater than either of these was Abelard (born 1079), who by his eloquence attracted great numbers of students to Paris. It is said that "few teachers ever held such sway as did Abelard for a time." He made Paris the center of the scholastic movement, attracting students from all parts of the world. He did more than any of his predecessors to give accepted ecclesiastical doctrines a rational expression. Scholasticism influenced the establishment of institutions of learning in England, Germany, Italy, and Spain, some of which later developed into great universities. Thomas Aquinas, Duns Scotus, and Occam may also be mentioned as great schoolmen. Of the first two Schwegler says,[3] "At the summit of scholasticism we must place the two incontestably greatest masters of the scholastic art and method, *Thomas Aquinas* (Dominican, 1225–1274) and *Duns Scotus* (Franciscan, 1265–1308), the founders of two schools, into which after them the whole scholastic theology divides itself,—the former exalting the

[1] "History of Philosophy," p. 186. [2] *Ibid.*, p. 185. [3] *Ibid.*, p. 186.

understanding (*intellectus*), and the latter the will (*voluntas*), as the highest principle, both being driven into essentially differing directions by this opposition of the theoretical and practical. Even with this began the downfall of scholasticism; its highest point was also the turning point to its self-destruction. The rationality of the dogmas, the oneness of faith and knowledge, had been constantly their fundamental premise; but this premise fell away, and the whole basis of their metaphysics was given up in principle the moment Duns Scotus placed the problem of theology in the practical. When the practical and the theoretical became divided, and still more when thought and being were separated by nominalism, philosophy broke loose from theology and knowledge from faith. Knowledge assumed its position above faith and above authority, and the religious consciousness broke with the traditional dogma."

Toward the end, another thing contributed to the downfall of scholasticism. The philosophical subtleties of discussion made the schoolmen lose sight of the main issue, and devote themselves to the most ridiculous questions.[1] Schwickerath remarks,[2] "It can not and need not be denied that the education imparted by the mediaeval scholastics was in many regards defective. It was at once too dogmatic and disputatious. Literary studies were comparatively neglected; frequently too much importance was attached to purely dialectical subtleties. . . . The defects of scholasticism became especially manifest in the course of the fourteenth and fifteenth centuries, when much time and energy were wasted in discussing useless refinements of thought." That it did a great deal of good will appear from the following summary: —

Summary of the Benefits of Scholasticism. — 1. It at-

[1] See K. Schmidt, "Geschichte der Pädagogik," Vol. II, p. 265, for subjects of these discussions. [2] "Jesuit Education," p. 46.

tempted to harmonize philosophy with Christianity, and may be called the first Christian philosophy.

2. It sought to base learning on reason and investigation, rather than on authority. In this we find the first impulse of that movement which later led to the founding of science.

3. Many universities were established through the scholastic influence, notably, Paris, Heidelberg, Bologna, Prague, and Vienna.

4. While it failed to establish them, it at least recognized the desirableness of a universal language for schools, and a universal church for man.

5. Although, with the exception of the universities which it founded, its direct work in education cannot be said to have been permanent, yet it imparted fresh vigor to educational endeavors.

6. Schwegler says,[1] "It . . . introduced to the world another principle than that of the old Church, the principle of the thinking spirit, the self-consciousness of the reason, or at least prepared the way for the victory of this principle. Even the deformities and unfavorable side of scholasticism, the many absurd questions upon which the scholastics divided, even their thousandfold unnecessary and accidental distinctions, their inquisitiveness and subtleties, all sprang from a rational principle, and grew out of a spirit of investigation, which could only utter itself in this way under the all-powerful ecclesiastical spirit of the time."

[1] "History of Philosophy," p. 189.

CHAPTER XX

CHARLEMAGNE

Literature. — *Ferris*, Great Leaders; *Emerton*, Introduction to the Middle Ages; *Guizot*, History of Civilization; *Wells*, The Age of Charlemagne; *Bryce*, The Holy Roman Empire; *Church*, The Beginning of the Middle Ages; *Lord*, Beacon Lights; *White*, Eighteen Christian Centuries; *Laurie*, Rise of the Universities; *Bulfinch*, Legends of Charlemagne; Encyclopaedia Britannica, Article on Charlemagne.

History, Character, and Purpose. — Charlemagne was not only the greatest ruler of the Middle Ages, but one of the greatest and wisest rulers the world has known. By birth and instinct he belonged to the Teutonic race, to which, as before stated, the world's enlightenment has been committed. Like Alexander the Great, Charlemagne united many peoples into one, until he ruled over the territory now included in France, Germany, parts of England, Austria, and Italy, — in fact, his empire comprised the richest part of central Europe. He designed to rebuild the Roman Empire, and was crowned "Emperor of Rome" by the Pope, in the year 800. While he protected the Pope and was loyal to him, he did not admit the papal supremacy in matters of State.

Two very important influences were wisely utilized by Charlemagne in his work of civilization, namely, the political ideas of the Teutons, and the adhering power of the Christian church. He cherished German customs, and left, in various parts of Germany, many monuments of his love for that people. He was of commanding presence, being seven feet in height, and of good proportions, blond in type, and of genial manners. His real capital was at Aix-la-Chapelle, but Rome was a nominal capital. Bulfinch says of Charlemagne: "Whether we regard him as a warrior or legislator, as a patron of learning or as the civilizer of a barbarous nation, he is entitled to our warmest admiration." If his successors had possessed the ability, enterprise, and breadth of view that characterized him, the world might never have known the period in history commonly called the "Dark Ages."

Personal Education. —When Charlemagne arrived at the estate of manhood and ascended the throne, he was ignorant of letters and lacked any considerable intellectual training. His education had been that of the knight who believed that skill in the use of arms and physical prowess were of far more importance than a knowledge of letters.[1] After he had come to the throne, and especially after he had conquered his foes and had leisure to study the welfare of his people, he realized his deficiencies, and sought to overcome them by diligent study.

He called to his court the most learned men of the world, received personal instruction from them, and had them read to him and converse with him while at his meals. In this way he overcame, in a measure, the defects of his early education. He thoroughly mastered Latin, became familiar with Greek, and learned also grammar, rhetoric, logic, music, astronomy, and natural history. He never learned to write well, owing to the late period of life at which he began, and to the clumsiness of the hand accustomed to wielding the sword rather than the pen.

[1] See "Feudal Education," Chap. XXII.

Among his instructors was *Alcuin of England*, the most celebrated teacher of his time. Charlemagne established the "School of the Palace," and placed Alcuin at its head. Here the children of the emperor as well as his courtiers were taught. He had his own daughters learn Latin and Greek. France is indebted to Alcuin for its polite learning. Alcuin was also the counselor of the emperor in the educational matters of the empire, and it was probably his influence that led Charlemagne to adopt such broad views concerning the culture of his people.

General Education. — We have seen that the prevailing idea was that education should subserve the interests of the Church. Charlemagne turned the current of thought toward the national idea. He believed in religious training, but wanted to found a great State, and therefore insisted that those things which encouraged intelligent patriotism should be taught. He protected the Church, but insisted that the Church was subordinate to the State, and that his will was law over both. Consequently he required priests to preach in the native tongues rather than in Latin, and decreed that monasteries that would not open their doors to children for school purposes should be closed. The priests, he insisted, should be able to read and write, should have a knowledge of the Holy Scriptures and of the chief doctrines of the Church, and should instruct the people in these things.

The seven liberal arts formed the basis of school instruction. Monks were not to remain in idleness and ignorance, but were required to teach, not only in the monasteries, but also outside of them. He also encouraged education among his nobles, and plainly intimated that merit and not noble birth would entitle them to favor. Charlemagne visited the schools himself, and required the bishop to report to him their condition. He thus became a superintendent of schools, being as familiar with the educational interests of his kingdom as he was with every other interest. He sought to teach first the priests and nobles, and after that the masses of his people. He introduced the practice of *compulsory education* for all children, and decreed that truant children be first deprived of food as punishment, and if that did not suffice, that they be brought before him.

Reading, writing, arithmetic, and singing were taught, especial attention being given to music, which was of use in the church services. The Apostles' Creed and the Lord's Prayer were also taught. In 801 Charlemagne decreed that women and children should receive instruction in the doctrines of religion, because he believed religion to be the foundation of a civilized nation.

Charlemagne's career shines out in brilliant contrast with the ignorance and superstition of his age. The world was not yet ripe for his advanced ideas, hence when the work lost the support of his strong personality, its effects soon became obliterated, and a retrogression of civilization resulted.

The clergy, who had entertained but little sympathy for the enterprises of the emperor, soon closed the monasteries to outside students, and returned to the same practices from which the authority and energy of Charlemagne had aroused them. His work was not wholly in vain, however, for he laid the foundations of the Prussian school system.[1]

Summary of Charlemagne's Work. — 1. He elevated the clergy by demanding greater educational qualifications of them and by insisting that they do their duty.

[1] Professor Masius, Lectures in the University of Leipsic.

2. He gave dignity to native tongues by requiring the priests to preach more frequently in the vernacular of the people, and thus helped to make the services of the Church of greater profit to the people.

3. He opened the cloisters to the purposes of education, and thereby greatly extended their usefulness.

4. He sought to perpetuate religion and insure the stability of his empire by making education compulsory and universal.

5. He believed in the education of women.

6. He laid the foundations of future school systems, and indicated certain principles that are still recognized as valid.

CHAPTER XXI

ALFRED THE GREAT

Literature. — *Ferris*, Great Leaders; *Lord*, Beacon Lights; *Mombert*, Great Lives; *Spofford*, Library of Historical Characters; *Green*, History of the English People.

History and Character. — Alfred became king of the West Saxons in 871 at the age of twenty-three. As a boy he had already shown remarkable energy and ability, and as a man he more than fulfilled the promise of his early years. England was divided into several kingdoms, the Danes having taken possession of the eastern part of the island. Alfred carried on war against them for many years with varying success, until he made peace by skillful diplomacy in giving them territory. He afterward showed remarkable statesmanship in winning them to peaceful acquiescence in his sovereignty, and thus he came to rule over united England.

He laid the foundation of England's naval greatness by building ships to defend the country against Danish pirates. Many stories are told of his simplicity, his perseverance, his strategy in defeating his enemies, and the love with which he inspired his people. Karl Schmidt says, "Alfred, as victor in fifty-six battles, as lawgiver, as king and sage, as Christian and man, as husband and father, is rightly called — 'The Great.'"

He was very methodical in his habits, and divided his

day into three equal parts of eight hours each: eight hours he gave to government, eight hours to religious devotion and study, and the other eight hours to sleep, recreation, and the recuperation of his body.

Education. — Alfred did not learn to read until twelve years of age. His mother then stimulated him by the promise of a book to that one of her sons who should first commit to memory a Saxon poem. With indomitable energy he mastered reading, learned the poem, and secured the prize. Throughout his life he gave much attention to literary matters. He translated many portions of the Bible, as well as other books, into Anglo-Saxon, and encouraged literary efforts in others.

Without doubt the intellectual activity of Charlemagne acted as a spur to Alfred's personal ambition and to his desire to elevate his people. Although he did not follow the example of Charlemagne in seeking universal education for his people, he did urge that the children of every freeman should be able to read and write, and should have instruction in Latin. The distinction thus made in the purposes of these two great rulers has been perpetuated till the present time, the Germans encouraging universal education, while the English have attended chiefly to the education of the higher classes. Alfred established many monasteries and made them centers of learning. It seems clear that he assisted in laying the foundations from which Oxford University grew. He left his impress upon the English people as no other ruler has done, implanting love for law, justice, freedom, national honor, and the domestic virtues which characterize that nation. His influence is felt upon English institutions to this day.

CHAPTER XXII

FEUDAL EDUCATION

Literature. — *Stillé*, Studies in Mediaeval History; *Bulfinch*, Legends of Charlemagne; *Emerton*, Mediaeval Europe.

EMERTON defines feudalism as "an organization of society based upon the absence of a strong controlling power at the center of the State."[1] It marks a step in the reorganization of society which was slowly going forward during the Middle Ages. It was an element in the movement toward freedom, in which men of large landed possessions gained the allegiance of vassals by gifts of land, in return for which the latter bound themselves to defend the former in case of attack. "The tie by which the higher freeman bound the lower one to himself was ordinarily a gift of the use of a certain tract of land, together with more or less extensive rights of jurisdiction over the dwellers thereon. By means of this gift he secured the service of the lesser man in war, and as war was the normal condition of things, such service was the most valuable payment he could receive."[2]

While it is true that the feudal lords were in many cases little else than robber chieftains, especially in the earlier history of the system, it would be false to history to picture them in general as being of that character. The

[1] "Mediaeval Europe," p. 478. [2] *Ibid.*, p. 480.

knights were chivalrous in battle, ever ready to fight for their religion, as shown in the crusades, to defend the weak, to show greatest respect for woman, and to maintain freedom. Fortified in an impregnable castle on some eminence, with his loyal retainers about him, the feudal baron was able to defy kings. The system marks a stage in the development of civilization, and when feudalism fell into decline its purpose had been fulfilled.

With such an independent manner of living, and such ideas of their own rights, it is not strange that the knights had a form of education peculiar to themselves, and this education is full of interest to the student. There was little in the schooling of the monasteries that could appeal to them, and their ideas of manhood were very different from those of the ecclesiastics. Prowess in the use of arms, skill in horsemanship, acquaintance with the chivalric forms of politeness and with knightly manners, were of far more importance to them than ability to read and write. Indeed, they despised book-learning as something beneath their own dignity, however suitable it might be for their vassals. In such a school as this Charlemagne grew up. It was a school of action rather than of thought; a school which looked to the present rather than the future.

The education of the knights was in striking contrast with the prevailing modes. Instead of the seven liberal arts, the seven perfections of the knight were taught,—horsemanship, swimming, use of bow and arrow, swordsmanship, hunting, chess-playing, and verse-making. Their purpose was to prepare for the activities of the life in which their lot was cast; that of the monasteries was to preserve learning to fit men for the duties of the Church, and to prepare them for the life to come. It must not be inferred, however, that the knight was unmindful of religion, for he was inducted into knighthood by most solemn religious ceremonies and vows.

The education of the knight was divided into three periods.

First Period. — The first seven years of the boy's life were spent in the home under the mother's careful direction. Obedience, politeness, and respect for older persons were inculcated, and stress was also laid upon religious training. By the development of strong and healthy bodies the boys were well prepared for the later education upon which they entered after the seventh year.

Second Period. — After the seventh year the boy was generally removed from home to the care of some friendly knight, in order that he might receive a stricter training. Here he remained till his fourteenth year, chiefly under the care of the lady whom he served as page. He was taught music, poetry, chess, and some simple intellectual studies, besides the duties of knighthood, especially in relation to the treatment of women, and to courtly manners.

Third Period. — At fourteen the boy left the service of his lady and became an esquire to the knight. He now attended his master upon the chase, at tournaments, and in battle. He was taught all the arts of war, of riding, jousting, fencing. It was necessary that he should have a watchful eye to avert danger, protect his master, and quickly anticipate his every wish. The service of this period completed his education, and at twenty-one he was knighted with imposing ceremonies. After partaking of the sacrament, he took vows to *speak the truth, defend the weak, honor womanhood, and use his sword for the defense of Christianity.*

This form of education was most potent in preserving knighthood for several centuries and was a powerful factor in shaping the destinies of Europe. It was faithfulness to the vow *to defend Christianity* that led finally to the overthrow of chivalry, as will appear in the study of the crusades.

Education of Women. — The girls remained at home and were taught the domestic arts, as well as the forms of etiquette which were practiced in this chivalric age, and which the peculiar homage paid to woman made necessary. They were also taught reading and writing, and were expected to be familiar with poetry. Daughters of the better families were sometimes collected in some castle, where a kind of school was organized, in which they were instructed in reading, writing, poetry, singing, and the use of stringed instruments, religion, and sometimes in French and Latin. Among no other class during the Middle Ages was such great attention paid to the education of women. It was the duty of mothers to see that their daughters were carefully prepared to sustain the peculiar dignity of feudal womanhood.

Criticism of Feudal Education. — 1. It honored woman and gave her the highest position afforded by any system during the Middle Ages.

2. It gave the world a splendid example of chivalry, teaching manliness, courage, devotion to the right as it was understood, and the espousal of the cause of the weak.

3. It contributed to literature through the compositions of the *Minnesingers*.

4. It counteracted the ascetic tendencies of the monastics by encouraging an active participation in life's affairs.

5. It restricted its advantages to the privileged class.

6. It despised intellectual training, while laying great stress upon physical prowess.

7. It lacked the elements of progress.

CHAPTER XXIII

THE CRUSADES AS AN EDUCATIONAL MOVEMENT

Literature.—*Michaud,* The Crusades; *Stubbs,* Mediaeval and Modern History; *Mombert,* Great Lives (see Godfrey); *Myers,* Mediaeval and Modern History; *Guizot,* History of Civilization; *Lord,* Beacon Lights; *Archer and Kingsford,* The Crusaders; *White,* Eighteen Christian Centuries; *Andrews,* Institutes of General History; *Ridpath,* Library of Universal History (article on the Crusades).

AMONG the most remarkable movements that took place during the Middle Ages were the crusades. The Saracens had overrun and conquered the Holy Land, and the Christian nations of the west attempted to recover from the hands of the infidels the soil made sacred by the life and death of Christ. For a long time the pilgrims who made journeys to the tomb of the Savior were undisturbed, as their pilgrimages were a source of profit to the Saracens. But when the Turks gained possession of Jerusalem, they began to persecute both the native Christians and those who came from abroad. Peter the Hermit, who had suffered from these cruelties at Jerusalem, returned to Europe, and by his crude eloquence and earnestness stirred the people almost to a frenzy. Obtaining the sanction of the Pope, he gathered an immense crowd of men, women, and children, and started for the Holy Land.

They encountered great hardships, many died of hunger, disease, and the hostility of the people through whose countries they passed, and the remnant who reached the Bosporus, were totally destroyed by Turkish soldiers.

The first successful crusade was organized by the feudal lords, who gathered an army of six hundred thousand men under the leadership of Godfrey of Bouillon. They had connected with their army one hundred thousand splendidly mounted men. After untold losses and horrors, which reduced their forces to sixty thousand men, they succeeded in taking Jerusalem. They established a Latin kingdom with Godfrey at the head, and thus accomplished the purpose for which they had set out. This crusade lasted from 1096 to 1099.

For about fifty years the Latin kingdom held its own; but it was constantly harassed by the Mohammedans, until it became necessary to organize a second crusade. The leaders in this were Conrad III. of Germany and Louis VII. of France. Jealousies soon arose between the rival leaders, who cared more for personal glory than for the purpose of the crusade. As a result, only a small portion of the three hundred thousand soldiers ever reached the Holy Land; and this crusade, which lasted from 1147 to 1149, resulted in failure.

Forty years later Saladin, a Mohammedan ruler, having captured Jerusalem, a third crusade was organized. This was led by Richard the Lion-Hearted of England, Frederick Barbarossa of Germany, and Philip Augustus of France. Barbarossa went overland, but Richard and Philip, profiting by past experiences, made the journey by water, thus accomplishing it with greater ease and fewer losses. The rivalries between the different nationalities engaged prevented successful warfare; but a truce was made with the humane Saladin,[1] whereby he guaranteed protection to the Christians, and thus the crusade came to an end. This crusade lasted from 1189 to 1192.

[1] See Lessing's "Nathan der Weise."

Other crusades followed from time to time for several centuries, with but little advantage gained over the conditions granted by Saladin.

Results of the Crusades.—This, in brief, is a historical account of the crusades.[1] It remains for us to note their educational value.

1. They drew various nations together by one common purpose.

2. They increased the knowledge of the manners, customs, culture, products, and civilization of the East.

3. They stirred up commerce, especially that of the Mediterranean, making Venice and Genoa great commercial centers.

4. They broke up the power of feudalism. Lord and vassal together entered upon enterprises of danger and suffering, which were great levelers of class distinction. In the enthusiasm of the holy cause, many feudal lords disposed of all their worldly possessions, and became as poor as their vassals. This broke up the feudal estates.

5. They widened the horizon of thought, made Europeans more liberal, and prepared the way for an intellectual and religious revival.

6. They emancipated philosophy from theology. As a result of movements inaugurated by the crusades, the university of Paris established the faculty of philosophy separate from that of theology.

7. G. W. Cox says, "By rolling back the tide of Mohammedan conquest from Constantinople for upward of four centuries they probably saved Europe from horrors the recital of which might even now make one's ears tingle."

[1] It would be impossible to give a full historical account of the crusades in a work of this kind. The reader is referred to any standard work on that subject.

CHAPTER XXIV

THE RISE OF THE UNIVERSITIES

Literature. — *Laurie*, Rise of the Universities; *Hallam*, Middle Ages; *Guizot*, History of Civilization; *Paulsen*, The German Universities; *Hurst*, Life and Literature in the Fatherland; *Brother Azarias*, Essays Educational.

WE have seen that the Church had almost entire control of education during the Middle Ages. Through her influence schools were established and maintained, learning was preserved, and the interests of civilization were promoted. She was also influential in the founding of universities, though not to her alone were these institutions due. Laurie says: —

"Now looking first to the germ out of which the universities grew, I think we must say that the universities may be regarded as a natural development of the cathedral[1] and monastery schools; but if we seek for an external motive force urging men to undertake the more profound and independent study of the liberal arts, we

[1] The cathedral schools were institutions connected with each cathedral for the purpose of training priests for their sacred office, but they were not limited entirely to priests. Instructions in the seven liberal arts was imparted, and also in religion. Parochial schools were established in many places for the purpose of training children in the doctrines of the Church. Thus, as early as the ninth century, the Church sought to extend the benefits of education to the people as well as to the priesthood. While the parochial schools were limited in their instruction, somewhat after the manner of the early catechumen schools, the changed conditions of Christianity permitted a much broader training than formerly.

can find it only in the Saracenic schools of Bagdad, Babylon, Alexandria, and Cordova. The Saracens were necessarily brought into contact with Greek literature, just when the western Church was drifting away from it; and by their translations of Hippocrates, Galen, Aristotle, and other Greek classics, they restored what may be quite accurately called the 'university life' of the Greeks."

The first universities, however, can hardly be said to have been inspired by the influence of the Church. Nor did the State assist in their establishment, though it afterward sanctioned them, and conferred upon them their peculiar privileges. The first universities grew out of organizations of scholars and students who joined themselves together for the purpose of study and investigation. The oldest institution of this kind was that of Salerno, Italy, which Laurie says was a "public school from A.D. 1060, and a privileged school from 1100." It taught medicine only, and was established by a converted Jew. It was entirely independent of both Church and State, and attracted students from many countries.

The next university was that of Bologna, Italy. It also had only one faculty, that of law. In 1158 Frederick I. recognized the institution by giving it certain privileges. It awakened widespread interest throughout Europe, so that by the end of the twelfth century it is estimated that twelve thousand students had flocked to Bologna, most of them from foreign lands. This is an indication that the revival of learning was quite general throughout the world.

But the greatest university of the Middle Ages was that of Paris, which attracted at least twenty thousand students. The university of Paris was evolved from a cathedral school, and it always retained a strong theological tendency. Philip Augustus gave it privileges as a corporation, and Pope Innocent III. recognized it as a high school of theology. The course of study was by no means narrow, as it was held that broad knowledge was essential as a preparation for theological study. Consequently it was not long before a philosophical faculty[1]—the first in history—was added as separate from the theological faculty. The greatest name connected with the university of Paris is that of Abelard. Early in the twelfth century he attracted great numbers of students, and it was his personality that made Paris the greatest university of the Middle Ages.

The university of Oxford, England, was founded in 1140,[2] that of Cambridge in 1200. The oldest German university is Prague, founded in 1348. Then follow: Vienna, 1365; Heidelberg, 1386; Cologne,[3] 1388; Erfurt,[3] 1392; Würzburg, 1403; Leipsic, 1409; Rostock, 1419; Greifswald, 1456; Freiburg-im-Breisgau, 1457; Trier, 1472; Tübingen, 1477; and Mainz, 1477. In France, after Paris, Toulouse, 1233; Orleans, Cahors, Caen, Poitiers, Nantes, and others during the fourteenth century. In the same century at Lund and Upsala in Sweden, Christiania in Norway, and Copenhagen in Denmark. Italy, Spain, England, Ireland, and Scotland also felt this wonderful impulse. These universities were usually modeled after that of Paris.

The European universities were early granted certain

[1] The complete university has four faculties, which embrace all human knowledge. The historical order of precedence is as follows: *Theology* (1259–60), *Law* (1271), *Medicine* (1274), and *Arts* or *Philosophy* (1281). The last includes all subjects not embraced in the first three. Thus all branches of science, history, language, mathematics, etc., belong to the "philosophical" faculty.

[2] Laurie, "Rise of the Universities."

[3] No longer in existence.

privileges, many of which are accorded to this day. Indeed, some of these privileges were assumed and allowed before the institutions had official recognition by charter. These educational associations acquired so much influence and power that princes and popes vied with each other to gain favor with them by granting them special privileges. One of the most important of these is that the government of the student body rests with the university faculty, both as to their life in connection with the university, and also outside of it. Thus to this day if a student is arrested by the police, his case is turned over to the authorities of the university for trial and punishment. This was an important concession largely growing out of the fact that a great many of the students were citizens of other countries than that in which the university was located. It will readily appear that this privilege alone would have a tendency to create a world for university students and professors apart from that of the citizens. Doubtless the moral tone among the former was often very low. Students took advantage of the situation created by their peculiar privileges, and disregarded laws which the citizens were obliged to obey. Conflicts between these two classes, therefore, were frequent and bitter.

The universities stimulated a desire for learning, created a respect for it, and began a movement toward free investigation, and for the promulgation of liberal ideas, which gains strength with each decade of the world's history. They have greatly contributed to the growth of knowledge, to the advancement of science, and to the elevation of mankind.

CHAPTER XXV

MOHAMMEDAN EDUCATION

Literature. — *Warner*, Library of the World's Best Literature (see article on the Koran); *Johonnot*, Geographical Reader; *Lane-Poole*, Story of the Moors in Spain; *Lord*, Beacon Lights of History; *Thalheimer*, Mediaeval and Modern History; *Stillé*, Studies in Mediaeval History; *Irving*, Mahomet and his Successors; *Church*, The Beginnings of the Middle Ages; *Andrews*, Institutes of General History; *White*, Eighteen Christian Centuries; *Myers*, Mediaeval and Modern History; *Mombert*, Great Lives; *Clarke*, Ten Great Religions; *Ferris*, Great Leaders; *Laurie*, Rise of the Universities; *Walker, John Brisben*, The Building of an Empire ("Cosmopolitan," Feb.-Sept., 1899); "North American Review," Vol. 171, p. 754.

We have thus far described the work of Christian education. Parallel with this and almost entirely independent of it grew the educational work of the Moslems. This was a very important movement most valuable to civilization.

History of Mohammedanism. — Mohammedanism dates from the time of the Hegira, or flight of Mohammed from Mecca, A.D. 622. From this date Moslems reckon their time, as the Christian world reckons from the birth of Christ. Mohammed first appeared as prophet when forty years of age. The religion of the Arabs was a most degraded one, and there was great need of the reformation which Mohammed undertook. The prophet was not well received at first, and, being obliged to flee from Mecca, he retired to a cave at Medina, where he meditated and studied. It was during this retirement that he wrote the Koran, the Bible of the Mohammedans. He claimed that the angel Gabriel appeared to him, giving him a new revelation, which was more significant than that of the Christians. Indeed, these so-called revelations were strangely suited to the varying ambition of the founder of this religion. The Koran teaches that as Jesus was greater than Moses, so Mohammed was greater than Jesus.

There is no doubt that the new religion was an improvement upon the degraded form of worship that Mohammed found among the Arabs, or that in the beginning of his activity he did much to purify and elevate his people. But as he gained great numbers of adherents, and as he acquired power, Mohammed became a warrior, and attempted by the sword to compel belief in his doctrines. Moslemism met with such wonderful success that already, during the life of Mohammed, all Arabia was conquered to this belief, while his successors spread his teachings into northern Africa, western Asia, Spain, and Turkey. They carried their triumphant arms into France, until they were checked by Charles Martel; they overran Austria and threatened the complete subjugation of southeastern Europe, until John Sobieski dealt them a crushing blow before the gates of Vienna, and forever destroyed their ambition for northern conquest; they occupied Spain for seven hundred years, and still retain Turkey as their sole European possession; they have extended their power over many parts of Asia and Africa, until now they number about two hundred million souls.

The five chief Moslem precepts are: —

1. Confession of the unity of God. "There is one God, and Mohammed is his prophet."

2. Stated prayer.

3. Almsgiving.

4. The fast of Ramadan, the ninth month of the Mohammedan year.

5. Observance of the festival of Mecca. Every Moslem is expected to make a pilgrimage to Mecca at least once in his lifetime.

Education. — When Mohammedanism became secure in its power, it turned its attention to education. The successors of Mohammed were called caliphs, and the caliphs of Bagdad and Cordova rivaled each other in fostering learning. Schools were established in all large Moslem cities and in many smaller towns. Their scholars translated the works of Aristotle and other Greek authors. They taught mathematics, astronomy, philosophy, and grammar. They originated the science of chemistry, and made great advances in the study of algebra and trigonometry. They also measured the earth, and made catalogues of the stars. Every branch of knowledge was studied, and students were attracted from all parts of Europe to their schools, especially to Cordova.

Students lived in colleges with the professors, and there was an atmosphere of culture and investigation not equaled in any of the Christian universities of the Middle Ages.

Spain reached the summit of Moslem education during the reign of King Hakem III. (961–976). This king fostered education, being himself a man of learning. He had a private library of six hundred thousand volumes.

Education was not confined simply to the higher schools and universities. There were also a great many elementary schools. The first work of these was to teach the Koran, which was used as a reading book. The Koran gives us the most perfect picture of the oriental mind that we possess. Children of the poor attended school from their fifth till their eighth year, when they were allowed to go to service. Children of the rich entered school at their fifth year and remained till their fourteenth or fifteenth year. After that, if parents could afford it, boys traveled until their twentieth year, under care of a tutor. This completed their education. Any person could teach who chose to do so, no authority fixing the qualifications of teachers.

The Mohammedan schools began to decline in the eleventh century. At the present time, but little attention is paid to education in any of the countries under the sway of Islam.

GENERAL SUMMARY OF EDUCATIONAL PROGRESS DURING THE MIDDLE AGES

1. Paganism gave way to Christianity, and the benign influence of the latter began to be felt in the recognition of the importance of the individual.

2. The Church undertook the direction of education, which, though necessarily limited chiefly to the ecclesiastics, had also a great influence upon the masses at large.

3. The Church Fathers were the leaders in intellectual as well as in spiritual matters, while monks and priests were the principal teachers.

4. The monasteries were the centers of educational activity, both in fostering scholarship and in preserving classic literature.

5. Secular courses of study were established, the most important being the "seven liberal arts."

6. Education was based on authority, and free investigation found but little encouragement, except among the scholastics.

7. The State assumed no part in the training of the young. Charlemagne's educational work is an exception

to this rule. He asserted the prerogative of the State to control education, recognized the necessity of universal education, and the principle of compulsory attendance.

8. The crusades checked the growth of feudalism, aroused the intellectual as well as the spiritual energies of the people, led to a broader conception of man's duty to his fellow-man, and prepared the way for greater religious and political freedom.

9. As an important result of the stimulated educational activity, both among Christians and Mohammedans, many universities were founded.

10. "The Middle Ages," says Emerson, "gave us decimal numbers, gunpowder, glass, chemistry, and gothic architecture, and their paintings are the delight and tuition of our age."[1]

[1] Emerson, Progress of Culture in "Letters and Social Aims," p. 204. Boston, 1895.

CHAPTER XXVI

THE RENAISSANCE

Literature. — *Williams*, History of Modern Education; *Quick*, Educational Reformers; *Bryce*, The Holy Roman Empire; *Andrews*, Institutes of General History; *Fisher*, History of the Reformation; *Reeve*, Petrarch; *Symonds*, Renaissance in Italy; *Seebohm*, Era of Protestant Revolution; *Spofford*, Library of Historical Characters; *Hegel*, Philosophy of History; *Draper*, Intellectual Development of Europe; *Azarias*, Philosophy of Literature; *Schwickerath*, Jesuit Education; *Dr. Ludwig Pastor*, History of the Popes, Vol. I, p. 54, etc.

As the fifteenth century drew to a close there were unmistakable evidences of the dawn of a better day, and the long period known as the "Dark Ages" was to be succeeded by a brighter and more glorious era. The sway of the Church over the consciences, lives, and material interests of men was disputed; the feudal system had begun to disintegrate; the world had been aroused to new enterprise by the discovery and exploration of distant continents, by the invention of paper, the printing press, gunpowder, and the mariner's compass; the Ptolemaic system of astronomy had been superseded by that of Copernicus; the great empires of the Middle Ages had disappeared, and upon their ruins had been constructed smaller nationalities which spoke a language of their own. The period in which these remarkable changes were taking place is known as that of the Renaissance. It cannot be confined to definite chronological limits, but is the period of transition from one historical stage to another, in which there was a "gradual metamorphosis of the intellectual and moral state of Europe." The Renaissance must be viewed as "an internal process whereby spiritual energies latent in the Middle Ages were developed into actuality and formed a mental habit for the modern world." It prepared the way for the Reformation, and introduced the era of wonderful progress upon which modern civilization has entered. It was the new birth, the regeneration (renascence) of the world.

A most important instrumentality for carrying forward the great work thus inaugurated was the Teutonic race. The despised northern barbarians, who had conquered Rome, had become civilized and Christianized, and were found to possess the sterling qualities which made them capable of bearing the great responsibilities of progressive civilization. The proud Roman Empire had at last succumbed to its internal weaknesses and vices, and had disappeared forever from the face of the earth.

With the greater enlightenment of men had come once more an appreciation of the value of the classic languages, and Greek, the language of the Eastern Empire, was no longer regarded with antipathy. The revival of learning, which had its inception in Italy and spread northward, found its most important expression in the new interest awakened in the classic languages. It is in this, the so-called humanistic phase of the Renaissance, that the student of education is chiefly interested. To this we turn our attention.

We have already alluded to the social conditions, the inventions, and discoveries, which prepared the way for the revival of learning. New and powerful impulses were shaping the progress of the world, and the leaders of the humanistic movement were not slow to utilize the instruments thus opportunely furnished them. Chief among these was the art of printing, which enabled them to multiply and distribute copies of the classics, that had been consigned to comparative oblivion.

Another important element must be considered if we are to understand this revival. We have seen that during the Middle Ages the ecclesiastics largely shaped the intellectual activity of Europe, that mystery was made of science, and that the authority of the Church was supreme on all questions of education as well as of religion. A new and vital doctrine was taught which had much to do with the intellectual and spiritual emancipation of man. This new doctrine may be stated as follows:—

Man is a rational, volitional, self-conscious being, born with capabilities and rights to enjoy whatever good the world offers.

This doctrine, it will readily appear, is capable of being perverted to an excuse for unbridled license, as was done by the Italians; or, rightly interpreted, of being productive of great good, as in the case of the Germans.

Another new doctrine taught was that there was goodness in man and his works even previous to the Christian era, and that a study of the writings of all who have contributed to human progress is essential to culture, and of value to mankind. This was an argument for the revival of the study of Greek, which had for centuries been neglected. Indeed, Gibbon tells us that in the time of Petrarch, "No more than ten votaries of Homer could be enumerated in all Italy."

Again, it was held that the gates of learning must be

opened to all and not limited to the clergy, the recluse, and the sage. Intellectual culture must be offered to all men, to make them better and happier, and is not to be confined to the few for the purpose of increasing their power and widening the breach between the classes. The Renaissance made learning popular, it created a passion for culture, it aroused and stimulated widespread desire for greater enlightenment. Some of the leaders in the movement, however, merited opposition because of their efforts to introduce not only the beauties of pagan art and literature, but likewise some of their licentiousness.

We may now turn our attention to a more detailed history of this revival and its effect upon different peoples, and to a brief study of some of its great leaders.

Humanism in Italy. — Italy was the first to catch the impulse of humanism. Dante, Petrarch, and Boccaccio in the fourteenth century inspired men with their new ideas, and set in motion influences which were attended with results often far from good. They revived the study of Latin and Greek classics, extracted manuscripts from their hidden archives, incited in society a passion for learning, and created a popular literature in their own vernacular. They implanted a love of freedom of thought in the Italian masses. Their enthusiasm for the new learning attracted scholars from Germany, France, and other countries, who spread the influence in their own lands.

The effect of humanism upon the Italian mind and life was pernicious in the extreme. It led to infidelity, to immorality, and to a return to many pagan practices. This was owing to two chief causes. First, the evil influence of many leaders of the Church, and second, the passionate nature of the Italian people. Karl

Schmidt says, "Humanism, but not morality, ruled in the Vatican." Brother Azarias, in speaking of this period, says:[1] "The clergy loved their own ease too well; they were too great pleasure-seekers and gold-coveters to attend to their flocks with that pastoral spirit of simplicity and good faith that is to be witnessed in the Church to-day. The bishops were no better. They looked for emoluments and court favor. Even the better class of ecclesiastics gave themselves up to the intellectual luxury of admiring Plato and imitating Cicero. While a general laxity of morals in all orders of religious life — among priest and monk, pope and cardinal — was bringing odium on the Church, and weakening her hold upon the people — especially upon the Teutonic races — the seeds of regeneration were germinating in her own body. She was even then the mother of sanctity. . . . The Catholic hierarchy at last realized that with themselves should begin the reformation they would see established; they therefore pronounced the most withering denunciations upon the clerical and religious abuses of the day."

The people interpreted the teaching of Petrarch that the world was made for man's enjoyment, as a plea for license and absence of restraint. Even monks and priests, who had been held to the rigid life of the cloister, imbued with this teaching, indulged in excesses that were subversive of both morals and religion.[2]

But without doubt there was a great intellectual movement in Italy. Draper says, "Between 1470 and 1500 more than ten thousand editions of books and pamphlets were printed, and a majority of them in Italy, demonstrating that Italy was in the van of the intellectual movement."

[1] "Philosophy of Literature," p. 123. [2] *Ibid.*

Humanism in Germany. — A far different result was attained among the Teutonic peoples. The best students of Germany went to Italy, and, becoming acquainted with the new education, returned to introduce it into their own universities. Being less directly under the influences that obtained in Italy, and possessing the moral stability which had brought the Teutonic race to the front, the Germans obtained good where the Italians had absorbed evil. The same principle, with different interpretation, under different conditions, and in different soil, brought forth far different fruit. Thus Petrarch's teaching was interpreted to mean that the good things of earth are not to be abused, and that man's acquirements are to be consecrated to his self-development and to the glory of God.

The German humanists revived the study of the classics, Greek, Latin, and Hebrew, until, at the beginning of the sixteenth century, these languages were taught in every German university. The Bible was studied in the original, and classic writings were redeemed from obscurity, printed, and given to the world. Heidelberg and Tübingen became centers of the humanistic movement, and Agricola, Reuchlin, and Erasmus were the great leaders.

Summary of the Influence of Humanism. — 1. It laid the foundation for future liberty of thought and conscience.

2. It revived the study of the classic languages, and gave them a place in education which they still hold.

3. It utilized the art of printing by placing the works of ancient authors in form to be used by the world.

4. It increased the number of students in the universities, and stimulated intelligence among the masses.

5. It changed courses of study, making them more practical.

6. It exerted an influence on schools of all kinds by giving better preparation to teachers.

7. It stimulated all forms of elevating activity, — in art, in science, in exploration, in invention.

8. It prepared the way for the Reformation, which broadened and perfected the work thus inaugurated.

CHAPTER XXVII

HUMANISTIC EDUCATORS

Literature.—*Spofford*, Library of Historical Characters; *Symonds*, Renaissance in Italy; *Reeve*, Petrarch; *Macaulay*, Essays; *Warner*, Library of the World's Best Literature (see articles on Dante, Petrarch, and Boccaccio); *D'Aubigné*, History of the Reformation; *Morris*, Era of the Protestant Revolution; *Leclerc*, Life of Erasmus; *Fisher*, History of the Reformation; *Mrs. Oliphant*, Dante; *Azarias*, Philosophy of Literature; *Schwickerath*, Jesuit Education.

THE mission of the humanistic leaders was to "awake the dead," for Greek had become in the fullest sense a dead language, and while classic Latin was still read, its spirit was not comprehended and therefore it also was practically dead. We have seen that the Italians were the first to catch the inspiration of this revival, and Germany, France, Spain, and England "were invited to her feast." The great leaders of Italy were Dante, Petrarch, and Boccaccio. It is not the purpose here to discuss these men in all of their intellectual activities, but simply to consider the part of their work that had a bearing on education.

THE ITALIAN HUMANISTS

DANTE (1265-1321)

Dante was born and educated in Florence. He was favored with a devoted teacher, Brunetto Latini, who was said to be "a great philosopher and a consummate master of rhetoric, not only knowing how to speak well, but to write well." Under him Dante became familiar with all of the great Latin poets, with philosophy, history, and theology. Dante always spoke of his teacher with great affection. Those were times of revolution and political disturbance, and Dante was readily drawn into politics. This caused his banishment and even endangered his life.

Dante's greatest work is the "Divine Comedy," which has made his name immortal. His was the first great name in literature after the long dark period of the Middle Ages. It is said of him that "he was not the restorer of classic antiquity, but one of the great prophets of that restoration." He brought the Italian language into use in literature and gave to it a dignity that it has never lost. Dante prepared the way for the humanistic movement and was therefore an important factor in this great revival.

PETRARCH (1304-1374)

The father of Petrarch was an eminent jurist, and he desired his son to adopt his profession, but Petrarch had neither taste nor capacity for Roman law. He was determined to be a man of letters. Like Dante, he too mixed in politics, and several important diplomatic positions were given to him. Though he succeeded in learning a little Greek late in life, Petrarch was not a Greek scholar. This did not hinder him from being a warm advocate of the claims of the Greek language as an important element of a liberal education. Although he possessed a manuscript of Homer, "Homer was dumb to him, or rather he was deaf to Homer."

Petrarch was the real founder of humanism. Being enthusiastic for the works of antiquity himself, he inspired the Italians with a remarkable zeal in the pursuit of classic lore; nor was his influence confined to the limits of his native country. He was the first to make a collection of classic works, and to bring to light the literary treasures which the monasteries had so carefully preserved for centuries. He inaugurated that great movement which "restored freedom, self-consciousness, and the faculty of progress to human intellect." He recognized that the most wonderful thing in the world is the human mind, the emancipation of which can be brought about only through its own activity. He was the first to appreciate the importance of Greek in human culture. Unlike Tertullian, Jerome, and Augustine, he believed that classic authors, together with the Holy Scriptures and the writings of the Church Fathers, produce the broadest intelligence. All of these have the same purpose, and all are necessary to human enlightenment. Petrarch broke down the unfruitful methods of the scholastics, and laid the foundations upon which modern education is based; namely, intellectual freedom, self-consciousness, and self-activity.

BOCCACCIO (1313-1375)

The third of the great Italian leaders in the humanistic movement was Boccaccio. At the age of twenty-five, while standing at the grave of Vergil, he decided to devote himself to a literary career. He admired the great work of Petrarch, and was proud that, "at his own expense, he was the first to have the works of Homer and other Greek authors brought to his native land; that he was the first to call and support a teacher of Greek; and that he was the first among all Italians who could read Homer in the original."

THE GERMAN HUMANISTS

The German mind is more earnest, disputative, and practical than the Italian, therefore the trend of German humanism was at first chiefly theological, and the study of the classic languages, especially Hebrew and Greek, was undertaken for the purpose of better understanding the Holy Scriptures. Only a few scholars, however, were interested, and not until a violent attack was made upon Reuchlin, was general attention attracted.

AGRICOLA (1443-1485)

RUDOLPHUS AGRICOLA was the first to prepare the northern countries for the reception of the classic revival. After studying for some time under the great Italian masters, he returned to Germany and accepted a professorship at Heidelberg, where he delivered courses of lectures on the literature of Greece and Rome. He lectured also at Worms at the request of the bishop, and drew around him a large number of students in both places. Hallam says of him, "No German wrote so pure a style, or possessed so large a portion of classic learning." He prepared the way for the introduction of humanistic teachings and some of his pupils became the great leaders of that movement among the Teutonic peoples.

The testimony of Erasmus concerning Agricola is as follows: "There was no branch of knowledge in which he could not measure himself with the greatest masters. Among the Greeks, he was a pure Greek, among the Latins a pure Roman. . . . Even when he spoke *ex tempore*, his speech was so perfect and so pure that one could easily believe that one heard a Roman rather than a German. United with his powerful eloquence was the broadest erudition. He had investigated all the mysteries of philosophy, and thoroughly mastered every branch of music. In his later years he devoted his whole soul to the mastery of Hebrew and to the study of the Holy Scriptures. He cared but little for glory."

REUCHLIN (1455–1522)

Reuchlin may properly be called the first great German humanist. He was educated at Freiburg, Paris, and Basel, and gave especial attention to the classic studies, which had almost disappeared from the university courses in Germany. He took his master's degree at Basel, and then began to lecture on classical Latin and Greek. Being a born teacher, he drew about him a great number of students, who became interested in classic studies. He made several visits to Italy, where he imbibed the humanistic theories of the Italians, though he was already far advanced in those theories before he went to Italy. In 1481 he was appointed professor at Tübingen, which thus became the first German university to teach humanistic doctrines.

At Linz, where he had been sent on an embassy, he made the acquaintance of the emperor's Jewish physician, with whom he began the study of Hebrew. This marks an important epoch in his history, as he is best known for his Hebrew Grammar and Lexicon, published in 1506, and for his championship of the Hebrew literature. Owing to the scarcity of classic text-books, Reuchlin was obliged to mark out courses for his students, and, in a measure, to supply text-books for them. Much of his work in the university had to be dictated, and students were obliged to copy their work from manuscripts. He published a Latin lexicon and prepared the manuscript of a Greek grammar which he never published, but from which doubtless he drew in his work with students.

In 1496 his friend Count Eberhard died, and Reuchlin's enemies succeeded in alienating the new prince, so he was glad to avail himself of the opportunity to go to the university of Heidelberg. Here he gave chief attention to Hebrew.

While in Heidelberg he became involved in an unfortunate controversy regarding Hebrew literature, a controversy which was forced upon him. John Pfefferkorn, a converted Jew, zealous for the conversion of his race, obtained an order from the emperor to confiscate and destroy all Hebrew works which opposed the Christian faith. Reuchlin was appealed to as the highest authority on Hebrew, and he urged that, instead of destroying the literature, two professors should be appointed in each university to teach Hebrew and thereby refute the Jewish doctors by making the students acquainted with the Bible. The struggle continued for years, and although the Church and even the universities were against him, Reuchlin was finally victorious, thereby saving a noble literature to the world. This was a great victory for humanism. A short time before his death Reuchlin returned to Tübingen, where he closed his illustrious career in 1522.

Reuchlin was the first to introduce Greek into Germany, and the first to recognize the necessity of a knowledge of Hebrew in interpreting the Holy Scriptures. He began a reform in the schools which prepared the way for a like movement in the Church, and in Luther he saw the man who was destined to carry both of these reforms to fulfillment. "God be praised," said he, "in Luther they have found a man who will give them work enough to do, so that they can let me, an old man, go to my rest in peace."

ERASMUS (1467-1536)

Erasmus was born at Rotterdam. Though not a German, he belonged to the Teutonic race. He has well been called a "citizen of the world," as he lived in so many countries, and came to be the most learned man of his time. He was left an orphan at an early age, and his guardians placed him in a convent. They wished to make a monk of him so that they could inherit his patrimony, but this plan was resisted by the boy for a long time. The life of the convent was very distasteful to him, and though he afterward took vows, he never was in sympathy with asceticism. Possibly the condition of the monasteries at that time may have had something to do with the repugnance of Erasmus to the monastic life. He was certainly greatly relieved when the Pope absolved him from his vows.

Erasmus was precocious as a child, and it was early predicted of him that he would be a great man, a prediction which he fully verified. Through the influence and help of the Bishop of Cambray, he was enabled to go to Paris for study, though the means furnished were not sufficient for his support. He took pupils and gave lectures, thereby supplying the deficiency in his funds. It is recorded that, in his eagerness for books, he said, "When I get money, I will first buy Greek books, and then clothing." He also studied at Oxford, and afterward at Turin, where he took the degree of Doctor of Divinity. Though many high offices in the Church, and many positions in universities, were offered to him, he refused them all, preferring to be an independent man of letters. Erasmus was recognized as the supreme literary authority of the world, and this lofty position was the summit of his ambition. Nothing could turn him aside from the path that led to that eminence, and, once attained, nothing could attract him away from it.

Basel had become the center of the new printing industry. This led Erasmus to choose that city as his home for the latter part of his life, and here he furthered the cause of humanism as no other man had done, by editing and giving to the world many of the classic treasures of the monasteries. He translated Greek works into Latin, thereby making them available to the world, as Latin was better understood than Greek. His edition of the Greek Testament was his most eminent service, though his "Colloquies" are better known. His "Praise of Folly" is a satirical work, in which he holds up to ridicule the ignorance and vice of the monks.

Though he never broke away from the Church, without doubt his sympathies were with the reformers. But neither the persuasions nor the denunciations of Luther could bring him to take a decided stand on either side. He thought that the reform could be wrought within the Church. He accepted the dogmas of the Church, and remained within it as long as he lived.

Erasmus was the exact counterpart of Luther. He appealed to the limited few, Luther to the masses; he to the educated and higher classes, Luther to the ignorant and lowly; he was a man of reflection, Luther a man of action. The apparent vacillation of Erasmus may have been due to ill health, to the influence of the Pope, to the ties of the Church in which he had been reared, to the satisfaction he found in his eminent literary position, and to his dislike for controversy.

Erasmus gives us some very valuable pedagogical teachings, which may be summed up as follows: —

Pedagogy of Erasmus. — 1. The mother is the natural

educator of the child in its early years. The mother who does not care for the education of her children is only half a mother.

2. Until the seventh year the child should have little to do but play, in order to develop the body. It must have no earnest work, but must be taught politeness.

3. After the seventh year earnest work must begin. Latin and Greek (which should be studied together) must be taught early so that right pronunciation and a good vocabulary may be attained.

4. The first subject to be learned is grammar. Language is necessary before a knowledge of other things can be gained.

5. Teachers should be better trained and better paid, and suitable places must be furnished for the schools.

6. The religious side of education must not be neglected.

7. Great attention must be paid to the cultivation of the memory: (*a*) by a proper understanding of the subject; (*b*) by logical order in thinking; (*c*) by comparison.

8. As the bee collects honey from many flowers, so knowledge is gathered from many sources.

9. The foundation of all training of children must be laid in the home. Parents should know what their children ought to be taught. Above all things children must be taught to *obey*.

10. The first care with girls is to inculcate in them religious feelings; the second to protect them from contamination; the third, to guard them from idleness.

CHAPTER XXVIII

THE REFORMATION AS AN EDUCATIONAL INFLUENCE

Literature. — *White*, Eighteen Christian Centuries; *Taylor*, History of Germany; *Draper*, Intellectual Development of Europe; *Guizot*, History of Civilization; *Lord*, Beacon Lights; *Seebohm*, The Protestant Revolution; *Gasquet*, Eve of the Reformation; *Spaulding*, History of the Reformation; *Bryce*, The Holy Roman Empire; *Morris*, Era of the Protestant Revolution; *Hurst*, History of the Reformation; *Lewis*, History of Germany; *Myers*, Mediaeval and Modern History; *Schiller*, The Thirty Years' War; *Hallam*, Literary History; *Kiddle and Schem*, Cyclopaedia of Education; *Dyer*, Modern Europe; *D'Aubigné*, History of the Reformation; *Yonge*, Three Centuries of Modern History; *Mombert*, Great Lives; *Schwickerath*, Jesuit Education.

Historical Conditions. — At the beginning of the sixteenth century we find the stage of political, religious, and educational activity transferred from the shores of the Mediterranean to the north of the Alps. We have seen the great work of civilization taken from the Greek and Latin races and committed to the Teutonic race. We have traced the humanistic movement from its birthplace in Italy to Germany, where it found a more congenial atmosphere and a more suitable soil. The world was ripe for a great revolution, which was destined to advance the interests of mankind with gigantic strides.

The invention of printing by Gutenberg, in the middle of the fifteenth century, must be mentioned as the primary material agency in forwarding this advance. It was said of this art that it would "give the deathblow to the superstition of the Middle Ages." It multiplied readers a hundredfold; it stimulated authorship; it revolutionized literature, because it made the preservation and dissemination of thought easy; it was a mighty influence in bringing about universal education, a principle for which the Reformation stood.

Another event of great importance was the discovery of America, which stimulated various European enterprises. Thus, at the beginning of the sixteenth century, the world awakened from its long sleep, and educational enterprise was born anew.

The German Reformation had been preceded by similar movements in other lands. Huss and Jerome of Prague, in Bohemia, Wyclif in England, Zwingli in Switzerland, the Waldenses in Italy, and the Albigenses in France, had raised their voices in solemn protest against clerical abuses,[1] and many of the reformers had paid for their temerity by martyrdom. But the German Reformation, under the leadership of Martin Luther, was destined to exert a mighty influence throughout northern Europe, and to set in motion impulses which were to shape all later history.

The chief rulers of Europe were Frederick the Wise of Saxony, known as Luther's friend, Henry the Eighth of England, Francis the First of France, and Charles the Fifth, king of Spain, Naples, Sicily, and Austria, and afterward emperor of Germany. Leo the Tenth was Pope, and he had great influence in temporal affairs. Emperor Charles the Fifth was the most powerful ruler of this period. Though a foreigner in manners, customs, and sympathy, and unacquainted with the German tongue, he became emperor of Germany by bribing the electors who had a

[1] See Brother Azarias, "Philosophy of Literature," pp. 122–124.

voice in selecting the ruler of that nation. It is said that he paid $1,500,000 to these corrupt electors, besides making many promises of future favors. He was treacherous, and never hesitated to break the most solemn pledges when his interests so demanded. Bayard Taylor says of him, "His election was a crime, from the effects of which Germany did not recover for three hundred years."

Intellectual Conditions. — These, then, were the external conditions which existed at the beginning of the sixteenth century. We have seen that the need of reformation was acknowledged on all sides. There were but few good teachers to be found, even in the Church which had so long been the mother of schools. Education was at such a low ebb, and the advantages offered by the schools were so poor, and of such a doubtful character, that but few persons cared to avail themselves of their privileges. Even the universities failed to educate. Luther says, "Is it not pitiable that a boy has been obliged to study twenty years or longer to learn enough bad Latin to become a priest, and read mass?" Again he says, "Such teachers and masters we have been obliged to have everywhere, who have known nothing themselves, and have been able to teach nothing good or useful."

There was need, then, of reform in education as well as in religion, and Luther took the burden of both upon his shoulders. As an educational reformer, he has earned for himself the world's gratitude. It must be admitted that Luther's main purpose was the reformation of the Church, and that his educational work merely grew out of the need of general intelligence as a necessary adjunct to that work. Of the existing conditions, Compayré well says, "With La Salle and the foundation of the Institute of the Brethren of the Christian Schools, the historian of education recognizes the Catholic origin of primary instruction; in the decrees and laws of the French Revolution, its lay and philosophical origin; but it is to the Protestant Reformation, — to Luther in the sixteenth century, and to Comenius in the seventeenth, — that must be ascribed the honor of having first organized schools for the people. In its origin, the primary school is the child of Protestantism, and its cradle was the Reformation." [1]

LUTHER (1483-1546)

Martin Luther was born at Eisleben, Germany, of poor and humble parents. He was brought up under the rigid discipline of the typical German home, in which the rod was not spared. Upon this point he writes, "My parents' severity made me timid; their sternness and the strict life they led me made me afterward go into a monastery and become a monk. They meant well, but they did not understand the art of adjusting their punishments."

When he was fourteen years of age, his parents, then in better circumstances, sent him to Magdeburg to prepare for the university. But the expense being too great, he was withdrawn from this school and sent to Eisenach, where he could live with relatives. Here he sang in the street for alms, and his sweet voice attracted the attention of Ursula Cotta, a wealthy lady, who took him to her own home and gave him an excellent teacher.

When eighteen years of age he entered the university of Erfurt, then a center of humanistic learning. He made

[1] "History of Pedagogy," p. 112.

Karl Schmidt, in speaking of the spirit of the Reformation, says, "These ideas form the basis of the common school, which up to this time had been sporadically established only in isolated places." "Geschichte der Pädagogik," Vol. III, p. 16.

marvelous progress in his studies until he took his degree. His father had intended him for the law, but Luther determined to devote himself to the Church, much to his father's disappointment. Accordingly he became an Augustinian monk when twenty-two years of age. Unlike many of his brethren, he kept up his studies while in the monastery, and was called to a professorship in the new university at Wittenberg in 1508, where he found an ample field for his remarkable powers. Two years later, he went as a delegate to the papal court at Rome, where his eyes were opened to the condition of the Church in her holiest sanctuaries. Returning to Wittenberg, he continued his studies and his lectures, and drew about him a great number of students. His lectures and his writings against the practices of the Church became so pronounced that he was summoned before the Diet of Worms and commanded to retract. This he refused to do in the memorable words: "Here I stand; I cannot do otherwise. God help me! Amen." On his return from Worms, fearing for his safety, his friends took him prisoner and confined him in the Wartburg castle at Eisenach. During the nine months of his confinement he translated the Bible into German.[1] Luther took great pains to make the language so pure and plain that it could be understood by the common people, to whom he appealed. He was never ashamed of his humble origin. When he came to be the honored friend and trusted ad-

[1] In 1877, Mr. H. Stevens published at South Kensington, a "List of Bibles in the Caxton Exhibition." He says: "Not only are there many editions of the Latin Vulgate long anterior to that time (1507 A.D.), but there were actually nine *German* editions of the Bible in the Caxton exhibition earlier than 1483, the year of Luther's birth, and at least three more before the end of the century." The general use of the printing press about this time made popular translations opportune, as it placed the Bible within the reach of all. It thus became a powerful instrument for universal education.

viser of princes and kings, he was wont to say, "I am a peasant's son; my father, grandfather, and remote ancestors were nothing but veritable peasants."

The language of Luther's translation of the Bible became the standard German, which was to supplant the many dialects.

His great watchword was, "Make the people acquainted with the Word of God." But the Bible was of little use to the masses so long as they could not read. Luther therefore set himself sturdily to the improvement of the schools, which were in a deplorable condition. He urged the principle of parental responsibility for the education of children. "Believe me," said he, "it is far more important that you exercise care in training your children than that you seek indulgences, say many prayers, go much to church, or make many vows." His pedagogy constitutes the foundation of the German common school system of to-day. Luther, then, must be remembered as the greatest educator of his time for two reasons.

1. *He gave the German people a language by his translation of the Holy Scriptures.*

2. *He laid the foundation of the German common school system.*

Luther's Pedagogy. — 1. Parents are responsible for the education of their children.

2. It is the duty of the State to require regular attendance at school of every child, and the parents must be held accountable for non-attendance.

3. Religion is the foundation of all school instruction.

4. Every child must learn not only the ordinary subjects taught at school, but also the practical duties of life, — boys, a trade; girls, housework.

5. Every clergyman must have pedagogical training

and experience in teaching before entering upon a pastorate.[1]

6. The teacher must be trained, and in that training singing is included.

7. Children must be taught according to nature's laws, — the knowledge of the thing must precede its name.

8. Due respect should be shown to the office of teacher, and by example and precept every teacher should be worthy of respect.

9. His course of study included Latin and Greek, history, mathematics, singing, and physical training, besides religion.

10. Every school should have a library.

11. It is the inherent right of every child to be educated, and the State must provide the means to that end.

The principles above stated are fundamental in the German school systems of the present time. Religious instruction, trained teachers, compulsory and universal education, are the central principles of the schools of Germany and of many other nations. Luther could not give his chief attention to education, but with deep insight he saw the necessity of it, and laid the foundations upon which later generations have built a marvelous structure, true to the design of its architect.

MELANCHTHON (1497-1560)

Philipp Melanchthon was the friend, colaborer, and adviser of Luther. Luther was a resolute, energetic, impulsive man; Melanchthon was quiet, reserved, and

[1] This was because the pastor had an oversight of the school, a practice still very common in Germany.

conciliating. There is no doubt that these two men of such opposite dispositions exerted a salutary influence upon each other, — Luther stimulated and encouraged Melanchthon; Melanchthon checked and restrained Luther. It is certain that each was helpful to the other, and that the great cause of the Reformation, to which they mutually consecrated themselves, was furthered by their friendship and union.

Melanchthon had excellent training as a boy, and early showed signs of unusual ability. At fifteen he took his bachelor's degree at Heidelberg University, and when only eighteen years of age Erasmus said of him, "What hopes may we not conceive of Philipp Melanchthon, though as yet very young, almost a boy, but equally to be admired for his proficiency in both languages! What quickness of invention! What purity of diction! What vastness of memory! What variety of reading! What modesty and gracefulness of behavior! And what a princely mind!"

After completing his course at Heidelberg, he went to Tübingen, where his studies were directed by Reuchlin, who was his kinsman. He gave public lectures at Tübingen on rhetoric and on various classic authors, attracting world-wide attention. In 1518 he was called to the Greek professorship at Wittenberg, where he made the acquaintance of Luther. Bishop Hurst says, "The life of Melanchthon was now so thoroughly identified with that of Luther that it is difficult to separate the two. They lived in the same town of Wittenberg. They were in constant consultation, each doing what he was most able to do, and both working with unwearied zeal for the triumph of the cause to which they gave their life."

His success at Wittenberg was assured from the first. Though youthful in appearance, being but twenty-one years of age, his pure logic, his profound knowledge of philosophy, his familiarity with the Scriptures, his perfect mastery of the classic languages, his fine diction, and his broad knowledge awoke enthusiasm at once. Wittenberg, possessing two such great men as Luther and Melanchthon, became the center of humanistic studies, not less than two thousand students being attracted to its university. Melanchthon was an inspiring teacher; among his pupils were men who afterward became leaders of thought in Germany, and who did much to shape the destiny of Europe.

Perhaps Melanchthon's greatest service to the schools was his publication of text-books, which were very much needed. He wrote a Greek grammar for boys when himself but a boy of sixteen. Grammar he defined as "the science of speaking and writing correctly," a definition that has been scarcely improved upon. Ten years later his Latin grammar was published, after being tested for some years in his classes. For more than one hundred years this was the principal Latin grammar in use, and there were not less than fifty-one editions of it.

He wrote also text-books on logic, rhetoric, and ethics. It will be seen that the trivium — grammar, rhetoric, logic — furnished the foundation of his literary activity, so far as the schools are concerned. He was active also in authorship of theological works, producing the first theological work of the Protestant Church, the "Loci Communes," which Luther placed next to the Bible for theological study.

The interest of Melanchthon for education made him the chief adviser and leader among the school men. His advice was constantly sought in the educational movements of Germany. After visiting the schools of Saxony, he drew up the "Saxony School Plan," which furnished the basis of various similar organizations throughout Germany. There were three fundamental principles in this system.

1. There must not be too many studies in the schools, and Latin should be the only language taught.

2. There must not be too many books used.

3. The children should be divided into at least three classes, or grades.

In the first grade, reading, writing, the Lord's Prayer, the Creed, prayers and hymns, and some Latin should be taught. In the second, the Latin grammar, Latin authors, and religion. In the third, completion of the grammar, difficult Latin authors, rhetoric, and logic. Williams calls this "Melanchthon's somewhat artless ideas of a proper school system," which he excuses as being "marked possibly by the crudity of a first effort at organization, but more probably controlled in form by the fewness of teachers in the schools of his time."

Melanchthon is also known as the first Protestant psychologist.

To sum up the educational work of Melanchthon, we find that he was a "born teacher," attracting and inspiring thousands of young men whom he instructed; that he was the author of many text-books for the schools, and of theological works; that he was an educational authority; that he outlined a complete school system; and that he was the adviser and friend of Luther in the work of the Reformation.

CHAPTER XXIX

OTHER PROTESTANT EDUCATORS

The educational work of Luther and Melanchthon bore remarkable fruit. Luther had urged parents to see to it that their children should be educated, and had appealed to magistrates to assist the Church in maintaining schools. He insisted upon compulsory education in the memorable words, "The authorities are bound to compel their subjects to send their children to school." As a result schools were organized in Nuremberg, Frankfort, Ilfeld, Strasburg, Hamburg, Bremen, Dantzic, and many other places. Eton, Rugby, Harrow, and other educational institutions were founded about this time in England.

Melanchthon's course of study (Schulplan) for Saxony had appeared in 1528, and in 1558 the school law of Würtemberg, by far the best yet enacted, went into force. Other German provinces adopted more or less efficient school systems, and for the first time in the history of Christian education, the duty of the State to assume the responsibility of the education of its subjects was recognized. Out of these primitive systems have grown the completer systems of the present, after more than three centuries of experiment, study, and struggle.

The Reformation taught the right of every person to an education, primarily, it is true, for religious ends, and it gradually came to be understood that the State must assume that duty. For the Church had neither the means nor the power to accomplish universal education. But it was not till the nineteenth century that this end was reached, whereby the advantages of education were offered to the child of every parent of whatever rank or station, and the State assumed full control of the schools.

This was the great work marked out by Luther and Melanchthon, and their pupils and disciples carried that work to its fulfillment. Among these immediate followers we may mention Sturm,[1] Trotzendorf, and Neander, who contributed to educational reform.

STURM[2] (1507–1589)

Johann Sturm is counted among the greatest schoolmen that the Reformation produced, though he belonged to the French rather than the German reformers. He received an excellent training in the schools of Germany, and completed his education at Paris, where he afterward became professor of Greek. He soon gained such a wide reputation that when only thirty years of age he was called to the rectorship of the *Gymnasium* at Strasburg, a position which he held for forty-seven years, and where he gained lasting fame. This fame rests not on his work as a teacher, but as an organizer and an executive. Paulsen doubts his having been a great teacher. He says, "He was a man who gave his attention to great things. He had his hands in universal politics; he was in the service of nearly all the European

[1] Though Sturm was not a Lutheran, he was a Protestant, being a follower of Calvin.

[2] See Quick, "Educational Reformers," and Williams, "History of Modern Education," p. 88.

potentates, drawing his yearly salary from all. . . . It is not probable that such a wonderful man was also a good schoolmaster."[1]

But his great work was the organization of the Strasburg *Gymnasium*, especially its course of study, which became the model for the Latin schools for many years. Sturm's counsel was sought by schoolmen all over Europe, and he came to be the recognized leader of educational forces. His school course took the boy at six years of age and provided at first a nine years', afterward a ten years' course, ending at the sixteenth year of age. He added a five years' course to this later, and evidently planned to found a university.[2]

Sturm believed that the mother should have charge of the child for the first six years of its life. In his ten years' course he required ten years of Latin, six of Greek, besides rhetoric, logic, religion, and music. He introduced the practice of translating Latin into German and then translating it back into Latin.[3] His course took no account of German, history, mathematics, or science. He thus sought to reinstate Greece and Rome, but entirely neglected those things which prepare for life. Williams says, "With regard to Sturm's

[1] "Geschichte des Gelehrten Unterrichts."

[2] Sturm's school course appeared in 1538. It was not the oldest school course of the Protestants. The oldest school course for a German school was prepared by Johannes Agricola and Hermann Talich in 1525 for the school at Eisleben, Luther's birthplace. Indeed, Paulsen thinks that Melanchthon had a hand in its preparation. He says ("Geschichte des Gelehrten Unterrichts," p. 182), "This is the oldest published school course of the Reformed Church, which, if not composed by Melanchthon, was without doubt outlined, or at least approved, by him." This was discovered in 1865 by F. L. Hoffmann in the Hamburg city library.

[3] See Ascham, p. 191, and Ratke, p. 210.

plan of organization, it should be borne in mind that it is the very earliest scheme that we have, looking to an *extended, systematic, well-articulated* course of studies for a school of several teachers, in which is assigned to each class such portion of the subject-matter of the course of instruction as is suited to the age and stage of advancement of its pupils."[1]

This course of study attracted the attention of all Europe. Karl Schmidt says that in 1578 "his school numbered several thousand students, among whom were two hundred of noble birth, twenty-four counts and barons, and three princes — from Portugal, Poland, Denmark, England, etc."

Paulsen, while not belittling the work of Sturm, thinks that the celebrated course has but little in it different from the courses of the Wittenberg reformers. He says, "If Melanchthon had had the planning of a school course for a large city, it would have been much the same (as Sturm's). The Saxon school plan of 1528 was effective only in small cities and country places. The basis of both (Melanchthon's and Sturm's) is the same, — grammar, rhetoric, dialectics, with music and religion. In the large schools, like those of Nuremberg and Hamburg, a beginning of Greek and mathematics was added."[2]

Sturm's course has the merit of definiteness, thoroughness, and unity. There seems to be some doubt as to his success in carrying it out. It is certain that but few students completed his course compared with the number who began it. Instead of sixty to seventy pupils in the last class, there were only nine or ten. The influence of Sturm, however, spread not only over Germany, but also reached to many other countries, and his Strasburg course of

[1] "History of Modern Education," p. 91.
[2] "Geschichte des Gelehrten Unterrichts," p. 197.

study shaped the work in the classical schools for many years.

TROTZENDORF (1490-1556)

Valentine Trotzendorf was born in poverty and beset by many difficulties in boyhood. His mother was a constant inspiration to him, and when he was disposed to give up the struggle, her words, "My son, stick to your school," led him to continue until he overcame the obstacles. When ready for the university he went to Leipsic, where he studied Greek and Latin for two years. In 1515 he became a teacher in a village near Leipsic, a position that he retained for three years. He then went to Wittenberg, where he studied under Melanchthon for five years, and became very intimate with that great teacher. His fame as a teacher was made at Goldberg, where he was thirty-five years rector of a school. Like Melanchthon, he believed that the fear of the Lord is the beginning of wisdom, and that the school is an adjunct of the Church. With Sturm, he laid great stress upon the classic languages, and insisted that his pupils should speak in the Latin tongue. As a teacher he possessed remarkable power. He loved to mingle with his pupils, converse with and question them, and he had great skill in drawing them out. In his instruction he employed many illustrations, and proceeded from the concrete to the abstract.

His discipline was unique and original. He introduced a practice before unknown, namely, that of self-government on the part of the students, an experiment that has been tried in recent years with excellent results in many American institutions for higher learning. Trotzendorf established a senate of twelve students, a consul, and other officers, who were made responsible for the government of the school. These constituted a court of which he was president. Offenders were brought before the tribunal and tried with great formality and dignity. This body sentenced the culprit to such punishment as his guilt merited, the master reserving to himself the right of being a court of final appeal. Besides the officers above named, there were others who were in charge of the boys in their domestic relations, — such as keeping guard over their punctuality, table manners, diligence in study, etc. It was considered a high honor to hold one of these offices. The scheme worked well under Trotzendorf; it taught self-government, and inculcated the spirit of freedom as well as an intelligent submission to law. Trotzendorf thus gives an example of school government which is quite in accord with the spirit of modern times. He also had his best pupils instruct the lower classes under his supervision, and thus prepared them to go forth as teachers. Teachers from his school were sought for by intelligent patrons of education in all parts of Europe.

NEANDER (1525-1595)

Michael Neander was another of Melanchthon's pupils who became great as a teacher. Neander was for forty-five years the sole teacher of a Latin school at Ilfeld. Though he never had many pupils, his school was pronounced by Melanchthon as "the best seminary in the country." He was a most successful teacher, and the students whom he sent to the university were found to possess the very best preparation, and always stood among the first. He was well versed in medicine and chemistry, and was one of the best Greek and Latin scholars of his time. Contrary to the practice of his contemporaries, he favored the teaching of geography, history, and the natural sciences.

His position in regard to the sciences places him in advance of other educators, and in this he was a follower of Melanchthon, who also believed that science should be taught.

Neander is celebrated also for the Greek and Latin textbooks which he wrote. Speaking of these books, Paulsen says, "What he especially emphasized is: as few and as short rules as possible, and these rules are to be progressive; at the proper time they are to be committed to memory. The pupil must also commit words, phrases, and sentences to memory, which is equally important." Lastly, he gave a careful outline of the work of a boy for every year from the sixth to the eighteenth. This was especially valuable for that period when parents and teachers alike had nothing to guide them except the monastic course of study, and when the world was giving birth to new theories in education as well as in religion.

Neander's whole life was concentrated on the work of teaching, and in the schoolroom he found his greatest joy. Here, also, he made a lasting impression upon his pupils and upon mankind. His father was mistaken when he addressed the boy, "Into a cloister with you; you will amount to nothing in the world."

Other great teachers in the schools and in the universities carried forward the educational work begun by the great reformers. Many cities had founded schools, and several of the German states had established school systems. The educational ideas of the Protestant Reformation had taken deep root, and were destined to spread over the whole world, gaining in force with each succeeding century.

The practical outcome of this great movement was the

establishment of schools in every village in Germany under the direction of the pastor, and where he was unable to teach, under his clerk or assistant. As the chief purpose was to prepare the children for entrance to the church by confirmation, religion was the center of the school course. But reading, writing, arithmetic, and singing were also taught.

The clerk of the church gradually became the schoolmaster, and while the relations of these two offices have materially changed, there is still a close official connection between the two, particularly in the country. In many cases the pastor is the local superintendent of the school, and the teacher is the clerk and chorister of the church. As fast as Lutheran churches were organized, schools were also established in connection with them. Nor were boys alone included in the work of education. Girls' schools were organized and an effort was made at universal education. Many provinces adopted advanced school laws, and the principle of compulsory education was recognized, though by no means successfully carried out.

Thus was born in the middle of the sixteenth century the common school, and thus was recognized the right of all men to an education, and a practical illustration of the means of securing it was given to the world.

CHAPTER XXX

THE JESUITS AND THEIR EDUCATION

Literature. — *Draper*, Intellectual Development of Europe; *Durrell*, A New Life in Education; *Dyer*, Modern Europe; *Fisher*, History of the Reformation; *Guizot*, History of Civilization; *Ferris*, Great Leaders; *Lord*, Beacon Lights; *Parkman*, The Jesuits in North America; *White*, Eighteen Christian Centuries; *Quick*, Educational Reformers; *Symonds*, Renaissance in Italy; *Hughes*, Loyola; *Larned*, History for Ready Reference; *Schwickerath*, Jesuit Education; *Châteaubriand*, The Genius of Christianity.

The Order. — The remarkable spread of Protestantism, however, was not to go on unchallenged. Already before the rupture of the Church, the need of a better-educated clergy had been acknowledged. We have seen that Luther and the Reformers laid great stress upon the education of the young as a means of propagating the new faith, and they had employed this means with great success. It is not to be gathered from this that the Roman Church had been unmindful of her duty in the training of the young. It has already been shown that the Church maintained education from the beginning of the Christian era down through the Middle Ages, that she never slackened in her zeal for this work, and that she held it to be her right and duty, as she does to this day, to train the young. At this very time she was maintaining many schools. But the "Order of Jesus" was destined to systematize education in such a degree as the Church had never witnessed.

It has been claimed that the founding of the "Society of Jesus" was a "Counter-Reformation," the purpose of which was to check the growth of Protestantism. Whatever may have been the effect of its work in this direction, it seems clear that such was not the purpose for which it was organized. Schwickerath shows that it is doubtful if the founder of the Jesuit order had ever heard the name of the German Reformer. He says,[1] "The Papal Letters and the Constitutions assign as the special object of the Society: 'The progress of souls in a good life and knowledge of religion; the propagation of faith by public preaching, the Spiritual Exercises and works of charity, and particularly the instruction of youth and ignorant persons in the Christian religion.'" It cannot be denied, whatever the original purpose of the Society, that it not only checked the onward march of Protestantism, but it even restored many provinces and communities to their fealty to the Mother Church. How well the last clause of the admonition above quoted was carried out will be seen when we remember that the Jesuits originated the most successful educational system of the sixteenth, seventeenth, and eighteenth centuries, a system having a definite end in view, and whose adherents by indomitable energy, by self-sacrifice, by oneness of purpose, secured remarkable success. Let us turn our attention to the founding of the "Order."

Loyola (1491-1556), the originator of the order, was a Spanish nobleman. While recovering from a severe wound received in battle, he read some religious books which made such a profound impression upon him that he resolved to consecrate himself to religious work. Not being an educated man, he devoted some years to study, and while at the university of Paris he gathered around him other young men who also were ready to consecrate themselves to the service of God. They formed themselves into the "Order of Jesus," with the avowed purpose at first of rescuing

[1] "Jesuit Education," p. 77.

Jerusalem from the hands of the infidels. This was not to be done by force of arms, as in case of the crusaders, but by peaceful means. This purpose was abandoned, but the zealous missionary spirit of the Jesuits endured. In 1540 Pope Paul III. recognized the new order and gave it the sanction of the Church. The organization was military in character, Loyola becoming its first general.

The Growth of the Society was remarkable from the outset. In 1600 it had 200 schools; in 1710, 612 colleges, 157 boarding or normal schools, 59 houses for novitiates, 340 residences, 200 missions, and 24 universities. The college at Clermont had, in 1651, 2000 students, and in 1675, 3000 students. These institutions controlled the education of the Catholic Church in all Europe, and many Protestant young men also were attracted to the Jesuit schools by their superior teachers and their thorough training.

The society became so strong that various attempts were made to check its power. It spread, however, to China and Hindustan, to the Indian tribes of North America, and to South America. Its spirit and its practices aroused the suspicion of princes and people, of many Catholics as well as Protestants. In 1773 the Jesuits were in possession of 41 provinces, and had 22,589 members, of whom 11,295 were priests. Since that time popes have suppressed them, rulers have expelled them from their countries, their property and power have been taken from them, until their influence has been greatly lessened and their progress checked.

Jesuit Education. — Unlike the monastics, the Jesuits mingled with the world; they assumed no peculiarities of dress, and held themselves ready to act as missionaries to the most remote parts of the world, as agents of the Church to which they so fully consecrated themselves, and as teachers of youth. They established schools everywhere, and placed them in charge of teachers of remarkable skill and pedagogical training.[1] We have seen that their efforts were chiefly directed to higher education, their schools being designed for boys not less than fourteen years of age. In general, primary education did not enter into their scheme. Schwickerath thinks that the "Jesuits could not undertake elementary education" because "they had never men enough to supply the demands for higher education."[2] This shows that they held higher education as of the greater importance, and the same author further adds: "Besides, the whole intellectual training of the Jesuits fitted them better for the higher branches." They reached sons of princes, noblemen, and others who constituted the influential classes,[3] but "the Constitutions expressly laid down that poverty and mean extraction were never to be any hindrance to a pupil's admission."[4] Instruction was free.

Their schools became the most efficient and the most popular means of education furnished throughout Europe, —and justly so, for their work was thorough, their teachers were competent and well trained, and their course of study comprehensive. It is worthy of especial note that all teachers of the Jesuit schools were carefully trained before they were allowed to give instruction. This is the first time in history that the necessity of special preparation for the work of teaching was recognized as an essential element in the work of education.

Every Jesuit school was divided into two departments,

[1] See Hughes, "Loyola," pp. 46, 113, 156, 282. Also Schwickerath, "Jesuit Education," p. 415.

[2] "Jesuit Education," p. 105. See also Hughes, "Loyola," pp. 4, 14, 43, 46, 68, 72, 82, and 86 (lines 12–23).

[3] See Hughes, "Loyola," pp. 72, 151.

[4] "Educational Reformers," p. 26.

the lower, *studia inferiora*, consisting of five classes, and the higher, *studia superiora*, requiring two or three years. Boys were admitted to the lower course at the age of fourteen, and the work consisted chiefly of the study of the humanities, while that of the advanced course embraced philosophy and theology.[1] With reference to these courses of study, Quick says, "The Jesuit system stands out in the history of education as a remarkable instance of a school system elaborately thought out and worked as a whole." Again, he says of the *Ratio Studiorum*:[2] "It points out a perfectly attainable goal, and carefully defines the road by which that goal is to be approached. For each class was prescribed not only the work to be done, but also the end to be kept in view." Surely these are most commendable features of any course of study. The work was remarkably thorough in every detail.

After the society had been in existence some forty years, Claudius Aquaviva became its General Superior. He at once began the study of the educational problem, using all the resources of his office in obtaining information, and employing his executive ability in producing an improved method of study. A committee of twelve most eminent churchmen was appointed in 1581 to study the question, and three years later a commission of six, representing different countries, began the labor of preparing a course of study. Their work, called the *Ratio Studiorum*,[3] completed in 1599, has remained, with some modifications, the guide of Jesuit institutions of learning.

Emulation. — Emulation was employed to stimulate pupils to work and to secure good conduct. Prizes,

[1] K. Schmidt, Vol. III, p. 230. [2] "Educational Reformers," p. 34.

[3] See Hughes, "Loyola," p. 141, for full description of this work and outline of the course. Also Schwickerath, "Jesuit Education," p. 191.

decorations, rewards, titles, were offered as a means of attaining desired ends. Emulation is a natural instinct in mankind, and it may be utilized to stimulate endeavor and "foster ambition." The principle ever to be kept in mind should be *excellency without degrading others*. Schwickerath thinks that such was the spirit in which the Jesuits employed this incentive.[1] He admits, however, that there are dangers connected with prizes, and, on the whole, that certain methods of fostering emulation recommended by the *Ratio Studiorum* are less suitable to northern countries and less in accordance with modern taste.

While corporal punishment was allowed, it was generally administered by an official disciplinarian. It was seldom used, however, the discipline being mild and humane.

Criticism of Jesuit Education. — As to the efficiency of the instruction in the Jesuit schools, opinions widely differ. Bacon and Descartes indorse it in highest terms, while Leibnitz, Voltaire, and others are equally strong in its condemnation. Bacon remarks, "As to whatever relates to the instruction of the young, we must consult the schools of the Jesuits, for there can be nothing that is better done." Leibnitz, on the other hand, says, "In the matter of education, the Jesuits have remained below mediocrity." Ranke, in speaking of the success of the Jesuit schools, says, "It was found that young persons learned more under them in half a year than with others in two years."

Mr. Quick says: "I have said that the object which the Jesuits proposed in their teaching was not the highest object. They did not aim at developing *all* the faculties of their pupils, but merely the receptive and reproductive faculties. When the young man had acquired a thorough

[1] See Hughes, "Loyola," p. 511.

mastery of the Latin language for all purposes, when he was well versed in the theological and philosophical opinions of his preceptors, when he was skillful in dispute, and could make a brilliant display from the resources of a well-stored memory, he had reached the highest point to which the Jesuits sought to lead him. Originality and independence of mind, love of truth for its own sake, the power of reflecting and of forming correct judgments, were not merely neglected — they were suppressed by the Jesuit system."[1]

Summary. — Summarizing the educational work of the Jesuits, the following would appear to us to be just: —

1. Their educational system was by far the most efficient and successful of any during the sixteenth, seventeenth, and eighteenth centuries.

2. This, however, applies only to higher education, as primary education was not undertaken by them.

3. They made their schools interesting, and learning pleasant. Their work was thorough, their consecration complete, their success as teachers marvelous, they being the greatest schoolmasters of their time.

4. They produced a course of study, the *Ratio Studiorum*, which lays principal stress upon the humanities and religious instruction.

5. They taught the necessity of trained teachers, and developed a remarkable power and tact in the work of instruction and school management.

6. They made use of emulation as a means of stimulating ambition, — a principle that tends to arouse the baser motives, and which is therefore to be used guardedly.

7. They were indefatigable in missionary enterprise, and zealous in the propagation of their principles, both religious and educational.

[1] "Educational Reformers," p. 35.

8. They stimulated authorship, advanced learning, and produced many great men.

9. They exerted a powerful influence upon the intellectual, social, and political movements of their time.

THE PORT ROYALISTS

Opposed to the Jesuits was another body of Catholics, sometimes called Jansenists from the organizer of the movement, and sometimes Port Royalists, because their chief school was at Port Royal near Paris. Their purpose was to check the progress of the Jesuits, to promote greater spirituality in the Church, and to revive the pure Catholicism of St. Augustine. Among their great leaders may be mentioned Pascal, Nicole, and Launcelot. The purpose of the Jansenists was very different from that of the Jesuits, and their methods were more modern. They gave preference to modern languages, while the Jesuits gave chief attention to the classic tongues. Their discipline, like that of the Jesuits, was humane, but firm.

Their greatest contribution to education is the *phonic method* of spelling. They also laid stress upon the use of objects, the development of the sense perceptions, especially in early childhood. One of their axioms was, "The intelligence of childhood always being very dependent on the senses, we must, as far as possible, address our instruction to the senses, and cause it to reach the mind, not only through hearing, but also through seeing." This appears to be the first instance in which *object teaching* was taught as a principle, a principle which Bacon, Comenius, Pestalozzi, and Froebel worked out, and which has been one of the most important factors of modern educational progress.

CHAPTER XXXI

OTHER EDUCATORS OF THE SIXTEENTH CENTURY

Literature.—*H. M. Skinner*, The Schoolmaster in Literature, The Schoolmaster in Comedy and Satire; *Gill*, Systems of Education; *Quick*, Educational Reformers; *Williams*, History of Modern Education; *Besant*, Rabelais; *Monroe*, Educational Ideal; *Collins*, Montaigne; *Emerson*, Representative Men; *Vogel*, Geschichte der Pädagogik; *Carlisle*, Two Great Teachers (Ascham and Arnold); *Azarias*, Essays Educational; *Davidson*, History of Education.

We have thus far discussed educators who were directly connected with the great Protestant and Catholic movements. There were others who were more or less independent of these movements. Among these we may mention Roger Ascham, Rabelais, and Montaigne.

ASCHAM (1515-1568)

Roger Ascham was the most celebrated English educator of the sixteenth century. He was educated at Cambridge, and studied three years in Germany. He had a thorough knowledge of the classic languages. For these reasons he was chosen tutor to Elizabeth, a position which he held for two years. Upon her accession to the throne, Ascham came to read with her several hours a day, and she retained her affection for her old teacher throughout his life.

His chief literary work is his "Scholemaster," which is the first educational classic in English. Dr. Johnson says of this book, "It contains, perhaps, the best advice that ever was given for the study of languages." This method was as follows, given in Ascham's words: "First, let him teach the child, cheerfully and plainly, the cause and matter of the letter (Cicero's Epistles); then, let him construe it into English so oft as the child may easily carry away the understanding of it; lastly, parse it over perfectly. This done, then let the child by and by both construe and parse it over again; so that it may appear that the child doubteth in nothing that his master has taught him before.

"After this, the child must take a paper book, and sitting in some place where no man shall prompt him, by himself let him translate into English his former lesson. Then showing it to his master, let the master take from him his Latin book, and pausing an hour at the least, then let the child translate his own English into Latin again in another paper book. When the child bringeth it turned into Latin, the master must compare it with Tully's book, and lay them both together, and where the child doth well, praise him, where amiss, point out why Tully's use is better.

"Thus the child will easily acquire a knowledge of grammar, and also the ground of almost all the rules that are so busily taught by the master, and so hardly learned by the scholar in all common schools. The translation is the most common and most commendable of all other exercises for youth; most common, for all your constructions in grammar schools be nothing else but translations; but because they be not *double* translations (as I do require), they bring forth but simple and single commodity; and because also they lack the daily use of writing, which is the only thing that breedeth deep root, both in the wit for good understanding, and in the memory for sure keeping of all that is learned; most commendable also, and that by the judgment of all authors which entreat of these exercises."[1]

Ascham often refers to his illustrious pupil in claiming merit for his system. He says, "And a better and nearer example herein may be our most noble Queen Elizabeth, who never took yet Greek nor Latin grammar in her hand after the first declining of a noun and a verb; but only by this double translating of Demosthenes and Isocrates daily, without missing, every forenoon, and likewise some part of Tully every afternoon, for the space of a year or two, hath attained to such a perfect understanding in both tongues, and to such a ready utterance of the Latin, and that with such a judgment as there be few now in both universities, or elsewhere in England, that be in both tongues comparable with her Majesty." Mr. Quick thinks that while Ascham may have thus flattered his royal pupil, there is no doubt that she was an accomplished scholar.

We have seen that Sturm made some use of double translation, but Ascham is entitled to full credit for the method, which he adopted from Pliny and perfected. Many teachers of language since that time have employed this method with excellent results.

RABELAIS[2] (1483-1553)

Though there is some obscurity as to the exact date of the birth of Rabelais, it is generally believed that he was born the same year as Luther, 1483. He was the son of a French innkeeper, and, after completing a classical course, was consecrated to the priesthood. His great ability and

[1] H. M. Skinner, "The Schoolmaster in Literature," p. 20.

[2] For special reference see Besant's "Rabelais."

independent thinking, and his humanistic tendency brought reproof from his superiors, and he was ordered to perform works of penance in his cell; but through the influence of powerful friends he was freed and allowed to go over to the Benedictines, with whom, however, he did not remain long. He became an independent preacher, and as such had many friends among the reformers, chief among whom was Calvin. His intimacy with Calvin led the more radical reformers to be suspicious of him, and not without reason. Walter Besant tells us that, "One hears he is a buffoon — he is always mocking and always laughing. That is perfectly true. He laughs at the pretensions of pope, cardinal, bishop, and priest; he laughs at monkery and monks; he mocks at the perpetual iteration of litanies; he laughs at the ignorance and superstition which he thinks are about to vanish before the new day of modern learning."[1] Nor was his sympathy with the reformers any more marked. Besant further adds, "It was at that time all important that, as in England, the scholars should range themselves on the Protestant side. Rabelais refused to do this. More, he set an example which deterred other scholars, and kept them, in sheer impatience, in the enemy's camp."[2]

The great literary work of Rabelais is embodied in a series of chronicles, the first of which is called "Gargantua" and the second, "Pantagruel." It is believed that these were popular names of giants in the Middle Ages. In these books we find Rabelais's pedagogy.[3] The giant Gargantua attends a school in which scholastic methods are employed. The author skillfully ridicules the methods, and shows the utter inefficiency of the instruction by contrasting the result in Gargantua and

[1] "Rabelais," 192. [2] *Ibid.*, 193. [3] "Schoolmaster in Comedy and Satire," 9–33.

Eudemon, a page of the king. Gargantua, a man of fifty-five, is introduced to Eudemon, a boy of twelve. The former is awkward, bashful, and does not know what to say, while the latter meets Gargantua cap in hand, with open countenance, ruddy lips, steady eyes, and with modesty becoming a youth. In reply to the polite and intelligent conversation of the lad, Gargantua "falls to crying like a cow, casting down his face, and hiding it with his cap." Compayré says, "In these two pupils, so different in manner, Rabelais has personified two contrasted methods of education: that which, by mechanical exercises of memory, enfeebles and dulls the intelligence; and that which, with large grants of liberty, develops intelligences and frank and open characters."

The deficiencies of the old education (the scholastic) being thus shown, Rabelais places his pupil under Ponocrates, Eudemon's teacher, who has produced such practical results. He then opens up his system of pedagogy in the plan pursued for the redemption of Gargantua.

Realism in Education. — Compayré's estimate of this pedagogy is as follows: "The pedagogy of Rabelais is the first appearance of what may be called *realism* in instruction, in distinction from the scholastic *formalism*. The author of 'Gargantua' turns the mind of the young man toward objects truly worthy of occupying his attention. He catches a glimpse of the future reserved to scientific education, and to the study of nature. He invites the mind, not to the labored subtleties and complicated tricks which scholasticism had brought into fashion, but to manly efforts, and to a wide unfolding of human nature." [1]

In comparing Rabelais with Lucretius, Walter Besant says, "Both, at an interval of fifteen hundred years, antici-

[1] "History of Pedagogy," p. 91.

pated the nineteenth century in its restless discontent of old beliefs, its fearless questioning, its advocacy of scientific research."[1] Compayré thinks that Rabelais is "certainly the first, in point of time, of that grand school of educators who place the sciences in the first rank among the studies of human thought."[2] It would seem, then, that the author of "Gargantua" is worthy of a most honorable place among educational writers. Rabelais began a movement, which was destined to revolutionize educational methods.

The educational scheme of Rabelais embraced the study of letters, of nature, of science, of morals and religion, of the physical well-being, — in short, of everything necessary, as Herbert Spencer would say, to complete living.

MONTAIGNE[3] (1533-1592)

Of a very different character from Rabelais was Montaigne. Rabelais was radical and extravagant, Montaigne conservative and discreet; Rabelais sought development of all the faculties alike, Montaigne gave preference to the training of the judgment; Rabelais would thoroughly master every branch of human knowledge, Montaigne was content to skim over the sciences. And yet, Montaigne must be recognized as an important factor in education, not only for his own teachings, but because undoubtedly Bacon, Locke, Rousseau, and other apostles of reform were greatly influenced by him. Bacon furthered Montaigne's theories concerning the importance of science, and by his inductive method rendered the world a far greater service than his great French contemporary. Locke

[1] "Rabelais," p. 187.

[2] "History of Pedagogy," p. 96.

[3] See Collins, "Montaigne."

enlarged upon Montaigne's ideas of physical training. Rousseau accepted a vital doctrine of Montaigne in the following words: "He (Émile) possesses a universal capacity, not in point of actual knowledge, but in the faculty of acquiring it; an open, intelligent genius adapted to everything, and, as Montaigne says, if not instructed, capable of receiving instruction."

Montaigne's father was a French nobleman, who fully appreciated the responsibility laid upon him in the education of his son. Doubtless his training had much to do in shaping the pedagogy of the illustrious son. It was wise, mild but firm, natural, and thorough. The tutors and servants who surrounded him were allowed to speak only in Latin. That tongue thus became as familiar as his native tongue. Indeed, it is said, that at the age of six he was so proficient in the language of Cicero, that the best Latinists of the time feared to address him. Nor was his knowledge confined to Latin alone. He was instructed in modern lore as well. At the age of six he was placed in the college of Guienne, where he remained seven years. His experience there, so contrary to that under which he had been brought up, led him to be utterly opposed to corporal punishment. Of the methods of discipline employed in the school, he says, "The discipline of most of our colleges has always displeased me. They are veritable jails in which youth is held prisoner. The pupils are made vicious by being punished before they become so. Pay a visit there when they are at their work; you will hear nothing but cries,—children under execution, and masters drunk with fury. What a mode of creating in these tender and timid souls an appetite for their lessons, to conduct them to their tasks with a furious countenance, rod in hand!—it is an iniquitous and pernicious fashion. How much more becoming it would be to see the classroom strewed with leaves and flowers than with blood-stained stumps of birch rods! I would have painted up there scenes of joy and merriment, Flora and the Graces, as Speusippus had his school of philosophy: where they are to gain profit, there let them find happiness too. One ought to sweeten all food that is wholesome, and put bitter into what is dangerous."[1]

Here we find a strong plea for humane forms of punishment and a severe criticism of the prevailing practice of flogging, a practice which did not cease until long after Montaigne's time. It is an equally forcible plea for beautiful and pleasant schoolrooms, decorated with works of art intended to awaken and cultivate the aesthetic sense of the children, while contributing to their happiness. It has been left to the educators of the end of the nineteenth century to take up and seriously act upon this suggestion made over three hundred years ago. "The purpose of education," said Montaigne, "is the training, not of a grammarian, or a logician, but of a complete gentleman." Education should be of a practical nature. The child must become familiar with the things about him. He must learn his own language first and then that of his neighbors, and languages should all be learned by conversation.

A decided weakness in his system is found in his ideas concerning women. He made no provision for their education, and, indeed, expressed great contempt for their abilities of either mind or heart.

Montaigne's chief literary work is his "Essays." Compayré pronounces Montaigne's pedagogy, "a pedagogy of

[1] Collins, "Montaigne," p. 14.

good sense," and further adds that he has "remained, after three centuries, a sure guide in the matter of intellectual education."

Observation and experience were to be abundantly employed, and visits to other lands, together with intercourse with intelligent men everywhere, were to "sharpen our wits by rubbing them upon those of others."

To sum up, we may say that the pedagogy of Montaigne teaches the training and use of the senses; the study of science; the learning of the mother tongue first by conversation, and then the language of our neighbors with whom we come in contact; the abolition of corporal punishment, and the beautifying of schoolrooms. This surely is no small contribution to education. His definition of education is worthy of note. He says, "It is not the mind only, nor the body, but the whole man that is to be educated."[1]

Summary of Educational Progress during the Sixteenth Century. — 1. Humanism had reached its climax and begun to decline. It stimulated invention and discovery; it revived classic literature and put it in such form that it could be used; it emancipated the mind; it prepared the way for later reforms; it produced great educators such as Petrarch, Erasmus, and Reuchlin.

2. The Reformation took up the educational work of humanism, and carried it forward. It instituted primary education, the education of the masses, compulsory education and parental responsibility therefor; it asserted the right and duty of the State to demand and secure universal education; it elevated and gave dignity to the office of teacher; it formulated several school systems, and laid the foundation of the present German school system. Among

[1] A good summary of Montaigne's educational ideas may be found in Collins's "Montaigne," p. 102.

its great educators were Luther, Melanchthon, Sturm, and Neander.

3. The Jesuits established a remarkable system of schools, noted for their thoroughness, for their singleness of purpose, for their rapid growth, and for their trained teachers. They gave little attention to primary education, but sought to reach the higher classes. Emulation was the principal incentive employed.

4. Opposed to the Jesuit education was that of the Port Royalists. They appealed to the intelligence of the children and cultivated the sense-perceptions. They invented the phonic method of spelling.

5. Sturm's celebrated course of study was introduced during this century at Strasburg.

6. The method of double translations in learning a language was taught by Ascham and Sturm.

7. In Rabelais we find the first appearance of *realism*, which bore rich fruit in later scientific education.

8. Montaigne opposed the use of the rod, and taught that the schoolroom should be made attractive. He also advocated the study of modern languages by conversation, and gave science an honorable place in the curriculum.

It thus appears that the sixteenth century surpassed many previous eras in its contributions to educational progress.

CHAPTER XXXII

EDUCATION DURING THE SEVENTEENTH CENTURY

Literature. — *Taylor*, History of Germany; *Guizot*, History of Civilization; *Schiller*, The Thirty Years' War; *Dyer*, Modern Europe; *Lewis*, History of Germany; *Macaulay*, History of England.

Political and Historical Conditions. — The seventeenth century was remarkable for the wars for religious supremacy. The Reformation had challenged the authority of the Church, aroused a questioning spirit, and instilled into men's minds a love for religious liberty. During the latter half of the sixteenth century, Europe had swayed back and forth between Protestantism and Catholicism, according as success in arms had favored one side or the other. The spirit of Protestantism had taken possession more especially of the common people, who formed the bone and sinew of the armies. Bitter animosities existed between the adherents of the papal church and the reformers, which found expression in bloodshed, rapine, and destruction of property.

England was torn asunder by civil war, which resulted in the death of Charles I. and the establishment of the Commonwealth under Cromwell, — the struggle between *Cavalier* and *Roundhead*, between established church and Puritan, ending finally in the revolution of 1688. The country was in a religious ferment during the greater part of this century, caused by a growing jealousy for the maintenance of the principle of the right to worship God according to the dictates of one's own conscience. Nor was the struggle less virulent or disastrous in continental Europe. The religious upheaval of the previous century culminated in the terrible conflict known as the Thirty Years' War; this lasted from 1618 till 1648, when the Peace of Westphalia secured religious liberty to all men. Northern Germany, Austria, France, Holland, Denmark, and Sweden, as well as minor countries, were involved in this great war.

Let Bayard Taylor paint the result of this fearful struggle. "Thirty years of war! The slaughters of Rome's worst emperors, the persecution of the Christians under Nero and Diocletian, the invasions of the Huns and Magyars, the long struggle of the Guelfs and Ghibellines, left no such desolation behind them. At the beginning of the century, the population of the German Empire was about 30,000,000; when the Peace of Westphalia was declared, it was scarcely more than 12,000,000! Electoral Saxony, alone, lost 900,000 lives in two years. . . . The city of Berlin contained but 300 citizens, the whole of the Palatinate of the Rhine but 200 farmers. In Hesse-Cassel, 17 cities, 47 castles, and 300 villages were entirely destroyed by fire; thousands of villages, in all parts of the country, had but four or five families left out of hundreds, and landed property sank to about one twentieth of its former value. . . . The horses, cattle, and sheep were exterminated in many districts, the supplies of grain were at an end, even for sowing, and large cultivated tracts had relapsed into a wilderness. Even orchards and vineyards had been wantonly destroyed wherever armies had passed. So terrible was the ravage that, in a great many localities, the same amount of population, cattle, acres of cultivated land, and general prosperity was not restored until the year 1848, two centuries afterward!

"This statement of the losses of Germany, however, was but a small part of the suffering endured. . . . During the last ten or twelve years of the war, both Protestants and Catholics vied with each other in deeds of barbarity; the soldiers were nothing but highway robbers, who maimed and tortured the country people to make them give up their last remaining property. . . . In the year 1637, when Ferdinand II. died, the want was so great that men devoured each other, and even hunted down human beings like deer or hares, in order to feed upon them.

"In character, in intelligence, and in morality, the German people were set back two hundred years. All branches of industry had declined, commerce had almost entirely ceased, literature and the arts were suppressed, and except the astronomical discoveries of Copernicus and Kepler, there was no contribution to human knowledge. Even the modern High German language, which Luther had made the classic tongue of the land, seemed to be on the point of perishing. Spaniards and Italians on the Catholic, Swedes and French on the Protestant side, flooded the country with foreign words and expressions, the use of which soon became an affectation with the nobility, who did their best to destroy their native tongue.

"Politically, the change was no less disastrous. The ambition of the house of Hapsburg, it is true, had brought its own punishment; the imperial dignity was secured to it, but henceforth the head of the 'Holy Roman Empire' was not much more than a shadow. . . . As for the mass of the people, their spirit was broken; for a time they gave up even the longing for the rights which they had lost, and taught their children abject obedience in order that they might simply live."[1]

The Educational Situation. — These political conditions had a marked influence upon education. Schools were abandoned, colleges gave up their charters, and people were content to allow their children to grow up in ignorance. Indeed, it was not to be expected that, in the midst of their poverty and sorrow, parents should care for education. And yet, some most important and wise school laws were enacted and put into force, which form the basis of the present German school system, as well as the school systems of many other countries. In 1619 the Duke of Weimar decreed that all children, girls as well as boys, should be kept in school for at least six years, — from six to twelve. This is the first efficient compulsory education law on record intended for all classes of children.

Besides Weimar, Würtemberg, Hesse-Darmstadt, Mecklenburg, Holstein, Hesse-Cassel, and other provinces were active in school work. They organized schools, appointed teachers, and formulated school regulations. In 1642, Duke Ernst of Gotha adopted a new school regulation which was a century in advance of the time, and this action was taken when the Thirty Years' War was at its height and in a territory sadly devastated by contending armies.

This law required every child to enter school at the beginning of his sixth year, and to remain in school until he could read his mother tongue, had mastered Luther's catechism, and was well grounded in arithmetic, writing, and church songs. A course of study was marked out, the schools were graded, and methods of instruction were outlined. The greatest defect in the system was the lack of

[1] "History of Germany," p. 409.

competent teachers. Discharged soldiers, worthless students, and degraded craftsmen who could read and write, and who possessed a little knowledge of music, continued for many years to be employed as schoolmasters. But little progress could be made under these adverse circumstances; and the only reason for encouragement was the fact that the duty of parents to keep their children at school was everywhere recognized.

The Innovators. — We must here mention also the Innovators or Reformers, whose period of educational activity falls chiefly within the seventeenth century. Among these appear the names of Francis Bacon, Ratke, Milton, Comenius, Rollin, Fénelon, and Locke. These men started movements which revolutionized education and laid the foundation of modern methods. The demands of the Reformers are summed up by Quick as follows: "First, that the study of *things* should precede, or be united with, the study of *words;* second, that knowledge should be communicated, where possible, by appeal to the senses; third, that all linguistic study should begin with that of the mother tongue; fourth, that Latin and Greek should be taught to such boys only as would be likely to complete a learned education; fifth, that physical education should be attended to in all classes of society for the sake of health, not simply with a view to gentlemanly accomplishments; sixth, that a new method of teaching should be adopted, framed 'According to nature.'"[1] In another chapter we shall study the life and work of some of these men.

[1] Quick, "Educational Reformers," p. 50.

CHAPTER XXXIII

EDUCATORS OF THE SEVENTEENTH CENTURY

Literature. — *Church*, Bacon; *Macaulay*, Essays; *Spofford*, Library of Historical Characters; *Lord*, Beacon Lights; *Montagu*, Life of Bacon; *Barnard*, English Pedagogy; *Quick*, Educational Reformers; *Williams*, History of Modern Education; *Laurie*, Life and Works of Comenius; *Comenius*, Orbis Pictus; *Barnard*, Journal of Education; *Milton*, Tractate on Education; *Pattison*, Milton; *Fowler*, Locke; *Leitch*, Practical Educationists; *Gill*, Systems of Education; *Schwegler*, History of Philosophy; *Courtney*, John Locke; *Vogel*, Geschichte der Pädagogik; *Compayré*, History of Pedagogy; *Fénelon*, Education of Girls; *Azarias*, Philosophy of Literature; *Monroe*, Comenius.

BACON[1] (1561–1626)

But little is known of the early years of Francis Bacon, but it is probable that he was well trained, as his father was a man of good education, and the boy was able to enter Cambridge when only a little over twelve years of age. His father was for many years Lord Keeper of the Seals, and this brought Francis in contact with court life, where his precocity made him a favorite with the queen. He thus early acquired that taste for the court, by which he climbed to the height of his ambition only to fall therefrom in ignominious defeat.

He remained at Cambridge only about three years. Lord Macaulay sums up the result of Bacon's university experience in the following words: "Bacon departed, carrying with him a profound contempt for the course of study pursued there, a fixed conviction that the system of

[1] For special reference see Macaulay's "Essays," Vols. II and III.

academic education in England was radically vicious, a just scorn for the trifles on which the followers of Aristotle had wasted their powers, and no great reverence for Aristotle himself."[1]

Some think that thus early, while not yet fifteen years of age, Bacon began to formulate that inductive system which made him a great benefactor of the human race. There seems to be but little proof of this; and, if it be so, he laid it aside until near the close of his life, and devoted himself to politics. After leaving Cambridge, he went abroad with the English ambassador at Paris, with whom he served until the death of his father compelled his return to England. Unexpectedly finding that his patrimony was gone, he began a career at the bar, and rose step by step, amid many discouragements, until he reached the height of his ambition, the Lord High Chancellorship of the realm. In reaching this position he resorted to many of the tricks of the politician, and sacrificed his best friends to further his selfish interests. Concerning his actions toward his benefactor, Essex, Macaulay says, "This friend, so loved, so trusted, bore a principal part in ruining the earl's fortunes, in shedding his blood, and in blackening his memory. But let us be just to Bacon. We believe that, to the last, he had no wish to injure Essex. Nay, we believe that he sincerely wished to serve Essex, as long as he could serve Essex without injuring himself."[2] Such seeming mitigation of Bacon's ingratitude serves only to bring the Lord Chancellor's cowardice more completely to light.

This lack of principle and greed for office, together with the luxurious tastes which kept Bacon constantly in debt, made him susceptible to corruption. Accordingly he ac-

[1] "Essays," Vol. III, p. 354. [2] *Ibid.*, Vol. III, p. 368.

cepted bribes; and, when exposed, his degradation from the highest office under the crown was most complete and humiliating. He was summoned before the bar of Parliament; and, finding the evidence against him complete, he admitted his guilt and pleaded for clemency. These are the words of his confession, "Upon advised consideration of the charges, descending into my own conscience and calling upon my memory to account so far as I am able, I do plainly and ingenuously confess that I am guilty of corruption, and do renounce all defense."

He was found guilty and condemned to imprisonment in the Tower during the pleasure of the king, and to a fine of £40,000; he was forbidden ever to sit in Parliament or come within the verge of the court, and was forever debarred from holding office. He never paid the fine, was released from the Tower after two days, was permitted to visit the court, and was summoned to the meetings of Parliament.[1] He never, however, took any part in public affairs. The king granted him a pension upon which he lived the remainder of his days. Thus disappeared from public life one of England's greatest statesmen, whose political career ended in disgrace. But during the remaining six years of his life, he wrote his principal works, which made him famous for all time, and which mark a new era in education as well as in the world's progress.

In 1620 his greatest work, the "Novum Organum," was published. In this appears his *Inductive Method*, a great educational discovery, which has been of inestimable value to mankind. It revolutionized science, and suggested the application of the forces of nature to

[1] For a full description of his trial consult Macaulay's "Essays." Also his biographer, Montagu, whose judgment of Bacon is much milder than Macaulay's.

the wants of man, thus opening to man's enterprise an illimitable field for research. In the three centuries since Bacon's discovery, science has made vast strides, and yet is only at the threshold of its possible development. The watchwords of the inductive method—experiment, investigate, verify—have led to the establishment of laboratories, to the founding of experimenting stations, and to the study of Nature herself. As Macaulay puts it, "Two words form the key of the Baconian doctrine, Utility and Progress." Again he says, "The philosophy of Plato began in words and ended in words. . . . The philosophy of Bacon began in observation and ended in arts."[1]

Macaulay depreciates the work of Bacon, and shows that he was not the original inventor of the inductive method, "which," he says with truth, "has been practiced ever since the beginning of the world by every human being."[2] Nor was he the "first person who correctly analyzed that method and explained its uses," as Aristotle had done so long before. But these facts do not detract from the glory of Bacon any more than the discovery of America by the Norsemen five hundred years before the time of Columbus detracts from his glory. The same process of reasoning would take all credit from every philosopher that has ever lived, for with equal truth it may be said that every mental process "has been practiced ever since the beginning of the world by every human being."

Bacon's teachings resemble those of Montaigne, though Bacon's work was far more important and complete than that of his French contemporary. His pedagogy may be summed up in these pregnant words from his own pen: "A judicious blending and interchange

[1] "Essays," Vol. III, p. 459. [2] *Ibid.*, Vol. III, p. 470.

between the easier and more difficult branches of learning, adapted to the individual capabilities and to the future occupation of pupils, will profit both the mental and bodily powers, and make instruction acceptable."

We find in Bacon, then, the beginning of a new era in education. It remained for Comenius, Locke, Rousseau, Pestalozzi, and their compeers to apply to specific educational systems the great truth contained in the inductive method; and to scientists and investigators of all kinds has been intrusted the mission of furthering, through this method, the marvelous scientific development which has almost re-created the world.

RATKE[1] (1571–1635)

Perhaps the first to urge the reforms which constitute the basis of educational theory was Ratke, a German, born in the province of Holstein. He originated a scheme by which he promised to teach any language, ancient or modern, in six months. He traveled throughout Europe, endeavoring to sell his discovery to princes and men of learning. Purchasers had to agree strictly to maintain the secret. Professor Williams speaks of this conduct as follows: "These were the acts of a charlatan peddling some secret quack nostrum."[2] Mr. Quick says, "He would also found a school in which all arts and sciences should be rapidly learned and advanced; he would introduce, and peacefully maintain throughout the continent, a uniform speech, a uniform government, and, more wonderful still, a uniform religion. From these modest proposals we

[1] Also Rateke, Radtke, and Ratich. Paulsen pronounces the last "an abominable mutilation of Latinization."

[2] "History of Modern Education," p. 141.

should naturally infer that the promiser was nothing but a quack of more than usual impudence; but the position which the name of Ratich holds in the history of education is sufficient proof that this is by no means a complete statement of the matter."[1]

Many thinkers fully believed that the schools were in bondage to the classic studies, that they did not prepare for life, and that science, which had begun to show signs of awakening, should have a place in education. The extravagant theories of Ratke, therefore, attracted attention. Opportunity was given him to put his theories into practice, first at Augsburg, then at Köthen, and finally at Magdeburg. In each instance he utterly failed, more from want of tact in dealing with men, — with those in authority, as well as with his teachers and pupils, — than from lack of soundness in theory. Of course much of his theory was worthless, especially that referring to the mastery of a language in six months, and that proposing uniformity in speech, government, and religion.

Ratke's method of teaching a language was not original with him, being similar to, though not so effective as, that advocated by Roger Ascham, more than a hundred years before (see p. 191), and suggested first by Pliny, fifteen centuries earlier. Ratke required the pupil to go over the same matter many times, to learn the grammar in connection with translation, and finally to translate back into the original. He proposed to follow the same course with all languages, and have all grammars constructed on the same plan.

The work which Ratke began was more successfully carried out by others who followed him, and thus fruit has been borne to these new and radical ideas.

[1] Quick, "Educational Reformers," p. 51.

Quick sums up Ratke's pedagogy in a few words, as follows:[1]—

1. Everything after the order and course of nature.
2. One thing at a time.
3. One thing again and again repeated.
4. Nothing shall be learned by heart.
5. Uniformity in all things.
6. Knowledge of the thing itself must be given before that which refers to the thing.
7. Everything by experiment and analysis.
8. Everything without coercion;[2] that is, by gentle means, and not by the use of the rod.

Others have worked out these principles until they have become thoroughly incorporated into every system of modern pedagogy.

COMENIUS[2] (1592–1670)

By far the greatest educator of the seventeenth century, and one of the greatest in educational history, was Johann Amos Comenius. He was born in Moravia, and belonged to the Protestant body known as the Moravian Brethren. His early education was neglected, a fact that was not without its compensation, for, not beginning the study of Latin until sixteen years of age, he was mature enough to appreciate the defects in the prevalent method of instruction. One of his most valuable services to education grew out of his attempt to remedy the defects thus discovered.

Of the schools he attended, he says, "They are the terror of boys, and the slaughterhouses of minds,—places

[1] "Educational Reformers," p. 53.

[2] Especial attention is called to Laurie's "Life of Comenius," and Monroe's "Comenius." For other works, see Appendix of Bardeen's edition of Laurie's "Comenius."

where a hatred of books and literature is contracted, where ten or more years are spent in learning what might be acquired in one, where what ought to be poured in gently is violently forced in, and beaten in, where what ought to be put clearly and perspicuously is presented in a confused and intricate way, as if it were a collection of puzzles, — places where minds are fed on words."[1]

In speaking of his own experience at school, he says, "I was continually full of thoughts for the finding out of some means whereby more might be inflamed with the love of learning, and whereby learning itself might be made more compendious, both in the matter of charge and cost, and of labor belonging thereto, that so the youth might be brought by a more easy method unto some notable proficiency in learning."[2]

The life of Comenius, which extended over nearly eighty years, was full of vicissitudes and trials. Briefly told, it is as follows: He was left an orphan at an early age, had poor educational advantages in childhood, began the study of Latin at sixteen, and completed his studies at Heidelberg at twenty-two, having previously studied at Herborn. After leaving the university, he was teacher of the Moravian School at Prerau for two years, and then having been ordained to the ministry, became pastor of Fulnek. Here he remained for a number of years, living a happy and useful life. In the meantime, the Thirty Years' War had broken out, the battle of Prague had been lost by the Protestants, and the town of Fulnek sacked. Comenius lost everything he possessed, and this misfortune was soon followed by the death of his wife and child. After hiding in the mountains for some time, he was banished from his native land, together with all the other Protestants. This

[1] Laurie, "Life of Comenius," p. 14. [2] Preface to the "Prodromus."

took place in 1627, when Comenius was thirty-five years old. Though he often longed to return to his fatherland, he was never permitted to do so.

He settled in Poland, and began by the study of the works of Ratke, Bacon, and other writers to prepare himself for the great task of educational reform. Of this experience he writes, "After many workings and tossings of my thoughts, by reducing everything to the immovable laws of nature, I lighted upon my 'Didactica Magna,' which shows the art of readily and solidly teaching all men all things."

He visited England, Sweden, and Hungary in the interests of education, and was invited to France, but did not accept the invitation. While living at Leszno, Poland, for a second time his house was sacked and all his property destroyed. Among other things, his work on Pansophia, and his Latin-Bohemian dictionary, on which he had labored for forty years, were burned. He closed his days at Amsterdam, Holland. In addition to the great honors bestowed upon him by the various countries that sought his advice on educational matters, he was made the chief bishop and head of the Moravian Brethren. Raumer forcibly sums up the life of Comenius as follows: "Comenius is a grand and venerable figure of sorrow. Though wandering, persecuted, and homeless, during the terrible and desolating Thirty Years' War, yet he never despaired, but with enduring courage, and strong faith, labored unweariedly to prepare youth by a better education for a happier future. Suspended from the ministry, as he himself tells us, and an exile, he became an apostle to the Christian youth; and he labored for them with a zeal and love worthy of the chief of the apostles." [1]

[1] Raumer, "Geschichte der Pädagogik."

Pedagogical Work. — The great educational works of Comenius are his "Gate of Tongues Unlocked," the "Great Didactic," and his "Orbis Pictus." Mr. Quick thinks that the "Great Didactic" "contains, in the best form, the principles he afterward endeavored to work out"[1] in his other educational writings. "The services of Comenius to pedagogy," says Professor Williams, "were of a threefold character, in each of which his merit was very great. First, he was the true originator of the principles and methods of the Innovators. Second, he was a great educational systematist. Third, he was the author of improved textbooks, which were long and widely famous."[2] This is a fair summing up of the remarkable activity of this man with the exception of the first point. Montaigne, Ratke, and Bacon had previously taught many of the fundamental truths which Comenius merely amplified and brought to practical fruition, and he himself acknowledged the influence of the last two men upon him. That the whole purpose of the life of Comenius was far nobler than that of Ratke or Bacon, there remains no room for doubt. Compayré says, "The character of Comenius equals his intelligence. Through a thousand obstacles he devoted his long life to the work of popular instruction. With a generous ardor he consecrated himself to infancy. He wrote twenty works and taught in twenty cities. Moreover, he was the first to form a definite conception of what the elementary studies should be."[3]

Bacon gave the inspiration and Comenius worked the truth into practical form; Bacon invented a new theory of scientific investigation, Comenius employed that theory in

[1] "Educational Reformers," p. 73.

[2] "History of Modern Education," p. 151.

[3] "History of Pedagogy," p. 122.

education; Bacon originated and Comenius applied. This does not detract from the merit of Comenius any more than his work detracts from the merit of Rousseau, Pestalozzi, or Horace Mann, all of whom gathered inspiration from him.

Summary of the Work of Comenius.—(1) He was the author of the first illustrated text-book, the "Orbis Pictus."[1] The cost of illustrations was for a long time a serious barrier to their general adoption in schoolbooks; but modern inventions and improvements have removed this obstacle, and many of the text-books of to-day are as valuable for their illustrations as for their text. The "Orbis Pictus" appeared in 1658.

(2) In his "Great Didactic," he presents a scheme for general organization of the school system which covers the first twenty-four years of life. It divides this time into four equal periods of six years, each as follows:—

1. *Infancy*, or the mother school, from birth up to six years of age.

2. *Boyhood*, the vernacular or national school, from six to twelve.

3. *Adolescence*, the *Gymnasium* or Latin school, from twelve to eighteen.

4. *Youth*, the university (including travel), from eighteen to twenty-four.

"The infant school should be found in every house, the vernacular school in every village and community, the gymnasium in every province, and the university in every kingdom or large province." This scheme, with variation of details, forms the basis of present school systems: first, the period in the home with the mother till six;

[1] See "Orbis Pictus," edited and published by C. W. Bardeen, Syracuse, N.Y.

second, the period of general education in the common school, from six to twelve or fourteen; third, the period of preparation for the professional schools, from twelve or fourteen to eighteen; and fourth, the professional or university course, from eighteen to twenty-four. The last is usually divided into a college and a university course.

(3) The educational principles of Comenius were revolutionary as to the school practices of the time. They have come to be almost universally accepted at present. We can here state only a few of the most essential.[1]

1. If we would teach and learn surely, we must follow the order of Nature.

2. Let everything be presented through the senses.

3. Proceed from the easy to the difficult, from the near to the remote, from the general to the special, from the known to the unknown.

4. Make learning pleasant by the choice of suitable material, by not attempting too much, by the use of concrete examples, and by the selection of that which is of utility.

5. Fix firmly by frequent repetitions and drills.

6. Let all things advance by indissoluble steps, so that everything taught to-day may give firmness and stability to what was taught yesterday, and point the way to the work of to-morrow."[2]

7. Let everything that is useless be eliminated from teaching.

8. Learn to do by doing.

9. Each language should be learned separately, have a definite time assigned to it, be learned by use rather

[1] Laurie's "Life and Works of Comenius," p. 77.
[2] *Ibid.*, p. 105.

than precept, — that is, the practice in learning should be with familiar things, — and all tongues should be learned by one and the same method.

10. The example of well-ordered life of parents, nurses, teachers, and schoolfellows is very important for children; but precepts and rules of life must be added to example.

11. As knowledge of God is the highest of all knowledge, the Holy Scriptures must be the alpha and omega of the Christian schools.

Comenius gives explicit directions as to methods of instruction, class management, discipline, courses of study, including a discussion of each branch, and moral and religious teaching. He presents these directions in the most remarkable and complete series of precepts and principles to be found in educational literature.[1]

MILTON (1608-1674)

John Milton was "the most notable man who ever kept school or published a schoolbook." While his fame rests on "Paradise Lost" and other great literary works, he deserves a place among educators for his "Tractate on Education," and for his sympathy with educational reform. He anticipated Herbert Spencer's celebrated definition, — "To prepare us for complete living is the function which education has to discharge," — in the following words: "I call, therefore, a complete and generous education that which fits a man to perform justly, skillfully, and magnanimously all the offices, both private and public, of peace and war."

He criticised the schools of his time and sought to

[1] For full discussion of the pedagogical principles of Comenius, see Professor Laurie's great work.

make them more practical. Like the earlier Innovators, and in harmony with the spirit that was rapidly growing, he thought that too much time was given to the study of Latin, and urged that science, music, physical culture, and language as a means of acquiring a knowledge of useful things, should receive more attention in the schools. Quick says, "A protest against a purely literary education comes with tremendous force from the student who sacrificed his sight to his reading, the accomplished scholar whose Latin works were known throughout Europe, and the author of 'Paradise Lost.'"[1]

Milton's experience in teaching was confined to a small boarding school, such as those usually resorted to for educating the sons of the better classes in England at that time. For pupils he began with two nephews, to whom were soon added a few other boys. These were sons of Milton's friends, and some of them came as boarders, others as day students. Milton seemed to like the work of teaching, and it was during this period that his "Tractate" was written. He probably taught school in this way for eight or nine years, and then was appointed to a small office under the government, which secured his living. The rest of his life was devoted chiefly to literary work.

Milton's "Tractate." — The principal lessons from this educational work are embodied in the following quotation: "The end then of Learning is to repair the ruines of our first Parents by regaining to know God aright, and out of that knowledge to love him, and to imitate him, to be like him, as we may the nearest by possessing our souls of true virtue, which being united to the heavenly grace of faith makes up the highest perfection."[2] This

[1] "Educational Reformers," p. 59. [2] "Tractate," p. 3.

rather cumbersome definition shows how fully Milton was possessed of the Puritan spirit, which then controlled England, and which magnified religious zeal.

Milton's scheme of education may be briefly summed up as follows:—

1. The school premises should consist of a spacious house with large school grounds, intended for about one hundred and thirty students from twelve to twenty-one years of age, who should receive their complete secondary and university education in the same school. This scheme, so unique in Milton's time, is practically carried out in France and the United States, where the connection between the lower and higher schools is direct. In England, the land of its inception, and in Germany, there is no such direct articulation between the lower and the higher schools.

2. The course of study embraces, first, the Latin grammar, arithmetic, geometry, religion, and Greek authors to be read in translation; second, Latin authors, geography, natural philosophy; third, Greek, trigonometry,—intended to prepare for fortification,—architecture, engineering, and navigation, anatomy, and medicine.

This course is supposed to be completed at about the age of sixteen. The harder topics now follow, together with the study of those subjects intended to teach ethical judgment. Milton says, "As they begin to acquire character, and to reason on the difference between good and evil, there will be required a constant and sound indoctrinating to set them right and firm, instructing them more amply in the knowledge of virtue and the hatred of vice." Then come Greek authors, Holy Writ, poetry, and "at any odd hour, the Italian tongue," ethics, and politics. He is consistent with his definition of education,—"that which fits a man to perform justly, skillfully, and magnanimously all the offices, both public and private, of peace and war," when he would train men to be "steadfast pillars of the State." He adds in his course also the study of law, including Roman edicts and English common law, a knowledge of Hebrew, and possibly Syrian and Chaldaic.

Nor were physical exercises omitted. Sword exercises, wrestling, military tactics, riding, etc., were to be daily practiced, each in its proper time. Finally, the young man, when about twenty-three years of age, should travel abroad, and thus, when mature enough to comprehend them, become acquainted with the geography, history, and politics of other countries. This was to be the final preparation for citizenship and service of country. Mr. Browning pronounces this a "magnificent and comprehensive scheme." The most serious criticism of it is, that it marks out much more than the average young man can accomplish.

LOCKE[1] (1632–1704)

John Locke was the son of a Puritan gentleman who took active part in the wars for religious freedom fought during the latter part of the seventeenth century. Without doubt the stirring scenes enacted and the great moral movements which occupied England had a great influence upon Locke's life. He was carefully trained at home until he was about fourteen years old, when he entered Westminster School, a Puritan institution, where he remained for six years. He then entered Oxford, and in due time took his bachelor's and master's degrees. In

[1] See Fowler's "Locke." Also Quick, Compayré, and Williams.

1660, when twenty-eight years old, he was made tutor of Christ Church, Oxford, where he lectured on Greek, rhetoric, and philosophy. He interested himself in theology, but never took orders; and he also studied medicine and for a time practiced it. His own health was precarious, he having suffered from chronic consumption nearly all his life. Nevertheless, he accomplished a tremendous amount of work. The friendship of the Earl of Shaftesbury gave Locke some political prestige. He lived in the family of that nobleman for many years, and was the tutor of his son and grandson.

Locke's great work, on which his fame securely rests, is the "Essay concerning Human Understanding," which stamps him as the greatest of English philosophers. This appeared in 1690. His most important educational work is entitled "Some Thoughts concerning Education." Compayré says, "From psychology to pedagogy the transition is easy, and Locke had to make no great effort to become an authority on education after having been an accomplished philosopher." Further, the same author says concerning the essential principles discussed in "Thoughts concerning Education," "These are: 1, in physical education, the hardening process; 2, in intellectual education, practical utility; 3, in moral education, the principle of honor, set up as a rule for the free self-government of man."

In Locke, for the first time, we find a careful set of rules as to the food, sleep, physical exercise, and clothing of children. While modern science rejects some of these, most of them are regarded as sound in practice. Plenty of outdoor exercise, clothing loose and not too warm, plain food with but little meat or sugar, proper hours of sleep, and beds not too soft, early retiring and rising, and cold baths, are means prescribed to harden the body and prepare it to resist the attacks of disease. "*A sound mind in a sound body*" is the celebrated aphorism which sums up Locke's educational theory.

As to moral education, Locke declares, "That which a gentleman ought to desire for his son, besides the fortune which he leaves him, is, 1, virtue; 2, prudence; 3, good manners; 4, instruction." In his course of study the idea of utility prevails. After reading, writing, drawing, geography, and the mother tongue are mastered, Locke, like Montaigne, would teach the language of nearest neighbors, and then Latin. Even the Latin tongue should be learned through use, rather than by rules of grammar and by memorizing the works of classic authors.

While his system of education was planned for sons of gentlemen, Locke urged the establishment of "working schools" for children of the laboring classes. This was in line with his utilitarian ideas, as the intent was not so much intellectual training, as the formation of steady habits and the preparation for success in industrial pursuits. Locke's plan was for a sort of manual training school, the first appearance of such a project in history.

Locke did not believe in universal education, nor in the public school. Only gentlemen were provided for in his formal scheme, and herein he followed the path marked out by Alfred the Great eight hundred years before, which England has not completely forsaken to this day. Since he had done all his teaching as a private tutor in the family of a gentleman, one can easily understand his advocacy of that form of instruction for the favored few. Locke's teachings in this respect are gradually losing their hold even in England, the most conservative of all countries in educational matters, and the latest great nation to accept the principle of universal education. During the last quarter of a century England has been earnestly seeking to give every child, whether of gentle or of humble birth, rich or poor, what his birthright demands, — a good common school education.

The influence of Locke upon education, then, has been very great. Williams remarks that "he inspired Rousseau with nearly every valuable thought which appears in the brilliant pages of his 'Émile.' He seems himself to have derived some of his most characteristic ideas from Montaigne, and possibly also from Rabelais."[1] Although Locke differed from other educational reformers in many respects, though he was somewhat narrow in his conception of education, owing to his environment, he opposed the dry formalism that characterized the educational practice of his time, and sought to emancipate man both intellectually and physically.

FÉNELON (1651–1715)

Fénelon was born of noble parents in the province of Périgord, France. During his early years his father attended very carefully to his education, and later his uncle, the Marquis de Fénelon, became his guardian. Though delicate in health, the boy showed remarkable aptness in learning. At the age of twelve he entered the college of Cahors, and thence went to the university of Paris. He was destined by his parents for the Church, for which, by natural temperament and pious zeal, he was well fitted. He preached at fifteen with marked success, and took up a theological course at St. Sulpice. At the age of twenty-four he was ordained priest. He desired to enter the

[1] "History of Modern Education," p. 181.

missionary field, first in Canada, and later in Greece, but had to abandon this purpose on account of ill health.

Saint-Simon, in his "Mémoires," describes Fénelon as a man of striking appearance, and says, "His manner altogether corresponded to his appearance; his perfect ease was infectious to others, and his conversation was stamped with the grace and good taste which are acquired by habitual intercourse with the best society and the great world."

For ten years Fénelon was at the head of the convent of the *New Catholics*, an institution which sought to reclaim Protestant young women to Catholicism. In this position, as well as in all his lifework, though himself an ardent Catholic, Fénelon's course was so temperate and just that he won the warmest admiration even of Protestants, who did not accept his faith. Among his friends were the Duke and Duchess of Beauvilliers, who had eight daughters and several sons. At their suggestion, and for the purpose of helping them in educating their daughters, he wrote his first and most important educational work, "The Education of Girls." Compayré pronounces this "the first classical work of French pedagogy." He further speaks of this book as "a work of gentleness and goodness, of a complaisant and amiable grace, which is pervaded by a spirit of progress."[1] It appeared in 1687.

In 1689, when thirty-eight years of age, Fénelon was chosen preceptor of the grandson of Louis XIV., the young Duke of Burgundy. In this position his remarkable powers as a teacher were brought to light, and he applied the theories which he had promulgated. The young duke, who was eight years of age, was of a passionate nature, hard to

[1] "History of Pedagogy," p. 165.

control, and yet, withal, of warm-hearted impulses. It is said that "he would break the clocks which summoned him to unwelcome duty, and fly into the wildest rage with the rain which hindered some pleasure." The "Telemachus"[1] of Fénelon, perhaps his greatest literary work, was composed at this time, as were also his "Dialogues of the Dead" and his "Fables." The inspiration of all these works was found in the charge committed to him — that of properly instructing his royal pupil. Fénelon thus created the material through which he interested the boy and taught him the intended lessons. The "Telemachus" was designed for the moral and political instruction of the prince; through his "Dialogues of the Dead" he taught history; and his "Fables" were composed for the purpose of teaching the moral and intellectual lessons which he wished to impart to his illustrious, but headstrong, pupil. Fénelon's success with the prince was phenomenal, as the passionate boy became affectionate, docile, and obedient.

The success of the experiment, however, was never put to the final test, as the duke died before coming to the throne. There seems to be no doubt that the cure was permanent, and it is not believed that, like Nero, he would have relapsed into his former viciousness and cruelty.

One naturally compares Fénelon with Seneca. To both were committed children, heirs apparent to thrones, — willful, cruel, disobedient, and hard to control. In Seneca's pupil the seeds of cruelty remained, to germinate into the awful tyrant; in Fénelon's the evil seemed to be permanently eradicated, and the result was a prince with generous impulses and noble intentions. And this result was largely owing to the difference in the teachers, — Fénelon, the gentle, but firm, patient, painstaking

[1] "Schoolmaster in Comedy and Satire," pp. 73–100.

conscientious man; Seneca, the more brilliant, but vacillating and timeserving sycophant.

Fénelon's Pedagogy. — 1. There must be systematic care of the body. Therefore regular meals and plain food, plenty of sleep, exercise, etc., are essential.

2. All instruction must be made pleasant and interesting. Play is to be utilized in teaching. In this he anticipated Froebel.

3. Let punishments be as light as possible. Encourage children to be open and truthful, and do not prevent confession by making punishments too frequent or too severe. Punishment should be administered privately, as a rule, and publicly only when all other means have failed.

4. Present the thing before its name, — the idea before the word. Study things, investigate. Employ curiosity. In this he was a disciple of Bacon and Comenius, and a prophet to Pestalozzi.

5. Allow nothing to be committed to memory that is not understood.

6. Girls, also, must share the benefits of education. Especial attention should be given to teaching them modesty, gentleness, piety, household economy, the duties of their station in life, and those of motherhood.

7. Morality should be taught early and by means of fables, stories, and concrete examples.

8. Proceed from the near at hand to the remote, from the known to the unknown. Thus in language, after the mother tongue, teach other living languages, and then the classics. The latter are to be learned by conversation about common objects, and by application of the rules of grammar in connection therewith. In geography and history one's own environment and country should be learned first, then other countries.

9. Example is of great importance to all periods of life, but especially to childhood. This Fénelon practically illustrated by his own life and by the concrete cases which he used. Voltaire says of Fénelon, "His wit was overflowing with beauty, his heart with goodness."

LA SALLE AND THE BROTHERS OF THE CHRISTIAN SCHOOLS[1]

In 1681, La Salle, a devoted priest of the Catholic Church, organized the *Brothers of the Christian Schools.*

The idea primarily was to awaken interest in elementary education. He perfected the work already done by Peter Faurier, Charles Demia, and others. The method of instruction, up to this time, had been largely individual. The pupils were called up to the teacher, one by one, or at most two by two, and, after the lesson had been heard, they were sent back to their seats to study. La Salle conceived the idea of grading together pupils of the same advancement, and teaching them simultaneously,—a practice now employed in primary schools everywhere. It is known as the *Simultaneous Method.* Brother Azarias says of this method, "Because we all of us have been trained according to this method, and see it practiced in nearly all of our public and many of our private schools throughout the land, and have ceased to find it a subject of wonder, we may be inclined to undervalue its importance. Not so was it regarded in the days of La Salle. Then a Brothers' School was looked upon with admiration. Strangers were shown it as a curiosity worth visiting."

[1] Especial reference is made to Brother Azarias, "Essays Educational."

La Salle laid down many explicit rules concerning punishment, methods of teaching, and school organization in a book called "The Conduct of Schools." While modern criticism would condemn many of these rules, we think, with Compayré, that "whatever the distance which separates these gloomy schools from our modern ideal, — from the pleasant, active, animated school, such as we conceive it to-day, — there is none the less obligation to do justice to La Salle, to pardon him for practices which were those of his time, and to admire him for the good qualities that were peculiarly his own."[1]

He established the first normal school in history at Rheims in 1684, thirteen years before Francke organized his teachers' class at Halle, and fifty years before Hecker founded the first Prussian normal school at Stettin. La Salle magnified the teacher's office, and urgently demanded professional training for instructors of the young. Brother Azarias forcibly sums up La Salle's great work in this respect as follows: "He is the benefactor of the modern schoolmaster. He it was who raised primary teaching out of the ruts of never ending routine, carried on in the midst of time-honored noise and confusion, and, in giving it principles and a method, made of it a science. He hedged in the dignity of the schoolmaster. He was the first to assert the exclusive right of the master to devote his whole time to his school work."[2]

Education, therefore, owes to La Salle three important contributions, — (1) the Simultaneous Method of Instruction, whereby a number of children of the same advancement are taught together; (2) the first Normal School, established at Rheims, France, in 1684; and (3) a dignifying of the teacher's profession by setting apart trained

[1] "History of Pedagogy," p. 276. [2] "Essays Educational," p. 238.

persons who should give all their time to the work of teaching.

Summary of the Educational Progress of the Seventeenth Century. — 1. School systems were established and compulsory attendance made efficient in Weimar, in 1619, in Gotha in 1642, and in many other cities, showing a growing recognition of the principle of universal education and the duty of the State to assume the responsibility for its attainment.

2. A school of educators, known as the "Innovators," laid emphasis on *sense-realism*, — the study of things, the contact with nature, the education that is of practical use.

3. Bacon laid the foundation of all future scientific research by his *inductive method*. This increased the riches of the world beyond calculation, taught how investigation is to be made, laid the foundation of modern science, and gave direction to all later education.

4. Ratke, though erratic and vulgar, instituted wholesome reforms in the teaching of languages, and promulgated theories which, under later reformers, bore rich fruitage.

5. Comenius, one of the greatest educators of all time, produced the first illustrated text-book, planned a general organization for schools in several countries, which is the basis of present systems, and proclaimed theories which are now universally accepted as the guide of modern pedagogical practice.

6. Milton, though primarily a literary man, lent the weight of his genius and his great name to school reform. He marked out a course of study which contemplates a unity of purpose from the elementary school to the university.

7. The great English philosopher, Locke, also found

time to devote to education. His principle, "*A sound mind in a sound body*," directed attention to physical education.

8. In the noble French priest, Fénelon, we find an example of theory practically applied. He gives, also, for the first time, a place in pedagogy to the education of girls.

9. In general, we find that the seventeenth century laid stress upon the principle of utility, gave great impulse to science, called attention to the care of the body, decreased the influence of classic studies, brushed away the fabric which superstition and conservatism had woven, produced some of the greatest educators that have ever lived, and laid the foundations on which modern education is built.

CHAPTER XXXIV

AUGUST HERMANN FRANCKE AND THE PIETISTS (1663–1727)

Literature. — *Rein*, Encyklopädisches Handbuch; *Strack*, Geschichte des Volkschulwesens; *Dyer*, Modern Europe; *Rein*, Am Ende der Schulreform? *Russell*, German Higher Schools.

PIETISM

Pietism is the name of a movement in Germany which sought to revive spiritual life in the Lutheran Church. In that church, religion had become purely a matter of intellect, instead of heart. Cold formality and adherence to the letter, rather than the spirit, had taken possession of the Protestant Church. Like the Jansenists in France, who had a similar purpose with reference to the Catholic Church, and later the Methodists in England, who sought to awaken religious zeal in the Church of England, the Pietists of Germany endeavored to vitalize religious life, and to lead men away from creeds promulgated by human agency, to the pure word of God. The Pietists differed from the orthodox Lutherans not in doctrine, but in insisting on the necessity of a change of heart and a pious life, instead of mere adherence to formal doctrine.

The Pietists founded the university of Halle, and this remained the center of the movement until it had run its course. Pietism had its inception during the latter part of the seventeenth century, and it extended through the first half of the eighteenth century. Its originator was Philipp Jakob Spener, a man of remarkable zeal and godly life. Though it met with bitter opposition on the part of the orthodox Lutherans, it certainly did great good, not only to its adherents, but to the Church at large, by awakening deeper spiritual life. Its influence was also great in reviving Biblical study in Germany, in improving the character of teachers, and in giving a spiritual direction to the studies of the schools. It has left an enduring monument in the great *Institutions* that it founded at Halle. The greatest of the Pietists was August Hermann Francke, who is celebrated, not only as a theologian, but as a philanthropist and teacher.

FRANCKE[1] (1663-1727)

Francke's early education was conducted by private teachers, though his parents, who were intelligent and God-fearing people, exerted a strong influence upon him. At thirteen he entered the highest class of the *Gymnasium* at Gotha, where he remained for one year. Here he was introduced to the reform teachings of Ratke and Comenius. Two years later he entered the university of Erfurt as a student of theology. He studied also at Kiel and Leipsic. While he gave particular attention to Hebrew and Greek, he also learned French, English, and Italian. He seemed to be gifted with a talent for learning languages, for during a short residence in Holland in later life he learned the Dutch language so well that he was able to preach in it. Under the instruction of a Jewish rabbi, he read the Hebrew Bible through seven times in one year. After spending some time as teacher in a private school, he returned to Leipsic as *Privat Docent*[2] in the university.

[1] Rein's "Encyklopädisches Handbuch," Vol. II, p. 336.

[2] The *Privat Docent* is the first step in the professor's career in the German university. He is allowed to lecture in the university, but receives no pay except fees from the students who hear him.

Having become acquainted with Spener and his teachings, Francke became an earnest Pietist. His success in lecturing and his zeal in religious work drew around him a large number of students. This awakened the envy of the old professors of the university, and they began a persecution which caused his dismissal. He then went to Erfurt and preached with remarkable success, drawing great crowds by his earnestness and eloquence. Persecution again followed him, and he was banished from the city.

About this time the new university of Halle called Francke to the chair of Greek and oriental languages and afterward to that of theology. He began his work in 1692, and remained in that position for nearly thirty-six years, until his death. As this position did not furnish enough to live upon, he became pastor of the church in the neighboring village of Glaucha. In his pastoral work he came in contact with poverty, drunkenness, and every form of immorality. Moved with pity, he collected small sums of money, which he distributed among the poor after catechising the children.

At Easter, 1695, he found seven guldens ($2.80) in the collection boxes, which he declared to be "A splendid capital with which something of importance can be founded; I will begin a school for the poor with it." This was the beginning of the great orphan asylum at Halle,— an enterprise the magnitude of which we shall describe later. Without visible income, with no means at command, but with a sublime faith in God and humanity, and an overwhelming sense of the ignorance and misery of the children about him, Francke began at once the great work; nor was his faith misplaced, as the result shows. He gathered together a few children and placed a student over them as a teacher. Soon the better class of citizens took an interest, and desired him to provide a school for their children. Two rooms were rented, one for those who could not pay and the other for those who could. This was the foundation of the *free school* and the *citizens' school* still connected with the *Institutions.* In the fall of 1695, Francke founded the orphan asylum. Money flowed in from all parts of the country as people began to understand the great work. Francke was thus able to branch out in many directions. He established a *Pedagogium* to prepare teachers for his and other schools; free meals were furnished to students who devoted a part of their time to teaching in the institutions; separate schools for boys and girls, a *Gymnasium,* a *Real-school,* a bookbindery and printing establishment, and many other institutions were founded.

The Institutions at Halle. — In a few years Francke had in successful operation a marvelous system, a work founded upon love of humanity and dependent upon philanthropy for its support. The results attracted attention from all Europe, and students came from many lands. "At the death of Francke in the year 1727, the following report of the *Institutions* was sent to King Frederick William I.: (1) In the *Pedagogism,* 82 scholars, 70 teachers and other persons; (2) in the Latin school, 3 inspectors, 32 teachers, 400 pupils, and 10 servants; (3) in the common school, 4 inspectors, 98 male teachers, 8 female teachers, 1725 boys and girls; (4) orphans, 100 boys, 34 girls, 10 overseers; (5) at the free table, 225 students, 360 poor children; (6) employed in the drug store, bookstore, etc., and other persons in the establishment, 82."[1] This makes a total of over 3200 persons instructed, sheltered, employed, or otherwise connected with these great *Institutions.* The

[1] K. Schmidt, "Geschichte der Pädagogik," Vol. III, p. 462.

foundations were so firmly laid that the progress has been steady from that time to this. At present there are no less than twenty-five different enterprises connected with the *Institutions*, among which may be mentioned a free school for boys, and one for girls; a common school for boys, and one for girls; a royal *Pedagogium;* a Latin school; a higher girls' school; a *Real-gymnasium;* a preparatory school for the high school; a *Real-school;* an orphan asylum for boys, and one for girls; a boarding house for students; a Bible house, which has distributed about 6,500,000 Bibles and religious works; a teachers' seminary (normal school) for each sex; a bookstore, a printing house, and a drug store.[1] About 3000 children receive instruction in the various schools, and about 118,000 have been recipients of the benefits since the *Institutions* were founded two hundred years ago. The cost is about one million marks a year, which is covered by endowments, by tuition fees, by profits from the productive departments (bookstores, printing establishment, etc.), and by moneys received from the State. Francke's idea of depending upon voluntary gifts has been abandoned.

All this work is the result of the energy of a man who began with a capital of less than three dollars, and a vast amount of faith to found "something of importance."

The Training of Teachers. — While Francke's greatest work for mankind was the *Institutions* mentioned above, we must notice one field of his activity that is of especial importance to us, — that of the training of teachers. We have seen that, on account of the scarcity of funds, he was obliged to rely upon students to do the work of instructing the children committed to his care. The young theologians made use of this opportunity as a stepping-

[1] See Rein, "Encyklopädisches Handbuch," Vol. II, p. 348.

stone to their future calling, the ministry, and Francke, perceiving this, sought to secure the most pious and gifted among his theological students for this work. He also established a pedagogical class (*Pedagogium*). After two years' membership therein, the student was allowed to teach provided he pledged himself to devote three years to teaching in the schools. This class met once a week for criticism and discussion under the leadership of the inspector of the school, and the various inspectors met Francke every evening for further instruction. The results soon attracted widespread notice, and created a great demand for Francke's teachers. Although this was very crude pedagogical training, it may be regarded as the inception of the normal school, which has now come to be an essential part of every educational system.

The Real-school. — A third service is credited by many to Francke, namely, the founding of the *Real-school*[1] of Germany. The best authorities give that credit to Professor Erhard Weigel of Jena. Whether or not the idea originated with Francke, he was ready to accept the necessity of such a change, and founded schools for higher learning in which Greek and Latin were not required, and in which more attention was given to modern languages and science.

[1] The *Real-school* is the great rival of the *Gymnasium* in Germany. The latter is the old established school which bases culture on the *Humanities*, — the classic languages, and literature. The *Real-school* is more modern and gives greater attention to the *Realities*, — to things of practical utility. Precedence is given to the modern languages, sciences, and arts. While the chief purpose of the *Gymnasium* is to prepare for the learned professions, that of the *Real-school* is to prepare for practical life. The relation of these two institutions to each other and to the university led to the *Berlin Conference* in 1890, at which it clearly appeared that the younger is outstripping the older and more conservative institution. See Russell, "German Higher Schools."

CHAPTER XXXV

GENERAL VIEW OF THE EIGHTEENTH AND NINETEENTH CENTURIES

Literature. — *Dyer*, Modern Europe; *Duruy*, The French Revolution; *Yonge*, Three Centuries of Modern History; *Andrews*, Institutes of General History; *Lord*, Beacon Lights; *Taylor*, History of Germany; *Guizot*, History of Civilization; *Draper*, Conflict between Religion and Science; *Schwickerath*, Jesuit Education.

THE history of the world since the seventeenth century has been crowded with events, and characterized by movements of greatest moment to mankind. It is not the purpose of this work to discuss political movements, to chronicle wars, or to study the great upheavals of society except in so far as they have a direct bearing upon educational questions.[1]

The political chains that fettered the nations of the world have gradually been broken until greater liberty has been secured, a more perfect acknowledgment of the rights of the individual brought about, and a more tolerant religious spirit fostered in every civilized land. These things have exerted a tremendous force in the intellectual emancipation of man. At last the long struggle of the centuries begins to bear legitimate fruit, and the supreme educational purpose of Christianity, that of asserting

[1] It must be freely admitted that such influences are powerful in shaping the destiny of man, and that they have had much to do with education, as we have often shown in the foregoing pages. We must, however, leave the tracing of the movements to each individual student.

and maintaining the importance of the individual, seems destined to complete realization. The noble truths of brotherly love, equality before God, and human rights were obscured during the long centuries, — obscured sometimes by the very institution whose chief aim is to scatter light and give gladness to men. It has remained for modern education to rediscover the educational principles which the Great Teacher promulgated, and which through the struggle of centuries failed of recognition, and bore indifferent fruit.

Among the many social and political changes that have taken place during the last two centuries, we may mention a few that have a direct influence upon education. Preceding centuries had prepared the way, — had broken the ground and sown the seed, and now the world was ready to reap an abundant harvest.

The great political events of this period may be briefly summarized as follows: —

1. *The abolition of human slavery.* — Great Britain, Spain, France, Russia, and finally our own country have forever removed the shackles of the slave within their borders. Perhaps the greatest of all emancipation acts was that of Russia, which, in 1861, without bloodshed and without serious disturbance, by royal decree, set free forty million serfs. The abolition of slavery in nearly all civilized countries is the greatest political triumph of Christian civilization. Without this there could never have come that higher intellectual emancipation which is the aim sought in all education.

2. *The extension of political rights.* — This is another victory that must be credited to the period under discussion. At the beginning of the eighteenth century there was scarcely a nation that acknowledged the right of the

individual to a part in government, or to personal freedom. Men were in vassalage to their immediate lord, who, in turn, was obliged to acknowledge the "divine right" of the king over him. With the exception of Switzerland, who for centuries had maintained her freedom, and of England, who had secured the rights of man only by much bloodshed, there was scarcely a people in the world that possessed the right of self-government. Even England had secured that right only in the latter half of the seventeenth century under the leadership of Cromwell. This right she did not concede to her colonies, however, until the American Revolution wrested her richest dependency from her, and forever established the principle of self-government for a sovereign people.

Immediately following the American Revolution came the French Revolution, which taught the Old World the ideas so heroically conceived, so bravely supported, and so successfully realized in the New World. Nor is this all. The same principle has compelled the rulers of most of the European nations to divide the responsibility of government with their subjects, and to grant their people enlarged powers but little short of absolute sovereignty.

3. *Science has been recognized as a powerful instrument of civilization.*—Through scientific discoveries there has been a wonderful accession to material wealth, invention has been stimulated, and progress has been made in all directions. The spirit of investigation has been fostered, old theories and superstitions have been abandoned, and truth has been established upon their ruins. In this direction more has been done by science during the eighteenth and nineteenth centuries than during the whole previous history of the world. Man has now become master of heretofore unknown forces which he may utilize

as a blessing for the human race. We shall see in later pages that scientific investigation has become the greatest educational principle of modern times.

4. *Religious freedom has been attained.*—The sixteenth and seventeenth centuries witnessed many struggles for religious liberty, which resulted in no decided victory. It was not until the last two centuries that complete religious freedom was gained. Men are no longer bound to accept ecclesiastical decrees without question, but every one may weigh and consider, and freely decide for himself. Civil law protects, civil society sustains, and public opinion justifies men in the exercise of personal liberty in religious matters.

By the realization of these great principles educational progress has been encouraged. The greatest obstacles have been removed, and the future opens with possibilities of universal brotherhood, universal peace, and universal education.

It remains for us to study some of the men who have contributed to the educational progress of the eighteenth and nineteenth centuries, to trace the chief movements in the intellectual development of the race, and to examine the school systems of the representative nations of the world at the present time.

CHAPTER XXXVI

MODERN EDUCATORS

Literature. — *Davidson*, Rousseau; *Graham*, Rousseau; *Morley*, Life of Rousseau; *Rousseau*, Émile; *Munroe*, Educational Ideal; *Vogel*, Geschichte der Pädagogik; *Quick*, Educational Reformers; *Weir*, The Key to Rousseau's Émile (article in *Educational Review*, Vol. XVI, p. 61); *Compayré*, History of Pedagogy.

ROUSSEAU (1712–1778)

JEAN JACQUES ROUSSEAU was born in Geneva, Switzerland. His father was a watchmaker, and upon him devolved the education of the boy, as the mother died in childbirth. Rousseau's father was a man of dissipated habits, careless of responsibility, and of very violent temper. He interested himself in his son far enough to teach him to read, and supplied him with the worthless novels which he himself was fond of reading. This unwise course doubtless had much to do in shaping the character of the boy. Probably it was the evil effects of this early literature that led Rousseau later in life to oppose teaching young children to read. Quick says, "Rousseau professed a hatred of books, which he said kept the student so long engaged upon the thoughts of other people as to have no time to make a store of his own."

Abandoned by his father at the age of ten, he was taken into the family of his uncle, who apprenticed him, first to a notary, and afterward to an engraver. At the age of sixteen he ran away, and began a life of vagabondage. While yet a young man, he became involved in intrigues, which, according to his own account in his "Confessions," were no credit to him. Madame de Warens, a young widow with whom he lived for some years, sent him to school at St. Lazare, where he studied the classics and music; but he soon lapsed again into vagabondage. He picked up a little music, and attempted to give lessons in it, but with small success. He also took a position as private tutor, but he had no talent for teaching. Later in life he married Thérèse le Vasseur, a woman from the common ranks of life. She bore him five children, all of whom he committed to foundling hospitals without means of identification. He did this because he was not willing that his own comfort or plans should be disturbed by the presence of children. Rousseau had reason to regret this heartless and unnatural course when, in later years, he sought in vain to find some trace of his children. Compayré says, "If he loved to observe children, he observed, alas, only the children of others. There is nothing sadder than that page of the 'Confessions,' in which he relates how he often placed himself at the window to observe the dismission of a school, in order to listen to the conversations of children as a furtive and unseen observer!"[1]

In 1749 Rousseau successfully competed for a prize offered by the Academy of Dijon on the subject, "Has the restoration of the sciences contributed to purify or to corrupt manners?" Rousseau entered this contest quite accidentally. He saw the notice of the contest in a newspaper, and decided at once to compete. Of this event he says, "If ever anything resembled a sudden inspiration, it was the movement which began in me as I read this.

[1] "History of Pedagogy," p. 286.

All at once I felt myself dazzled by a thousand sparkling lights; crowds of vivid ideas thronged into my mind with a force and confusion which threw me into unspeakable agitation; I felt my head whirling in a giddiness like that of intoxication. A violent palpitation oppressed me; unable to walk for difficulty of breathing, I sank under one of the trees of the avenue, and passed half an hour there in such a condition of excitement that when I rose I saw that the front of my waistcoat was all wet with tears, though I was wholly unconscious of shedding them. Ah, if I could have written the quarter of what I saw and felt under that tree, with what clearness should I have brought out all the contradictions of our social system; with what simplicity should I have demonstrated that man is good naturally, and that by institution only is he made bad."

This essay made him famous, and its publication was the beginning of a remarkable literary career. His principal literary works are his "Confessions," in which he declares that he conceals nothing concerning himself; the "Social Contract," an anti-monarchic work, which many believe incited the French Revolution; "Héloïse," a novel overstrained in sentiment and immoral in its teachings, but "full of pathos and knowledge of the human heart"; and "Émile," his greatest work, which contains his educational theories. The "Emile"[1] was an epoch-making book, which excited great interest throughout Europe. It is said that the philosopher Emanuel Kant became so absorbed in reading it that he forgot to take his daily walk.

Pedagogy.—(*a*) Rousseau's first principle is, "Everything is good as it comes from the hands of the Author of nature; everything degenerates in the hands of man." It follows, then, that education has only to prevent the

[1] "Schoolmaster in Literature," pp. 40–63.

entrance of evil, and let nature continue the work begun. It is to be a negative, as well as a natural, process. The fallacy of this principle is very forcibly shown by Vogel[1] as follows: "The very first sentence of 'Émile,' that man by nature is good, is a fundamental error; for by nature, that is, from birth, man is neither good nor bad, but morally indifferent. Only when the individual possesses mature self-consciousness does he have a correct idea of good and evil. If man by nature is good, it is inexplicable how evil can originate within him. External things may, indeed, furnish motives to evil, but are never in themselves evil; the evil arises rather from the conduct of the individual toward outside objects. If, then, evil does not come from without, and is not by nature already within the heart, it is impossible that there shall be such a thing as evil."

(*b*) The first education is physical and it begins at birth. As the physical wants of the child are natural they should be satisfied, but the clothing should be of such character as not to interfere with the perfect freedom of the body. Great care must be taken to distinguish between the real wants of the child and its passing whims. To gratify the latter because of the crying of the child will tend to form bad habits. In this connection may be taught the first moral lessons. It thus becomes important that the speech, gestures, and expressions of the young child shall be carefully studied. This is the first suggestion of the necessity for child study. The idea was later developed by Pestalozzi and Froebel, and is one of the most important features of recent pedagogical activity.

(*c*) The child's second period begins with his ability

[1] "Geschichte der Pädagogik," p. 127. See also Compayré, "History of Pedagogy," p. 286.

to speak and continues till the twelfth year. No attempt must be made to educate the child for his future, but he must be allowed to get the full enjoyment of childhood by freedom to play as he will. Let him run, jump, and test his strength, thereby acquiring judgment of the material forces about him, and learning how to take care of himself. Leave him free to do what he will, let him have what he wishes, but, as far as possible, he should be led to depend upon himself to satisfy his wants. Give him perfect freedom, for freedom is the fundamental law of education. If he disobeys, do not punish him,—disobedience works its own punishment; therefore, do not command him. The training of the senses is the important work of this period; therefore, there should be as little moral training as possible, and absolutely no religious training. The only moral idea for the child to learn is that of ownership. He is to be prevented from vice in a negative manner, that is, by never being allowed to meet it. "The only habit that a child should be allowed to form is to contract no habit."

He is to have a preceptor devoted entirely to him, not to instruct or control him, but to lead him to discover and experience for himself. In regard to his intellectual instruction, Rousseau says of *Émile* at twelve years of age, "that he has not learned to distinguish his right hand from his left." Books are entirely proscribed, and, indeed, they are useless to him as he cannot read; the only intellectual knowledge the child receives is that which comes from things through his own experience.

This is a brief outline of the erratic, impossible, and inconsistent training that Rousseau provides for *Émile* during this period when the foundation of character in the child must be laid. Gréard says, "Rousseau goes beyond progressive education to recommend an education in fragments, so to speak, which isolates the faculties in order to develop them one after another, which establishes an absolute line of demarkation between the different ages, and which ends in distinguishing three stages of progress in the soul. Rousseau's error on this point is in forgetting that the education of the child ought to prepare for the education of the young man."

(*d*) The third period extends from the twelfth to the fifteenth year. It is the period of intellectual development. With no habits of thought or study, being little else than a robust animal, in three years *Émile* is to obtain all needed intellectual training. True, Rousseau excludes everything that is not useful, and places limitations even on that. For example, he naturally lays great stress upon the physical sciences which are to be taught in connection with things themselves, — out of doors, by travel, and in actual life; but he allows no history, or grammar, or ancient languages. No books are permitted save "Robinson Crusoe," which Rousseau finds entirely suitable for *Émile*. A trade is to be learned during this period.

While in general we condemn Rousseau's scheme of education, there is much in his methods that is most excellent. On this point Compayré comments as follows: "At least in the general method which he commends, Rousseau makes amends for the errors in his plan of study: 'Do not treat the child to discourses which he cannot understand. No descriptions, no eloquence, no figures of speech. Be content to present to him appropriate objects. Let us transform our sensations into ideas. But let us not jump at once from sensible to intellectual objects. Let us always proceed slowly from one sensible notion to another. In general, let us never substitute the sign for the thing, except when it is impossible for us to show the thing.'"[1]

(*e*) The fourth period of education begins at fifteen, the period of adolescence. At this time, "*Émile* will know nothing of history, nothing of humanity, nothing of art and literature, nothing of God; but he will know a manual trade." Rousseau himself says, "*Émile* has but little knowledge, but that which he has is really his own; he knows nothing by halves." He has a mind which, "if not instructed, is at least capable of being instructed." The remaining work to be done in the education of *Émile* consists in training the sentiments of affection, the moral and the religious sentiments. The feeling of love for his fellow-beings is now to be cultivated. The error of this is shown by Compayré, who says, "For fifteen years Rousseau leaves the heart of *Émile* unoccupied. . . . Rousseau made the mistake of thinking that a child can be taught to love as he is taught to read and write, and that lessons could be given to *Émile* in feeling just as lessons are given to him in geometry."

In morals Rousseau taught that the first duty of every one is to take care of himself; we must love ourselves first of all, and find our greatest interest in those things that best serve us. We must seek that which is useful to us and avoid what harms us, instead of loving our enemies and doing good to those that hate us, as taught by Christ. We must love those who love us, while we must avoid and hate those who hate us.

As to religion, *Émile* does not yet know at fifteen that he has a soul, and Rousseau thinks that perhaps the eighteenth year is still too early for him to learn that fact; for, if he tries to learn it before the proper time, he runs

[1] "History of Pedagogy," p. 298.

the risk of never really knowing that he possesses an immortal soul. But as religion furnishes a check upon the passions, it should be taught to the boy when eighteen years of age. He is not to be instructed in the doctrines of any particular sect, but should be allowed to select that religious belief which most strongly appeals to his reason. Modern investigation has proven the utter fallacy of Rousseau's teachings in this respect. Indeed, it seems to be established that the most orthodox period of the child's life occurs before the fifteenth year, the time when Rousseau would begin his religious training. Conformable to this truth, many sects confirm children and receive them into the church at or before the fifteenth year.[1]

(*f*) Having brought *Émile* to the period of life at which he is to marry, Rousseau proceeds to create in Sophie the ideal wife. It is not the education of women as such that Rousseau discusses, but their education with reference to man. He says, "The whole education of women should be relative to men; to please them, to be useful to them, to make themselves honored and loved by them, to educate the young, to care for the older, to advise them, to console them, to make life agreeable and sweet to them,—these are the duties of women in every age." Consequently the sole instruction woman needs is in household duties, in care of children, in ways to add to the happiness of her husband. Her own happiness or development does not enter into Rousseau's scheme. This is the weakest part of his educational theory. The world is gradually awakening

[1] See address of Professor Earl Barnes, Proceedings of the National Educational Association for 1893, p. 765. Also article by Dr. G. Stanley Hall in *Pedagogical Seminary*, Vol. I, p. 196. Note also the religious development of Laura Bridgman.

to the fact that woman's intellectual capacity is not inferior to that of man, and the prejudices of ages are slowly disappearing.

Rousseau's pedagogical theories made a profound impression throughout Europe, and though often inconsistent, extravagant, and visionary, they set the world to thinking of the child and his psychological development. A new direction was thus given to educational theory and practice, and upon this basis Pestalozzi, Froebel, and other modern educators have built. Rousseau must, therefore, be reckoned among the greatest pedagogical writers of modern times. Karl Schmidt pronounces the "Émile" "a Platonic republic of education,—nevertheless, Rousseau's work is a great universal achievement, the importance of which Goethe recognizes when he calls the book the *nature-gospel* of education."[1]

[1] "Geschichte der Pädagogik," Vol. III, p. 559.

CHAPTER XXXVII

MODERN EDUCATORS (*Continued*)

BASEDOW[1] (1723–1790)

THE name of Basedow is connected with what is known as the *Philanthropinic* experiment. He was born at Hamburg, his father being a wigmaker. Not being appreciated in his home, the son ran away and bound himself out as servant in the household of a gentleman. Through the influence of this man, who discovered his extraordinary abilities, he was reconciled with his father, and returned home. He was sent to the *Gymnasium* at Hamburg, and afterward, through the assistance of friends, went to the university of Leipsic, where he studied theology. Here he lived a rather wild life, and upon the completion of his studies was found too unorthodox to take orders. Accordingly, he became tutor (Hauslehrer) to the children of Herr von Quaalen. In this position he showed great aptitude and originality in the instruction of children. His method of teaching included conversation, adaptation of play, and use of the woods, fields, plants, birds, and other works of nature.

"Owing to his original manner of teaching, Basedow obtained the best results. In teaching Latin, for instance, he began by pointing to objects and giving their Latin

[1] Special References, Williams, "History of Modern Education"; Quick, "Educational Reformers," pp. 144, 288; Lang, "Basedow" (Teachers' Manuals, No. 16).

names. His pupils, in a very short time, learned to speak Latin almost as well as their native language. Basedow himself learned French, after the same manner, of the governess of the house."[1]

He next became Professor of Morals and Polite Literature at Soröe, Denmark, where his unorthodox writings again led him into trouble. He was removed to the *Gymnasium* at Altona. Rousseau's "Émile" produced a profound impression upon him, as it had done upon many other thinkers in Europe, and many of his theories are probably traceable to that book. Basedow was convinced of the need of a radical reform in the schools of Germany, and set himself the task of effecting it.. Bernsdorf, the Danish minister of education, became interested in his writings, and, together with several of the crowned heads of Europe, assisted him in bringing out his "Elementary Book" (Elementarbuch), which foreshadowed his plans. It was modeled after the "Orbis Pictus" of Comenius. The interest of these distinguished patrons shows how urgent was the need of an educational reform. Basedow also made the acquaintance of the great literary men of the time, chief among whom was Goethe. In temperament he was misanthropic and peevish, owing in part, doubtless, to ill health brought on by overwork and worry.

The Philanthropin. — Indirectly through Goethe, Prince Leopold of Dessau was attracted to Basedow. The prince determined to found an institute in which the plans of the great educator could be carried out. The institute, called the Philanthropin, was established, and became celebrated throughout Europe. Quick says: "Then, for the first and probably for the last time, a school was started in which use and wont were entirely set aside, and every-

[1] Lang, "Basedow," p. 6.

thing done on 'improved principles.' Such a bold enterprise attracted the attention of all interested in education, far and near; but it would seem that few parents considered their own children *vilia corpora* (vile bodies), on whom experiments might be made for the public good. When, in May, 1776, a number of schoolmasters and others collected from different parts of Germany, and even from beyond Germany, to be present by Basedow's invitation at an examination of the children, they found only thirteen pupils in the Philanthropin, including Basedow's own son and daughter."[1]

The main purpose of the Philanthropin was to give Basedow an opportunity to carry out his new educational ideas. A prominent feature of the undertaking was that it should be a model institute "for the preparation of teachers in the theory and practice of the new education." The institution was to be a "school of true humanity. Its name was to give evidence of its object—the education of youth in accordance with the laws of nature and humanity." In it Basedow was to exemplify his ideas of education. The best of teachers were to be employed, the best appliances furnished, and the instruction was to be founded entirely on sense-perception. The Philanthropin was opened in 1774, and at once awoke universal interest.

But this school, conceived in love for humanity, founded with the noblest of purposes, and exemplifying much of sound educational philosophy, was destined to be short-lived. It was abandoned in less than twenty years. This downfall was owing to several causes, some of which may be mentioned. 1. The institution was purely secular in character, and the world was not yet ready for this. Parents were suspicious of a non-sectarian school, the idea of

[1] "Educational Reformers," p. 150.

which was so contrary to that of the traditional church-school. Hence the small number of pupils in the Philanthropin, even at the height of its prosperity under Basedow.

2. Altogether too many subjects were included in the course. Quick outlines the work undertaken as follows: "(1) Man. Here he would use the pictures of foreigners and wild men, also a skeleton, a hand in spirits, and other objects still more appropriate to a surgical museum. (2) Animals. Only such animals are to be depicted as it is useful to know about, because there is much that ought to be known, and a good method of instruction must shorten rather than increase the hours of study. Articles of commerce made from the animals may also be exhibited. (3) Trees and plants. Only the most important are to be selected. Of these the seeds also must be shown, and cubes formed of the different woods. Gardeners' and farmers' implements are to be explained. (4) Mineral and chemical substances. (5) Mathematical instruments for weighing and measuring; also the air pump, siphon, and the like. The form and motion of the earth are to be explained with globes and maps. (6) Trades. The use of various tools is to be taught. (7) History. This is to be illustrated by engravings of historical events. (8) Commerce. Samples of commodities may be produced. (9) The younger children should be shown pictures of familiar objects about the house and its surroundings."[1]

There are very many suggestive ideas in Basedow's course, which have been adopted in modern schools; but the trouble was that he demanded too much, and he himself acknowledged later in life that "he had exaggerated notions of the amount boys were capable of

[1] "Educational Reformers," p. 151.

learning," and accordingly his curriculum was very much shortened.

3. Another reason for the failure of the Philanthropin was Basedow's indiscriminate condemnation of everything that had been done before, and of all who failed to agree with him. This awoke the antagonism of teachers everywhere. All reformers are apt to be radical in their own views and denunciatory of the opinions of others. Had there been less to criticise in Basedow himself, he would doubtless have triumphed over all opposition. But his educational theories and practices did not produce the results which he predicted for them, and his opponents were quick to mark every weakness that his system betrayed.

4. More fatal still, perhaps, was the unfitness of Basedow for the directorship of the institution. He was capricious, lacking in self-command and proper balance, visionary, and often suspicious of the teachers under his direction. Such causes prevented the experiment at Dessau from fulfilling the bright hopes of Basedow and the friends who assisted him in starting the enterprise.

Basedow retired after four years' leadership, and the institution continued for a few years with varying success, under such men as Campe, Salzmann, and Matthison. Yet, when the Philanthropin was closed in 1793, the teachers, dispersed throughout Germany, carried the new gospel wherever they went, arousing fresh interest in education and doing much for its advancement.

Quick thinks that Basedow's system possessed great merits "for children, say, between the ages of six and ten." Kant was greatly disappointed at the result. Rousseau's "Émile" had awakened his interest in education, and he looked to the experiment at Dessau for an exemplification of the new ideals. His estimate of the work accomplished is as follows: "Experience shows that often in our experiments we get quite opposite results from what we had anticipated. We see, too, that since experiments are necessary, it is not in the power of one generation to form a complete plan of education. The only experimental school which, to some extent, made a beginning in clearing the road, was the Institute at Dessau. This praise at least must be allowed, notwithstanding the many faults which could be brought up against it—faults which are sure to show themselves when we come to the results of our experiments, and which merely prove that fresh experiments are necessary. It was the only school in which teachers had liberty to work according to their own methods and schemes, and where they were in free communication both among themselves and with all learned men throughout Germany."[1]

Writings.—Basedow's chief educational writing is the book called the "Elementary." The "Book of Method" was the first to appear, and was really the first part of the "Elementary." Concerning the "Book of Method," Lang says, "This famous manual was undoubtedly the greatest of Basedow's educational writings. . . . It was full of valuable suggestions. It set educators to thinking, and has been a powerful motor in bringing about a change in school instruction."

The "Elementary," containing Basedow's complete scheme of education, has been called the "Orbis Pictus of the eighteenth century." The general opinion is that Basedow obtained the root ideas of this work from Comenius, Locke, and Rousseau. There is but little that is original in his pedagogical principles, but he made an effort to carry out the progressive teachings which had

[1] Kant, "Ueber Pädagogik."

entered into the theories of advanced thinkers but had not been worked into practice. Still, the problem of education became through Basedow better understood, and he is deserving of a place among the great educators of the world for his experiment at Dessau toward the solution of that problem. The experiment was crude, but it has borne fruit in modern schools and their methods, in better school buildings and apparatus, in trained teachers, in milder forms of discipline, in the improved study of nature, and in a broader and more philanthropic view of man's duty to his fellow-man.

CHAPTER XXXVIII

MODERN EDUCATORS (*Continued*)

PESTALOZZI (1746–1827)

Literature. — *De Guimps*, Pestalozzi, his Life and Works; *Krüsi*, Life, Work, and Influence of Pestalozzi; *Quick*, Educational Reformers; *Von Raumer*, Life and System of Pestalozzi; *Durrell*, New Life in Education; *Gill*, Systems of Education; *Skinner*, The Schoolmaster in Literature; *Barnard*, Pestalozzi and Pestalozzianism; *Vogel*, Geschichte des deutschen Volksschulwesens; *Rein*, Encyklopädisches Handbuch der Pädagogik.

JOHANN HEINRICH PESTALOZZI was born in Zurich, Switzerland, January 12, 1746. His father was a physician of great intelligence, and his death before the boy reached his sixth year deprived the latter of a wise counselor. The character of the mother is shown by the dying appeal of Pestalozzi's father to his servant Bäbeli: "For God's sake and in the name of mercy do not forsake my wife. When I am dead she will be helpless, and my children will fall into the hands of strangers."

Bäbeli replied, "I will never leave your wife, if it should please God to take you hence. I will remain with her till death, if she wishes me to do so," a promise which she faithfully kept. Krüsi thinks that, "The sacrifices of a mother for her children do not show more nobility of soul than was displayed by this poor, uneducated girl, who gave up all her worldly interest for a family not her own." Who can say that Pestalozzi himself was not inspired to his long life of devotion to the interests of the lowly by the unselfish consecration of this lowly woman to his family?

Pestalozzi did not care for companions of his own age. He was peculiarly a mother's boy, content to grow up dreamy and impractical at her quiet hearthstone. Consequently he was awkward and reserved, easily imposed upon, and lacking in self-reliance. These qualities remained with him as long as he lived, and caused him many painful failures. On the other hand, the pious example of his mother and the tranquil life he led with her made the boy reflective and imaginative, while his soul became filled with great thoughts for the well-being of mankind. His grandfather, a country pastor, whom he often visited, by his simple, godly life exerted a great influence in shaping Pestalozzi's religious character.

Schooling.—At school he was the butt of ridicule among the scholars because of his awkwardness, his simplicity, and his ingenuousness. His comrades dubbed him "Harry Oddity of Follyville," a nickname that carried no reproach with it, but was intended to express good-natured appreciation of his characteristics. Mr. Quick tells us that "his good nature and obliging disposition gained him many friends. No doubt his friends profited from his willingness to do anything for them. We find that when, on the shock of an earthquake, teachers and scholars alike rushed out of the schoolhouse, Harry Oddity was the boy sent back to fetch out caps and books." While not brilliant as a scholar, he was by no means dull. He was more ready in grasping the *content* than the *form* of the subject. Consequently all through life he never overcame his weakness in some of the commonest requirements of education.[1]

[1] In regard to the criticisms made against him at Burgdorf, Pestalozzi says: "It was whispered that I myself could not write, nor work accounts, nor even read properly. Popular reports are not always entirely wrong. It is true I could not write, nor read, nor work accounts well."

Life Purpose. — After completing the work of the elementary schools, he entered the university of Zurich, where he sustained himself with credit. Even while yet a boy he joined a league of students which was intended to resist injustice. Of himself and his fellow-students, he says, "We decided to live for nothing but independence, well-doing, and sacrifice for love of country."

Speaking of society as he saw it, he says, "I saw the unfortunate condition of all mankind, especially of my own countrymen, in all its hollowness. I saw indulgence despoiling the highest moral, spiritual, and civil interests, and sapping the lifeblood of our race as never before in the history of Europe. I saw finally the people of our nation steeped in poverty, misery, and universal want. From youth up the purpose of my life has been to secure to the poor of my country a happier fate by improving and simplifying their educational privileges. But the only sure foundation upon which we may hope to secure national culture and elevate the poor is that of the home where the love of father and mother is the ruling principle. Through the unselfishness, truth, strength, and purity of their love, parents kindle faith in their children. This leads to that implicit obedience which is based on confidence and love."

Love for humanity, desire to ameliorate suffering, and thorough unselfishness furnished the key to Pestalozzi's purpose and lifework.

The Christian Ministry. — It was this lofty purpose that led him first to attempt the work of the Christian ministry, a work which his aged grandfather encouraged. But he failed in his first sermon, and at once decided that he had mistaken his calling. Krüsi[1] says that "he stopped short in his sermon and made mistakes in the Lord's Prayer. This may have been due to embarrassment, which made the young minister forget the sermon which he had been obliged to commit to memory. More likely, however, it was an exalted idea of the proper qualifications of a clergyman, compared with his own humble merits, which induced him to exchange the study of theology for that of law."

The Law. — His motive in devoting himself to law was the same that had led him to the ministry, — his desire to be a blessing to his fellow-beings. He saw the peasantry cheated and imposed upon because of their ignorance, and determined to become their champion. Krüsi thinks that his study of the law must "have produced negative results by showing him the insufficiency of human legislation to do away with abuses, unless supported by principles of charity and justice." He therefore gave up this enterprise also.

Farming. — The advice of a dying friend, Bluntschli, "Never embark in any operation which might become dangerous to your peace of mind, because of the simplicity and tenderness of your disposition," may have had its effect upon Pestalozzi. He now entered upon his third venture. Having induced a wealthy firm in Zurich to advance him money, he bought about one hundred acres of unimproved land in the canton of Aargau, where he proposed to raise madder as a means of profit. Once more his real purpose was philanthropic, as he intended to show the poor peasants improved methods of farming whereby they could obtain better results for

[1] "Life, Work, and Influence of Pestalozzi," p. 17.

their labor and thereby be enabled to live more comfortably. He named the place Neuhof.

Marriage. — At this time he had just passed his twenty-first year. We pause to mention an event that had much to do with his happiness and with his later life. He had made the acquaintance of Anna Schulthess, a young lady of considerable means, and sought her hand in marriage. His letter to her, proposing marriage, is remarkable for its frankness, for the ingenuous confession of his own weaknesses, and for its correct estimate of himself. A few quotations from this letter must suffice.[1] "My failings, which appear to me the most important in relation to the future, are improvidence, want of caution, and want of that presence of mind which is necessary to meet unexpected changes in my future prospects. I hope, by continued exertions, to overcome them; but know that I still possess them to a degree that does not allow me to conceal them from the maiden I love. . . . I am further bound to confess that I shall place the duties toward my fatherland in advance of those to my wife, and that, although I mean to be a tender husband, I shall be inexorable even to the tears of my wife, if they should ever try to detain me from performing my duties as a citizen, to their fullest extent. My wife shall be the confidant of my heart, the partner of all my most secret counsel. A great and holy simplicity shall reign in my house. . . . My dear friend, I love you so tenderly and fervently that this confession has cost me much, since it may even take from me the hope of winning you."

Anna was not discouraged by the picture which the man she loved drew of himself, and she consented to become

[1] Both Quick and Krüsi give this letter in full.

his wife. They were married in his twenty-fourth year, and thus began a long period of happy wedded life that extended over fifty years. Quick tells us that "the forebodings of the letter were amply realized, . . . and yet we may well believe that Madame Pestalozzi never repented of her choice."

Neuhof. — But to return to Pestalozzi's experiment in farming, matters had not progressed well. The Zurich capitalists became suspicious, and after an investigation decided to withdraw their support, thus precipitating failure. Of this Pestalozzi himself says, "The cause of the failure of my undertaking lay essentially and exclusively in myself, and in my pronounced incapacity for every kind of undertaking which requires practical ability." One cannot fail to admire the energy and courage of the man, who, conscious of his own weakness, still persevered in great enterprises until he achieved success.

It was not for himself, but for humanity, that Pestalozzi labored, and no discouragement could daunt, no failure defeat, no lack of appreciation or misunderstanding check, the ardor of his zeal for the great work that absorbed his life. Around him were men and women in poverty and misery, whose children were growing up in vice and ignorance, to perpetuate the evils under which their parents suffered. With the spirit of his divine Master, Pestalozzi sought to elevate and bless those around him.

Accordingly, after the failure caused by the withdrawal of the financial support heretofore mentioned, he started again at Neuhof, using his wife's money. He opened an "industrial school for the poor," which Krüsi calls "the first school of its kind ever conceived, and the mother of hundreds now existing on both sides of the Atlantic." This was in 1775. He gathered fifty children together, and fed, clothed, housed, and taught them without compensation; in return for this they were to work in the fields in summer and at spinning in the winter. But this experiment also was doomed to bring disappointment. The children were lazy, shiftless, and dishonest; their work was of little use to Pestalozzi, because of their lack of skill and their bad habits. They would often run away as soon as they were well fed and had a new suit of clothes. Parents were unappreciative and dissatisfied, demanding pay for the labor of their children. Was there ever a more discouraging situation than this which Pestalozzi had to confront, when people demanded pay for accepting the philanthropic and unselfish measures taken for the good of their children and for their own elevation?

This could not continue long, and in 1780 Pestalozzi was obliged to close his school. He found himself badly in debt, with his wife's property gone. But even under these overwhelming misfortunes he says, "My failure showed me the truth of my plans," and this has long since been verified, both in his ideas of farming and in the industrial school.

Authorship. — The next eighteen years, though passed by Pestalozzi in extreme poverty, were not unfruitful. He began to write pamphlets and books, the first book being, "The Evening Hours of a Hermit," which appeared in 1780. His second book, "Leonard and Gertrude,"[1] was published the year following. It created great interest and brought Pestalozzi immediate fame. The government of Berne presented him a gold medal, which, however, he was obliged to sell to procure the necessities of life for his family. In "Leonard and Gertrude" Pestalozzi gives a homely and touching picture of life among the lowly, and

[1] "Schoolmaster in Literature," pp. 83-110.

shows how a good woman uses her opportunities for uplifting and educating, first her own family, and then her neighbors. In this work she is aided by the village schoolmaster and the magistrate, who are inspired by her example and leadership. Pestalozzi wrote several other books during this period, but none to equal "Leonard and Gertrude."

Stanz. — In the meantime, the French Revolution broke out, and Pestalozzi, influenced by the writings of Rousseau, became an ardent champion of the new order of things. He seems to have acquired considerable political influence, as the Directors of the Government of Switzerland thought it necessary to win him to their cause by giving him a political office. They therefore asked him what office he wanted, and he replied, "I want to be a schoolmaster." Accordingly, when the French had pillaged the inhabitants and burned their homes, Pestalozzi was sent to Stanz, — the only village left in the canton of Nidwalden, — to establish a school.[1] Now for the first time he found himself in the calling for which his whole nature had yearned, for which he was peculiarly suited, and in which he was destined to become famous.

At the age of fifty-three Pestalozzi began his work at Stanz. The government gave him an empty convent in which to hold his school, and, before it was ready for occupancy, children flocked to it for admission. The devastation of the land by the French and the consequent lack of the necessities of life among the people increased the difficulties of Pestalozzi's task. His own description of the beginning of his work is full of eloquence. Speaking of the school, he says, "I was among them from morning till evening. Everything tending to benefit body and soul I administered with my own hand. Every assistance,

[1] See Krüsi, p. 28, for an account of his appointment.

every lesson they received, came from me. My hand was joined to theirs, and my smile accompanied theirs. They seemed out of the world and away from Stanz; they were with me and I with them. We shared food and drink. I had no household, no friends, no servants around me; I had only them. Was their health good, I enjoyed it with them; were they sick, I stood at their side. I slept in their midst. I was the last to go to bed and the first to rise. I prayed with them, and taught them in bed till they fell asleep." How true is the saying that, "He lived with beggars in order that beggars might learn to live like men."

Thus living with them, teaching them, inspiring them to be good, devoting his whole thought to their welfare, Pestalozzi, who was described as "either a good-natured fool, or a poor devil, who was compelled, by indigence, to perform the menial office of schoolmaster," began a work that has revolutionized educational method.

But the same discouragements that had met him at Neuhof attended him at Stanz. Parents brought their children to the asylum only to be clothed, and then removed them upon the slightest pretexts. Nevertheless, the work of Pestalozzi at Stanz was not a failure, though the school was rendered houseless by the French soldiers in 1799, and had to be abandoned after less than five months' existence. Krüsi comments upon this period of Pestalozzi's life as follows: "Let those who now witness the mighty changes that have taken place in education pay grateful tribute to the man who first took up arms against the hollow systems of the old school routine, and who showed the path to those delightful regions of thought, in whose well-tilled soil rich harvests will ever be reaped by the patient laborer.

"To the philanthropist and friend of education, Stanz will always be a hallowed spot, exhibiting, as it does, the picture of this venerable teacher sitting among the outcast children, animated by the very spirit of Christ, and by a great idea which not only filled his own soul, but also inspired those who witnessed his labors."[1]

Burgdorf.—But Stanz proved the turning point in Pestalozzi's career. He was soon chosen assistant teacher at Burgdorf. His experience at Stanz, without books and without appliances, had compelled him to invent methods of interesting the children. He was thus brought to the use of objects, and here we have the beginning of practical object teaching. It was not long, however, before the head master of the school became jealous of him because he secured the attention and affection of the pupils, and Pestalozzi's dismissal was obtained on the ground that he did not know how to read and spell correctly, a charge which, as we have seen, was without doubt true. As to his method of teaching, Ramsauer, one of his pupils, tells us that "there was no regular plan, not any time-table. . . . As Pestalozzi, in his zeal, did not tie himself to any particular time, we generally went on until eleven o'clock with whatever we commenced at eight, and by ten o'clock he was always tired and hoarse. We knew when it was eleven by the noise of the other school children in the street, and then we usually all ran out without bidding good-by." Certainly no one will commend such schoolroom practice, and at first glance Pestalozzi would seem to merit only censure; but his enthusiasm, his zeal for the good of his fellow-beings, and his consciousness of possessing the truth triumphed over his lack of system as well as over other obstacles. The school committee of Burg-

[1] "Pestalozzi," p. 36.

dorf appreciated this, as is shown by their report. "He (Pestalozzi) has shown what powers are hidden in the feeble child, and in what manner they can be developed. The pupils have made astonishing progress in some branches, thereby proving that every child is capable of doing something if the teacher is able to draw out his talent, and awaken the powers of his mind in the order of their natural development."

Upon his dismissal from this position he united with Hermann Krüsi in founding a private school. Pupils increased in numbers, and at last Pestalozzi was on the road to success as well as fame. He gathered a strong corps of teachers about him, who not only contributed to the success of the institution, but sat at the feet of their recognized master, and loyally supported his measures. During his life at Burgdorf, he issued his work entitled "How Gertrude teaches her Children" (1801), in which he attempts to give his system of education. "A work," says Professor Hunziker,[1] "whose contents in no way meet the demands of the subtitle." (The full title is, "How Gertrude teaches her Children; an Attempt to direct Mothers how to teach their own Children.")

Yverdon.—In 1804 Pestalozzi was obliged to vacate his quarters at Burgdorf, and after some hesitation he moved his school to Yverdon, into an old fortress, "which," says Krüsi, "having stood many a siege of invading armies, was now captured by a schoolmaster; and it was henceforth to become more formidable in its attack upon ignorance, than it had before been in its defense of liberty." At Yverdon Pestalozzi was enabled to carry out the principles of education which he had so long held, and this place must be recognized as the Mecca of Pestalozzianism.

[1] "Encyklopädisches Handbuch der Pädagogik," Vol. V, p. 315.

His success at Burgdorf had drawn to him the attention of the world, and now educators, philosophers, and princes began to study his theories, while many visited the institution to witness its peculiar workings. Without doubt the many visitors seriously disturbed the work, as Pestalozzi took great pains to show what his pupils could do, especially when men of influence came. During the first five years there was great prosperity, the number of students reaching one hundred and fifty. Pestalozzi usually arose at two in the morning, and commenced literary work; and his example was followed by his teachers, one of whom testifies, "There were years in which not one of us was found in bed after three o'clock, and summer and winter we worked from three to six in the morning."[1]

At first the teachers were thoroughly united, cordially carrying out the teachings of "Father Pestalozzi." But after a time private ambitions and personal jealousies crept in and destroyed harmony. Many of the best teachers left and the school was closed.[2] In 1825, after an existence of twenty years, the institute at Yverdon was abandoned, and once more Pestalozzi saw the apparent failure of his hopes. He died two years later, at the age of eighty-one.

Mr. Quick comments upon this event as follows: "Thus the sun went down in clouds, and the old man, when he died at the age of eighty,[3] in 1829,[4] had seen the apparent failure of all his toils. He had not, however, failed in

[1] "Encyklopädisches Handbuch," Vol. V, p. 319.

[2] Krüsi, whose father was associated with Pestalozzi, gives a full account of these dissensions. He also tells many interesting incidents connected with Pestalozzi and his school at Yverdon, p. 45.

[3] Should be eighty-one.

[4] 1827.

reality. It has been said of him that his true function was to educate ideas, not children, and when twenty years later the centenary of his birth was celebrated by schoolmasters, not only in his native country, but throughout Germany, it was found that Pestalozzian ideas had been sown, and were bearing fruit, over the greater part of central Europe."[1]

Professor Hunziker says of Pestalozzi's influence, "Eighty years have passed since Pestalozzi was laid in the grave. The social thinker, who pointed out the way of reform for humanity in his 'Leonard and Gertrude,' who attempted to solve the enigmas and inequalities of social life in his 'Inquiries concerning the Course of Nature in the Development of Mankind,' is almost forgotten. But the name of Pestalozzi shines brighter than ever in the field of pedagogics. In every branch of education we hear the warning cry, return to Pestalozzi! Let the watchword for the future be: *Pestalozzi forever!*"[2]

Summary of Pestalozzi's Work. — No one can study the history of Pestalozzi without discovering the secret of his educational purpose. It is revealed in every enterprise he undertook, in every book he wrote, in his whole lifework.[3] Let us briefly sum up the work he accomplished: —

1. He showed how the theories of Comenius and Rousseau could be applied. By this a decided impulse was given to educational reform, and the way was prepared for the wonderful educational revival of the present century.

2. His greatest pedagogical principle is that education consists in the harmonious development of all the human powers.

[1] "Educational Reformers," p. 183.
[2] "Encyklopädisches Handbuch," Vol. V, p. 320.
[3] "In him the most interesting thing is *his life*." — QUICK.

3. Development should follow the order of nature. While he doubtless borrowed this thought from Rousseau, unlike Rousseau he held that the order of nature requires the child to be taught with other children.

4. All knowledge is obtained through the senses by the self-activity of the child.

5. Instruction should be based on observation, especially with young children. Hence objects must be freely used. There are three classes of object lessons, — those applying to *form*, to *number*, and to *speech*. Mr. Quick says, "By his object lessons Pestalozzi aimed at, — (1) enlarging gradually the sphere of the child's intuition, that is, increasing the number of objects falling under his immediate perception; (2) impressing upon him those perceptions of which he had become conscious, with certainty, clearness, and precision; (3) imparting to him a comprehensive knowledge of language for the expression of whatever had become or was becoming an object of his consciousness, in consequence either of the spontaneous impulse of his own nature, or of the assistance of tuition."

6. The mother is the natural educator of the child in its early years. "Maternal love is the first agent in education; . . . through it the child is led to love and trust his Creator and his Redeemer." It follows, therefore, that mothers should be educated.

7. He illustrated his principles in his methods of instruction. He employed the phonic method in spelling;[1] made use of objects in teaching number; graded the work according to the capacity of the children; taught drawing, language, composition, etc., by use, thus illustrating one of the aphorisms of Comenius, — "*We learn to do by doing.*"

[1] Not original with Pestalozzi, — see Port Royalists.

8. But the greatest lesson that Pestalozzi taught is embodied in the word *love*. He loved little children, he loved the distressed and lowly, he loved all his fellow-men. By the spirit which actuated him, by the methods of instruction employed, by a life of disappointment and apparent failure, by the appreciation of his service after he had gone to his rest, by the accelerated growth of his teachings throughout the world, he more closely resembles the Great Teacher than any other man that has ever lived. Dr. Harris says, "He is the first teacher to announce convincingly the doctrine that all people should be educated, — that, in fact, education is the one good gift to give to all, whether rich or poor."[1] Hence there is no character in educational history more worthy of study and more inspiring to the teacher than Johann Heinrich Pestalozzi.

[1] For statement of his principles, see Compayré, p. 438; Williams, p. 312; Krüsi, p. 169.

CHAPTER XXXIX

MODERN EDUCATORS (*Continued*)

FROEBEL (1782–1852)

Literature.—*Lange*, Collected Writings of F. Froebel; *Kriege*, Friedrich Froebel; *Bowen*, Froebel and Education by Self-activity; *Herford*, The Student's Froebel; *Froebel*, Education of Man; *Quick*, Educational Reformers; *Munroe*, Educational Ideal; *Williams*, History of Modern Education; *Marenholtz-Bülow*, Reminiscences of F. Froebel; *Rein*, Encyklopädisches Handbuch der Pädagogik.

FRIEDRICH WILHELM AUGUST FROEBEL was born at Oberweisbach, a village in the beautiful Thüringian Forest of Germany. The first ten years of his life were spent at home under the instruction of his father, who was a Lutheran clergyman and had six villages under his pastorate. The many cares of his office prevented the pastor from giving his son much attention, and as the stepmother neither understood the boy, nor took much interest in him, he spent most of his time in the woods, with birds and flowers as his companions, and received far less rudimentary training than most boys of his age. But at the age of ten an important change took place in his life. He went to live with his mother's brother, who sent him to school for four years. Here he was taught the elementary branches and a little Latin. He tells us of the profound impression made upon him the first day of school by the text of Scripture that the children repeated. It was, "Seek ye first the kingdom of God." He says,

"The verse made an impression on me like nothing before or since. Indeed, this impression was so lively and deep, that to-day every word lives fresh in my memory with the peculiar accent with which it was spoken; and yet since that time nearly forty years have elapsed." His progress in the school does not seem to have been very great.

At fourteen he returned to his father's home, and soon thereafter was apprenticed to a forester. Here he was entirely in his element, and he tells of four aspects of this life: "The homelier and more practical life; the life spent with nature, especially forest nature; the life of study, devoted to mathematics and languages, for which he found a good supply of books ready to hand; and the time spent in gaining a knowledge of plants, in which he was much helped by books on botany lent him by a neighboring doctor."[1] But he obtained little help from the forester, so at the end of three years Froebel withdrew, and soon thereafter entered the university of Jena. He seems to have studied hard during the year and a half he spent at Jena, but to have accomplished little. He became involved in debt, and was imprisoned for nine weeks in the university "Carcer."[2] After his liberation, he left the university.

As Teacher. — Meeting with little success in various enterprises in which he engaged, he at last drifted to Frankfurt-am-Main, where he made the acquaintance of Dr. Gruner, head master of the Model School. Dr. Gruner quickly discovered Froebel's talent, and urged him to accept a position under him as teacher. Froebel reluctantly consented, but in speaking later of his first experi-

[1] Bowen, "Froebel," p. 11.

[2] For a part of this debt Froebel's brother, also a student, was responsible. The amount of the debt was less than twenty-five dollars.

ence in the schoolroom, he says, "It seemed as if I had found something I had never known, but always longed for, always missed; as if my life had at last discovered its native element. I felt as happy as the fish in the water, the bird in the air."

Although Froebel succeeded at once in his new profession, thereby justifying Dr. Gruner's opinion of him, he felt that he needed special preparation for the work of teaching. Accordingly, in 1808, after two years' experience in teaching, having in the meantime visited Pestalozzi at Yverdon, and having read his works, he gave up his position and joined the institute at Yverdon.

He took with him three of his pupils to tutor, and "it thus happened," he tells us, "that I was there both as teacher and scholar, educator and pupil." Froebel spent two years at Yverdon, and his testimony concerning Pestalozzi is interesting. He says, "He set one's soul on fire for a higher and nobler life, though he had not made clear or sure the exact road toward it, nor indicated the means whereby to attain it." This sums up in a word the secret and extent of Pestalozzi's power. Dittes thinks that "the origin of the kindergarten is due to the pedagogical revival of Pestalozzi." Froebel himself, speaking of his experience at Yverdon, says, "I studied the boys' play, the whole series of games in the open air, and learned to recognize their mighty power to awaken and to strengthen the intelligence and the soul as well as the body." Here we find the first suggestion of the kindergarten, which has made Froebel famous.

After leaving Yverdon, Froebel spent about two years at the universities of Göttingen and Berlin in furthering his preparation for educational reform, to which he had devoted himself. In 1813 war for German liberty broke out, and Froebel, with many other students, enlisted. It is not the purpose here to follow his fortunes as a soldier, but while in the army he made the acquaintance of two young men who afterward became associated with him in educational enterprise, — Wilhelm Middendorff and Heinrich Langethal.

His First School. — In 1816 Froebel opened his first school at Griesheim, under the high-sounding title of "Universal German Educational Institute." At first he had his five nephews as his only pupils. Soon after, the school was removed to Keilhau, near Rudolstadt, in the Thüringian Forest. Here he was joined by his old friends Middendorff and Langethal. This institution continued for a number of years with some success, until 1833, when Froebel removed to Burgdorf, Switzerland. The Prussian government, far from giving encouragement to the institution at Keilhau, had regarded it with suspicion. A commission was sent by the government to examine the institution, and although the report was highly complimentary to Froebel's work,[1] the persecution did not cease. In 1851 the government prohibited kindergartens, as forming "a part of the Froebelian socialistic system, the aim of which is to teach children atheism"; and this decree was in force till 1860!

Indeed, to this day, Prussia does not regard the kindergarten as an educational institution, nor does she give aid to it as such. The kindergarten is officially recognized as a sort of *day nursery*, its teachers are not licensed, — hence have no official standing, — and "everything that pertains to the work of the elementary schools, every specific prepara-

[1] The sole recommendation of the commission that might be interpreted as a criticism was that the boys should have their hair cut! See Bowen's "Froebel," p. 26, for the full report of the visiting commission.

tion for the work of the latter, must be strictly excluded, and these schools can in no way be allowed to take the character of institutions of learning. Especially can neither reading nor arithmetic be allowed a place in them."[1]

But Froebel received more encouragement in Switzerland. He admitted children from four to six years of age, and organized a teachers' class to study his theories. Although Froebel did not remain long in Switzerland, that land proved congenial to his ideas, and the kindergarten has flourished there from his time to the present. Great credit is due to this country, which extended its hospitality to the two great educational modern reformers, Pestalozzi and Froebel!

The Kindergarten. — Mr. Herford says of Froebel's institution at Burgdorf, that, "Here we recognize the rise of the kindergarten, not yet so named."[2] The name came to Froebel a few years later as an inspiration. He had returned to Keilhau and opened a school in the neighboring town of Blankenburg. For a long time he had been pondering over a suitable name for the new institution. "While taking a walk one day with Middendorff and Barof to Blankenburg over the Steiger Pass, Froebel kept repeating, 'Oh, if I could only think of a good name for my youngest born!' Blankenburg lay at our feet, and he walked moodily toward it. Suddenly he stood still as if riveted to the spot, and his eyes grew wonderfully bright. Then he shouted to the mountain so that it echoed to the four winds, 'Eureka! *Kindergarten* shall the institute be called!'"

But, like Pestalozzi, Froebel was wholly incapable of financial management, and the institution at Blankendorf

[1] Rescript from the Prussian Minister of Education, April 7, 1884.

[2] "The Student's Froebel," XV.

had to be closed. He devoted the remainder of his life to lecturing upon his theories in different parts of Germany. He appealed to mothers, and endeavored to instruct them in the duty of training young children. He taught that the mother is the natural teacher of the child, and that it is her duty to fit herself for the sacred responsibility that God has placed upon her. His greatest disciple among women was Baroness Bertha von Marenholtz-Bülow, who materially helped him while he lived, and, since his death, has published one of the best accounts of his life and work.[1]

The "Education of Man." — Froebel gives his philosophy of education in his "Education of Man," but his most popular work is "Songs for Mother and Nursery." His greatest contribution to the work of educational reform is the kindergarten, an institution that has been ingrafted upon the school systems of many lands, and that is destined to become ever increasingly potent for good. In no country in the world has the kindergarten taken so strong a hold and made so great progress as in America. The purpose of the kindergarten, according to Froebel himself, is, "to take the oversight of children before they are ready for school life; to exert an influence over their whole being in correspondence with its nature; to strengthen their bodily powers; to exercise their senses; to employ the awakening mind; to make them thoughtfully acquainted with the world of nature and of man; to guide their heart and soul in the right direction, and to lead them to the Origin of all life, and to unison with Him." If conducted in the spirit of its originator, how is it possible for such an institution as the kindergarten to find enemies anywhere among true educators?

[1] "Handbuch der Froebelischen Erziehungslehre," "Reminiscences of Friedrich Froebel, Child and Child-nature."

CHAPTER XL

MODERN EDUCATORS (*Continued*)

HERBART (1776–1841)

Literature.—*De Garmo*, Herbart and the Herbartians; *Felkin*, Introduction to Herbart; *Van Liew*, Life of Herbart and Development of his Pedagogical Doctrines; Yearbooks of the Herbart Society; *Lange*, Apperception; *Rein*, Outlines of Pedagogics; also, Encyklopädisches Handbuch der Pädagogik; *Willmann*, Herbart's pädagogische Schriften.

It is probable that no system of pedagogy is attracting so much attention and awakening so much interest at the present time as that of Herbart. Professor Rein says, "He who nowadays will aspire to the highest pedagogical knowledge, cannot neglect to make a thorough study of Herbart's pedagogy." Johann Friedrich Herbart was born at Oldenburg, May 4, 1776. His grandfather was rector of the *Gymnasium* at Oldenburg for thirty-four years; his father was a high official under the government; but his mother seems to have wielded the most influence over him. She watched over his studies with greatest care, and, indeed, studied Greek herself to spur him on. Though gentle and mild, she was firm in discipline. The father was satisfied to leave the direction of the education of his son to her. There was, however, little sympathy between the father and mother, and there were frequent family dissensions, that must have had a bad influence on the lad. These disagreements finally led to a separation. A tutor employed for Herbart at this period developed in him a speculative tendency and taught him the power of forcible expression. Herbart learned to play on several musical instruments, and at the age of eleven displayed considerable talent as a pianist.

When twelve years of age he entered the *Gymnasium* at Oldenburg, and six years later completed the course. He entered the university of Jena in 1794 and became a student of Fichte, who was sure to inspire a young man of Herbart's philosophical bent. His attention seems to have been directed to educational questions, though he had not yet decided to be a teacher.[1]

As Teacher. — After three years at Jena, Herbart became tutor (Hauslehrer) in the family of Herr von Steiger, governor of Interlaken. This was his only experience in teaching children. "Herbart's experience as a teacher," says De Garmo, "would seem too small a thing to mention — some two or three years in a private family in Switzerland with three children aged respectively eight, twelve, and fourteen. Yet to a man who can see an oak tree in an acorn, who can understand all minds from the study of a few, such an experience may be most fruitful." It is certain that Herbart often drew upon this experience in his later writings. While in Switzerland he visited Pestalozzi, with whom he was deeply impressed. Opinions differ as to the harmony of theory between Pestalozzi and Herbart. Professor Rein thinks that, "In the ideas of Pestalozzi are found the outlines of Herbart's pedagogical structure."

Having decided to devote himself to academic teaching, he gave up his position in Switzerland and went to Bremen for further study. During the two years spent

[1] Professor Rein indicates that Herbart discussed educational questions at this period. See "Encyklopädisches Handbuch," Vol. III, p. 468.

there, he wrote several essays on educational subjects, but gave his chief attention to the study of Greek and mathematics.

As Professor. — In 1802 he took the first step in his academic career as *Privat Docent* at the university of Göttingen. This with him was a period of great literary activity.[1] In 1809, he was called to the chair of philosophy at Königsberg once occupied by Kant. He calls this "the most renowned chair of philosophy, the place which when a boy I longed for in reverential dreams, as I studied the works of the sage of Königsberg."[2]

His Practice School. — Here he established a pedagogical seminary, having a practice school in which the students instructed children under the criticism of Herbart himself. Concerning his pedagogical activity at Königsberg, Herbart says, "Among my many duties, the consideration of educational questions is of especial interest to me. But it is not enough to theorize merely; there must be experiment and practice. Furthermore, I desire to extend the range of my own experience (already covering ten years) in this field. Therefore, I have long had in mind to teach daily for one hour a few selected boys in the presence of such of my students as are familiar with my pedagogical theory. After a little, these students are to take up the work I have begun, and give instruction under my observation. In time, in this way, teachers would be trained, whose method by means of reciprocal observation and discussion must be perfected. As a plan of teaching is valueless without a teacher, and indeed a teacher that is in sympathy with that plan, and is master of the method, —

[1] For list of works produced, see De Garmo's "Herbart and the Herbartians," p. 17.

[2] Felkin's translation of "Science of Education," p. 16.

so perhaps a small experimental school, such as I have in mind, would prepare the way for future greater undertakings. There is a word from Kant, 'first experimental schools and then normal schools!'"[1]

This was the first practice school in connection with the chair of pedagogy in a university; the idea, however, does not seem to have taken very deep root, as, with the exception of the celebrated practice school at Jena, under Professor Rein, there is not one now in Germany. Most professors of pedagogy conduct a *Seminar*, in which some practice work with children is done, but none of them maintain a practice school.

Literary Activity. — Herbart's literary activity at Königsberg was great. He worked out his psychological system, and wrote also on philosophy, history, and pedagogy. But his greatest works in the latter field are his "A B C der Anschauung,"[2] and his "Allgemeine Pädagogik,"[3] both of which appeared while he was still at Göttingen.[4] In 1833, after twenty-four years in Königsberg, he returned to Göttingen, where his lifework was completed in 1841. Upon his retirement from Königsberg, the practice school was closed. Ten years later, a pupil of Herbart, Karl Volkmar Stoy, established the practice school at Jena, of which mention has already been made. Two schools of Herbartians exist in Germany, the Stoy school, which attempts to follow Herbart very closely, and the Ziller school, which is freer in its interpretation of him. The chief exponent of the latter is Professor Wilhelm Rein of

[1] Willmann's "Herbart," Vol. II, p. 3.

[2] "The A B C of Observation."

[3] "General Pedagogy."

[4] The best collection of his works is that by Willmann, "Herbart's Pädagogische Schriften," which has not been translated into English.

Jena, the place which is at present the center of Herbartian activity. In America this movement is under the direction of the National Herbart Society.

His Pedagogical Work. — Aside from the educational movements organized by Herbart and his followers, the credit is due to him of being the *first to elevate pedagogy to the dignity of a science*. Professor Rein says, "Herbart has rendered an undisputed service in that he has elevated pedagogics to the rank of a science. No one has ever repented of having become familiar with Herbart's teachings, for, in any case, he has thereby added richly to his own attainments. The development of our people will be fortunate if the education of the youth shall be intrusted more and more to those who stand and work upon the lines laid down by Comenius, Pestalozzi, Herbart.

"The pedagogic thinking of Herbart has indeed borne rich fruit in Germany. Other peoples, also, have been blessed by his teachings. Thus Herbart, whose span of life did not reach to the middle of this century, lives in the present. He created the basis of a science of education, which furnishes a safe starting point for all pedagogical theories, and which bears in itself the most fruitful germs for future development."[1]

Modern Herbartians have carried forward that development far beyond its original outline. The terms "many-sided interest," "apperception," "concentration," "culture-epochs," "the formal steps of instruction," "correlation," and "harmonious development," are phrases that have become common in educational literature. The limits of this volume do not permit a discussion of these subjects. Indeed, many of them belong more properly to the dis-

[1] "Encyklopädisches Handbuch der Pädagogik," Vol. III, p. 485.

ciples of Herbart, rather than to Herbart himself.[1] Herbart's ideal was that education should aim to produce well-rounded men, fit for all the duties of life; men well developed physically, intellectually, morally, and spiritually. He himself was not one-sided, being an enthusiastic teacher as well as psychologist and philosopher.

[1] For discussion of these subjects see the Yearbooks of the Herbartian Society, and other works referred to on page 278. For the completest list of references to Herbartian literature, see "Encyklopädisches Handbuch," Vol. III, p. 485.

CHAPTER XLI

MODERN EDUCATORS (*Continued*)

HORACE MANN (1796–1859)

Literature. — *Mrs. Mary T. Mann*, Life of Horace Mann; *Hinsdale*, Horace Mann; *Winship*, Horace Mann, the Educator; *Lang*, Horace Mann; *F. W. Parker*, Article in Educational Review, Vol. XII, p. 65; *Wm. T. Harris*, Educational Review, Vol. XII, p. 105; *Martin*, Education in Massachusetts.

COLONEL PARKER says, "It would be difficult to find a child ten years of age in our sixty-five millions who does not know of Abraham Lincoln or George Washington; but the third, at least, in the list of the builders of the American republic is not known to millions of intelligent people. Washington and Lincoln represent the highest types of heroism, patriotism, and wisdom in great crises of republic-building; Horace Mann, the quiet inner building, the soul-development of the nation." [1]

Horace Mann was born at Franklin, Massachusetts, May 4, 1796. Inured to the hard work of the farm, with but a few weeks' schooling in the winter, never blessed with very rugged health, left at the age of thirteen by the death of his father with the responsibilities of a man, it is no wonder that he "retained only painful recollections of the whole period which ought to be, with every child, a golden age to look back upon." [2]

[1] *Educational Review*, Vol. XII, p. 65.

[2] Mrs. Mann, "Life of Horace Mann," p. 10

When nearly twenty years of age, through the influence of Mr. Barrett, an eccentric teacher who came to the village, he decided to go to college, and in six months he prepared for the sophomore class of Brown University. This preparation was a tremendous undertaking which broke down his health for life. He now had an opportunity to satisfy the cravings for knowledge, which the hardships of his early life had not been able to stifle. He was graduated with the highest honors of his class and decided to study law. He spent two years at Brown University as tutor, meanwhile privately studying law, and then resigned that position to enter the law school at Litchfield, Connecticut. Two years later, at the age of twenty-seven, he was admitted to the bar.

As Statesman. — He was called upon to serve his state in the legislature, and later as representative in Congress.[1]

The year 1837 marks a new epoch in the educational history of Massachusetts. "Although Massachusetts had had schools for nearly two centuries, the free school had been, to a great degree, a charity school the country over. . . . Horace Mann, like Thomas Jefferson, saw clearly that there could be no evolution of a free people without intelligence and morality, and looked upon the common school as the fundamental means of development of men and women who could govern themselves. He saw clearly that the whole problem of the republic which was presenting itself to intelligent educated men rested upon the idea of public education."[2]

As Educator. — Accordingly, having secured the passage of a law establishing a State Board of Education,

[1] Mr. Mann completed the term made vacant by the death of John Quincy Adams, and was reëlected for the two succeeding terms.

[2] Colonel Parker in article cited.

Mr. Mann was made its secretary at a salary of one thousand dollars a year. To accept this work, he gave up a lucrative law practice, fine prospects of political preferment, and probable fortune, as well as professional fame. He entered upon an educational campaign full of discouragement, colossal in its undertaking, and sure to arouse bitterest animosities. Of this period Colonel Parker says, "The story of his early struggles in this direction has not yet been written. When it is, it will reveal a profound depth of heroism rarely equaled in the history of the world." Mr. Mann visited all parts of the state, lecturing to parents and stimulating the teachers. He was often received with coldness, sometimes with active hostility.

His Annual Reports. — But he persevered until the whole state was awakened. He continued in this work for twelve years, and presented its results in his Annual Reports, the most remarkable documents of American educational literature.[1] In the meantime, he visited Europe, studied the schools, and gave the results of his investigations in his celebrated Seventh Annual Report.

Mr. Martin summarizes the work of Horace Mann during these twelve years as follows: "In the evolution of the Massachusetts public schools during these twelve years of Mr. Mann's labors, statistics tell us that the appropriations for public schools had doubled; that more than two million dollars had been spent in providing better schoolhouses; that the wages of men as teachers had increased sixty-two per cent, of women fifty-one per cent, while the whole number of women employed as teachers had increased fifty-four per cent; one month had been added to the average length of the schools; the ratio of private

[1] For an analysis of these Reports, see Dr. Harris's article in *Educational Review*, Vol. XII, p. 112

school expenditures to those of the public schools had diminished from seventy-five per cent to thirty-six per cent; the compensation of school committees had been made compulsory, and their supervision was more general and more constant; three normal schools had been established, and had sent out several hundred teachers, who were making themselves felt in all parts of the state."[1]

Love for the Common Schools. — He believed most fully in the common school, declaring that, "This institution is the greatest discovery ever made by man. . . . In two grand characteristic attributes, it is supereminent over all others: first in its universality, for it is capacious enough to receive and cherish in its parental bosom every child that comes into the world; and second, in the timeliness of the aid it proffers, — its early, seasonable supplies of counsel and guidance making security antedate danger."

In his first Annual Report Mr. Mann asserts that, "The object of the common school system is to give to every child a free, straight, solid pathway, by which he can walk directly up from the ignorance of an infant to a knowledge of the primary duties of man." Horace Mann could hardly have anticipated the kindergarten for the infant years, and the high school at the end of the course, as they now stand in the common school systems of our country. And yet, what has already been accomplished in our educational scheme fulfills the prophecy implied in his words.

The best known and most important of Mr. Mann's written documents is his Seventh Annual Report, in which he gives an account of European schools. Concerning this Mr. Winship says, "He had made a crisis, and his Seventh Report was an immortal document; opposition to

[1] "Education in Massachusetts," p. 174.

the normal schools was never more to be heard in the land, and oral instruction, the word method, and less corporal punishment were certain to come to the Boston schools."[1]

After severing his connection with the State Board of Education, Mr. Mann served in Congress from 1848 to 1853, and was defeated in his candidacy for governor of Massachusetts. At the age of fifty-six he accepted the presidency of Antioch College at Yellow Springs, Ohio, a position which he held until his death in 1859. He closed his last address to the graduating class at Antioch with these noble words: "*Be ashamed to die until you have won some victory for humanity.*" He himself had won many great victories for humanity, — in the improvement of the common school systems of his native country; in the establishment of free schools; in the founding of normal schools where teachers might be trained; in the adoption of milder means of discipline; in the improvement of schoolhouses; in the better support of schools; in better methods of instruction; and in the inspiration he gave to teachers for all time. Therefore he at least had no need to be "ashamed to die."

[1] "Horace Mann," p. 76.

CHAPTER XLII

THE SCHOOL SYSTEM OF GERMANY

Literature. — *Parsons*, Prussian Schools through American Eyes; *Klemm*, European Schools; *Prince*, Methods in the German Schools; *Seeley*, The German Common School System; *Russell*, German Higher Schools; *Bolton*, Secondary Education in Germany.

WE have traced the historical development of education to the present time. It now remains for us to examine briefly the educational systems of a few leading countries, in order that comparisons may be made, lessons drawn, and the present condition of education clearly set forth.[1]

The plan of discussion to be followed in each of the four systems considered will embrace, 1, *Administration*; 2, *School Attendance*; 3, *the Schools*; 4, *Support of Schools*; 5, *the Teachers*.

Administration. — Each German state is independent in its school system, though there are many features in common, and there is a mutual understanding on most educational questions between the various states, which makes their systems practically uniform. The system here described is that of Prussia, which, being the largest, most

[1] It will, of course, be impossible within the limitations of this work to give more than a mere outline of these systems. The reader will find full discussions in the works referred to in the Literature. Particular attention is called to the Reports of the United States Commissioner of Education from the year 1895 to the present time.

populous, and most influential of the states comprised within the German Empire, as well as the foremost in educational development, may well be taken as a type.

There is a minister of education whose jurisdiction extends over the whole kingdom. He represents the school interests in the Prussian diet or *Landtag*, listens to appeals, distributes school moneys, and is the general educational executive officer. Each of the thirteen royal provinces has a school board whose presiding officer is *ex officio* the royal president of the province. With him are associated other royal counselors, and pedagogically trained men,—school superintendents and principals. This board consists of men of highest integrity and intelligence. Their duties extend to the higher institutions of learning, and to institutions for the unfortunate; they have charge of the school finances of their provinces, adopt the school books that are used in the higher schools, and appoint teachers in the normal schools. They report annually to the minister, and as much more frequently as he may require.

The thirteen royal provinces are subdivided into the so-called *governments* (*Regierungen*), of which Prussia contains thirty-six. These *governments* have an administrative school board similar to that of the province, with duties within their territory corresponding to those of the provincial board. They come into close touch with the schools, have a voice in the appointment of teachers and in the selection of text-books for the elementary schools. Their work is especially with the common schools, while that of the provincial boards is with the higher schools.

The *governments* are subdivided into districts. There is a district school board similar to that of the larger territories mentioned, but the chief and most important school officer of the district is the school inspector. The district inspector is always a man of pedagogical training and experience. He is appointed for life and devotes his whole time to the schools in his district. His efficient and wise inspection of the schools insures their success. The district school board erects school buildings, determines the amount of the teachers' salaries, oversees their pensions, enforces compulsory attendance laws, decides upon taxable property, fixes boundary lines, and provides for the finances.

Finally, there is the local school board for each separate school. These men have charge of the external matters of the school such as the direct enforcement of attendance, the repairs, supplies, etc.; but they may not interfere with the teacher in his work. In the country villages they have a voice in the choice of the teacher. The teacher may appeal to them in matters that need immediate attention.

In the administration of the schools men of the highest character are chosen without reference to their political leanings. There are usually teachers among the number, on the principle that those who have made the most careful study of education are the most competent to administer it.

School Attendance. — Every child in normal health is required to attend school between the ages of six and fourteen for every day that the school is in session. Parents are held responsible for the attendance of their children, and may be fined or imprisoned for non-fulfillment of the requirements of the law. In case parents are unable to secure the attendance of their children, the latter are placed in reform schools. The law is carried out with great strictness and wonderful efficiency. For example, in 1893, out of 5,299,310 children of school age in Prussia, there were only 945 unexcused absentees, — that is, 2 in

10,000. All parents expect their children to be in school every day, and the children grow up fully impressed with the idea that they are to attend school regularly. The chief reason for the efficiency of compulsory attendance in Germany lies in the fact that it covers every school day, and therefore does not allow the formation of habits of truancy.

The Schools. — The common school (Volksschule) of Germany reaches every child, as we have seen. In villages the sexes are taught together; but in cities they are generally separated. The school hours are from eight to eleven in the forenoon, for six days in the week, and from two to four for four days in the week, Wednesday and Saturday afternoons being holidays. These hours may be varied to suit local conditions. The school is in session for about forty-two weeks each year. Each teacher is required to give about twenty-eight hours of service per week, while the pupils must attend from sixteen hours (for beginners) to twenty-eight. The common schools of Prussia are now practically free. The common school is intended for the common people, and it is not followed by a high or secondary school. This is the greatest weakness of the German school system. It perpetuates the class system, and effectually prevents the child from rising above his station.

The sole opportunity for the child of the lower classes to receive a higher education is through the normal school, and even this privilege is limited to a small number of the pupils who show special ability. We may mention also the *Continuation* schools, which are held evenings and Sundays. These schools are rapidly multiplying and becoming more efficient, as many of them are held in the daytime. They furnish an opportunity for the child who has completed the common school to review his work, and also to add some subjects that will be of utility in his lifework.

In general, there are three classes of secondary schools, — the *Gymnasium*, the *Realgymnasium*, and *Oberrealschule*. Each prepares for the university, and each has nine classes; namely, *Sexta*, *Quinta*, *Quarta*, *Untertertia*, *Obertertia*, *Untersecunda*, *Obersecunda*, *Unterprima*, and *Oberprima*. These schools differ chiefly in the amount of classics they offer, the *Gymnasium* laying stress upon the classics and the *Realschule* upon the realities.[1] Neither of these schools succeeds the common school, and the boy who is to pursue one of these courses of study must begin at not later than nine or ten years of age.[2] Thus, if a professional life is chosen for a boy, he cannot attend the common school, — at least not for more than the first three or four years, — but must be sent to one of the schools above mentioned, for they alone prepare for the university, and without a university course he cannot enter a profession. The university is the crowning institution of the German school system.

Support of Schools. — About one half of the expense of the schools is paid from the general state fund, one third from local taxation, and the balance comes from income from endowments, church funds, tuition, etc. The general tendency is to make the schools free, according to the recommendation of the minister of education, but some communities still continue to charge tuition. In these cases, there are poor schools for those who cannot pay tuition, thus affording school privileges to all.

[1] In addition to these schools, there are also the Progymnasium, the Realprogymnasium, and the Realschule, which, as their names indicate, are modified forms of the principal types. These schools do not offer the full nine years' course. See footnote on p. 236 for explanation of the work of these schools.

[2] Russell's "German Higher Schools" fully describes these institutions.

The Teachers. — All teachers of the Prussian common schools are normal graduates, or have had an equal pedagogic preparation.[1] Graduates of the university seldom enter the common school work; they teach in the secondary schools, in private schools, and as tutors. The common school teachers generally come from the common schools. If a child shows special aptness for teaching, the attention of the school inspector is called to him, and, with consent of his parents, he is sent to a preparatory school for three years. His work there is entirely academic in character. At seventeen he enters the normal school and has another year of academic work, after which he begins his technical work. His normal course is three years, the last year being given almost entirely to professional work. Each class in the normal school contains from thirty to thirty-six students, thus making the total number of students in a German normal school about one hundred. As only about thirty can enter from the whole district, it will appear that the opportunities for children to extend the common school course are very limited.

After completing the normal course, the graduate is provisionally appointed to a position for three years. He is now under the oversight of his former principal, as well as of the district inspector. If he proves successful in teaching, he is required to pass a final examination, chiefly on pedagogical questions, and then has a life tenure, and can be removed only on the ground of inefficiency or immorality. The average tenure of office with teachers is

[1] In 1893 there were only 241 teachers out of 71,731 in Prussia, who were outside of the above requirement. These 241 were old teachers who began before the law was so strict, and who, because of their efficiency, are retained. In a few years this band will entirely disappear, and all will be normal graduates.

twenty-five years. The salary is often very low, but with free rent, fuel, and light, the schoolmaster's income is by no means inadequate. His salary increases with the years of service, and his prospective pension also increases year by year.[1]

The German schoolmaster is a state officer. He commands, by virtue of his position, the respect which his character, his self-sacrifice, his efficiency, and the great work that he is doing deserve. "It is the schoolmaster that has won our battles," said Von Moltke; and it is he that is preparing Germany for the arts of peace as well as those of war.

The Prussian school system is the most efficient in the world, at least so far as the education of the masses is concerned. It has practically obliterated illiteracy in the kingdom, more than 99½ per cent of the recruits received into the army in 1893 being able to read and write. Many countries have materially improved their school systems by adopting some of the lessons taught by Prussia.

The three most important features of the German school system are: —

1. *Only professionally trained teachers can be employed.*
2. *Such teachers are appointed to permanent positions.*
3. *The attendance of every child during the entire school year is compulsory.*

[1] For full statement of salaries and pensions, see "German Common School System," pp. 172, 195. Though the German teacher's salary is much smaller than that of the average American teacher, taking into account the greater purchasing power of money in Germany, the simple habits, and fewer demands upon the purse, the German teacher is fully as well off as the American.

CHAPTER XLIII

THE SCHOOL SYSTEM OF FRANCE

Literature. — *Parsons*, French Schools through American Eyes; *Richard*, The School System of France; *Weigert*, Die Volksschule in Frankreich; *Schroeder*, Das Volksschulwesen Frankreichs; United States Commissioner's Reports.

Administration. — France, like Germany, has a minister of education who sits in the cabinet of the president. The work of his office is divided into three departments, *higher*, *secondary*, and *primary*, and at the head of each there is a director. There are two advisory bodies in charge of education. One has general oversight of all the school interests of France. The other is divided into three boards, appointed by the minister himself, for supervision of the three departments above mentioned. The general board consists of sixty members, fifteen appointed by the president of the republic, and the others appointed by the board itself whenever vacancies occur. This body meets once a year to hear reports, to pass upon the general school policy, and to legislate for the schools. Out of its membership is chosen an executive committee that meets once a week, and upon which devolves the chief management of educational affairs. This committee is answerable to the general board, to which it renders an annual report. Men of the highest character and intelligence constitute this board.

The whole of France is divided into seventeen parts called *académies*. These divisions do not coincide with the political divisions, but are made merely for convenience in school administration. Each *académie* has a school board to which is committed the general oversight of all educational interests within its territory, and particularly the care of the higher schools.

A narrower division is into *départements*. There are ninety of these in France and Algiers. Each is governed by an educational council which has charge of the elementary schools. The principal officer of a *département* is a school inspector, a trained educator who devotes all his time to the schools. In each *département* there is a normal school for each sex, though in a few instances two *départements* combine to maintain one normal school.

The *département* is subdivided into *arrondissements*. Each has an executive officer and a council in close touch with the schools. Lastly there are the *cantons*, whose school board has direct control of each individual school.

In this manner from the highest to the lowest division there are executive officers with well-defined duties — all working together in perfect harmony and with great efficiency. Trained teachers often sit in these councils as members and advisers. Thus the highest pedagogical training of the republic is utilized to obtain the best administration of the school interests.

School Attendance. — School attendance is compulsory upon children from six to thirteen years of age for every school day. As in Germany, the child is not compelled to attend the public school, but must receive instruction for the required time and in a manner approved by the State. It is the right of the child to be educated, and the State asserts its prerogative to secure that right to the child, whatever be the attitude of the parent. But the manner of securing it is left to the parent if he chooses to exercise that privilege. Although France has had compulsory education only since 1882, the law is effective, and grows more so each year. In 1895, 91 per cent of all the children of school age attended school regularly.

The Schools. — In the arrangement of her schools, and the perfect articulation between them from the *mother* school to the university, France has the most perfect system in the world. The *mother* schools (*écoles maternelles*) take children from two to six years of age and care for them from early morning till evening, thereby permitting parents to go out to service. They combine the idea of the day nursery and the kindergarten. These schools, in communes of 2000 or more, are supported by the State, as are other schools.

Instead of the *mother* school, sometimes the *infant* school (*école infantine*) takes the child from four to seven and prepares him for the primary school. This school is more nearly like the kindergarten than the *mother* school. It is supported wholly by the State and is a part of the school system, its work being entirely in sympathy with that which follows. In this respect, France has taken a more advanced step than any other nation.

With the lower *primary* school (*école primaire élémentaire*), which covers the period of from six to thirteen years of age, begins compulsory education. The sexes are always taught separately except in villages of less than five hundred inhabitants. The pupils all dress in the same garb. The school is in session five days in the week, Thursdays being free. There is no religious instruction in the schools. A peculiar and very important factor is a book of registration for each child, in which specimens of work in each subject are entered once a month for the whole school course. This book is kept at the school, and furnishes an accurate indication of progress to parents or inspectors.[1]

Following the *lower primary* school is the *higher primary* (*école primaire supérieure*), which has two courses, one for pupils who wish to review their elementary work and add some subjects, with the view of better preparing for the ordinary walks of life; and the high school course for those who wish to prepare for academic life. The former is indefinite in length; the latter requires five years, thus being completed at the eighteenth year. Here appears another superiority over the German system, in which, it will be remembered, there is no connection between the common and the high school.

These high schools prepare for the normal school and for the university. There are also many other kinds of schools under State support, — such as technical schools, apprentice schools, schools of mines, etc. In the advantages offered to young men for perfecting themselves in a trade or calling, France surpasses all other countries.

Finally there are the State universities, fifteen in number, the professors of which are appointed by the State. While the State pays all salaries, the maintenance of the buildings depends upon fees, endowments, and such local support as is obtainable. These institutions are open to students from the higher primary schools, thus making a complete system from the lowest school to the highest, and offering remarkable advantages to all. All degrees are given by the State, thereby securing perfect uniformity.

Support of Schools. — All of the schools above mentioned, from the *mother* school to the university, are free.

[1] See Parsons, "French Schools through American Eyes," p. 82.

The expenses are distributed as follows: (1) The State pays the salaries of all teachers, administrators, and inspectors, and all the expenses of the normal schools. Thus it will be seen that the bulk of the expense of education is borne by the State in general. (2) The *départements* erect the normal school and furnish the apparatus and supplies for the same. (3) The *communes* pay for the needed supplies, for the janitor, and for other local necessities of the elementary schools. They may also tax themselves to increase the salaries of teachers beyond the State allowance. Each community thus has the power to decide whether it will be content with an average school, merely fulfilling the State requirements, or whether it will have a superior school taught by the best teachers obtainable.

The Teachers.—There are two classes of normal schools in France, the elementary, of which there are eighty-seven for men and eighty-five for women,—practically one for each sex in each of the departments,—and the higher, of which there is one for men, one for women, and one for kindergartners. Nearly all teachers are graduates of normal schools, and as no candidates for positions are considered unless they hold a normal certificate, in the near future all the teachers of France will be professionally trained.

Candidates for admission to the normal school must be at least sixteen years of age, of good moral character, and of fair abilities. They must pledge themselves to teach for not less than ten years.[1] The elementary course covers three years. After graduation, the young teacher is appointed provisionally until he has taken a final examination, which must be within ten years. If he has been successful in

[1] This is no hardship, as they fully expect to devote their lives to teaching.

the schoolroom, as well as in this second examination, he becomes a permanent teacher, and can be removed only for immorality.

The course in the advanced normal school takes three or more years, depending upon the preparation with which the candidate enters. Only those between eighteen and twenty-five can be admitted. These schools train principals, superintendents, inspectors, and teachers for the elementary normal schools. They are the model schools of France, and shape the educational practice of the republic. Graduates from the elementary normal schools are not debarred from entering the higher normal schools; thus ambitious teachers are encouraged to prepare themselves for higher work.

No other country in the world does so much as France to assist young teachers in their preparation. In all of the normal schools mentioned, tuition, board, room, and books are free. And when the young teacher has been graduated, the State recognizes its own work by giving him the preference in appointments.

There are five classes of teachers in the elementary schools, the lowest being the fifth. The young graduate teacher begins in the lowest class and works his way up. The annual salaries for the different classes are indicated by the following table: —

Classes of Teachers	Men	Women
Fifth Class	$200.00	$200.00
Fourth Class	240.00	240.00
Third Class	300.00	280.00
Second Class	360.00	300.00
First Class	400.00	320.00

Additional allowances are made in large schools, and the *communes* often supplement the above amounts.

The annual salaries of principals are as follows: —

Principals	Higher Primary	Normal Schools	
	Both Sexes	Men	Women
Fifth Class	$360.00	$700.00	$600.00
Fourth Class	400.00	800.00	700.00
Third Class	450.00	900.00	800.00
Second Class	500.00	1000.00	900.00
First Class	560.00	1100.00	1000.00

The assistants in these schools receive: —

Assistants	Higher Primary	Normal Schools	
	Both Sexes	Men	Women
Fifth Class	$240.00	$500.00	$440.00
Fourth Class	280.00	540.00	480.00
Third Class	320.00	580.00	520.00
Second Class	380.00	620.00	560.00
First Class	440.00	680.00	600.00

In addition to these amounts there is also a small allowance for rent.

After thirty-five years of service, the teacher may retire upon three fourths of his salary as a pension.

Without doubt France has outstripped all other nations in educational progress during the last twenty-five years, — the period in which her school system has been constructed. The three great signs of advance in French education are *the establishment of free schools* (1881); *compulsory education and the secularization of the schools* (1882); and *the restriction of teachers to lay persons* (1886).[1] The strong features of the French school system may be stated as follows:—

1. *Completeness and harmony of the system*, covering the period from early childhood till the prescribed education is finished.
2. *Thoroughly trained teachers.*
3. *Two kinds of normal schools* to meet the various educational requirements of teachers.
4. *Liberal support* of schools of all kinds.
5. *Admirable administration* of the schools.

[1] Previous to this the members of religious orders could teach in the public schools.

NOTE.—In 1902 the government still further restricted the teaching by religious orders. It is now proposed not only to forbid all teaching by these orders, but also to sequestrate the property of such congregations as exist solely for teaching purposes. This will close about 3500 schools of the Christian Brothers which have existed for a long time, and necessitate the organization by the government of corresponding school facilities to supply their place. Five years are allowed to effect the change.

CHAPTER XLIV

THE SCHOOL SYSTEM OF ENGLAND

Literature. — *Sharpless*, English Education; *Craik*, Education and the State; *Barnard*, English Pedagogy; *Clark*, The State and Education; *Gill*, Systems of Education; *Balfour*, Educational Systems of Great Britain and Ireland; United States Commissioner's Reports for 1889 to 1902.

NEARLY a thousand years ago Alfred the Great encouraged education of the higher classes to the exclusion of the masses — a principle that has governed education in England until within recent times. Statistics taken in 1845 showed that only one in six of the inhabitants could read, one in four write, and one in fifty cipher as far as the Rule of Three. Since 1870 important changes have been made, and the number of children in the elementary schools of England has increased from 1,500,000 in 1870 to nearly 6,000,000 in 1902.[1]

"The principal features of the law of 1870 were (1) the obligation assumed by the government to secure school provision for all children of ages 5 to 14; (2) the recognition or creation of local agencies (private or church managers or elected boards) for the execution of this purpose; (3) provision for securing efficient instruction by means of an annual grant from the treasury to be distributed to the local managers upon the results of examination and inspection by government inspectors; (4) the creation of a central agency to carry out the provisions on the part

[1] The total enrollment in 1902 was 5,881,278, or 18.08 per cent of the population.

of the government and of new local agencies or school boards which every school district must elect except upon satisfactory evidence that schools efficient and adequate to the needs of the district were otherwise provided; (5) the admission of private and public elementary schools to a share in the government grant upon the same conditions; (6) the requirements that board schools should be strictly non-sectarian and the children of private schools protected from enforced sectarian instruction by a conscience clause."[1] The most important modifications of this law are the laws of 1899 and 1903. The law of 1899 has reference to the general administration of education in England and Wales, while that of 1903 entirely changes the local management of schools and extends the sphere of public education to secondary as well as elementary schools.

Administration. 1. *General.* — Under the provisions of the law of 1899 the general administration of educational affairs is committed to a board of education consisting of a president, appointed by the crown, lord president of the council, the principal secretaries of state, the first commissioner of the treasury, and the chancellor of the exchequer — not less than five nor more than fifteen members. By means of a sufficient number of royal inspectors who are trained educators, whose duty it is to visit the schools and report thereon, the board of education is able to reach every school in the kingdom. There is also a consultation committee, two-thirds of whom are "persons representing universities and bodies interested in education," whose office is to advise the board of education.

2. *Counties and County Boroughs.* — By the terms of the law of 1903 the council of every county and of

[1] Report of the United States Commissioner of Education for 1896–1897, Vol. I, p. 12.

every county borough are constituted a "local education authority," which controls secular instruction in all elementary schools within its district, and performs the duties of former school boards and school attendance committees. They may also establish high schools. In boroughs of over 10,000 and cities of over 20,000 inhabitants a special board or "local education authority" is allowed.

3. *Local Managers.* — All public undenominational (board) schools have a body of six managers, four of whom are appointed by the "local education authority" and two by the minor local authority. All public denominational (voluntary) schools shall also have six managers, four of whom are foundation managers and two are appointed by state authority. A greater number of local managers may be chosen, but the above proportion of members must hold.

School Attendance. — The school age is from five to fourteen, and the local authorities are required to compel attendance for that period excepting in case where the pupil has obtained the educational certificate of exemption, which cannot be given before the child is twelve years of age. The average attendance in 1902 reached nearly 83 per cent of the enrollment. England has stringent laws in regard to the employment of children in factories, mines, etc., which are well enforced.

The Schools. — We have already mentioned the *board* and the *voluntary* schools which supply the principal means of elementary education. The voluntary schools are under the fostering care of the Church, and their enrollment includes more than half of the children. Secondary education is carried on chiefly in private schools, though the law of 1903 permits the establishment of high schools to follow elementary education. The private secondary schools are of two general classes, "grammar" and "public" schools. The former are intended for the middle classes, their main purpose being to prepare for civil service, while the latter are the great endowed schools like Rugby, Eton, etc.

Support of Schools.—The expense of the elementary schools is met by parliamentary grants, by local taxes, and by endowments. Parliamentary grants cover about 62 per cent of the total, and the balance is made up from the other sources. Formerly both denominational and undenominational schools participated alike in the government grants, but the former were compelled to make up the balance needed by private subscriptions, school pence, etc., while the latter were allowed to levy a local tax for this purpose. Under the law of 1903 both may share alike in the local tax, thereby removing the necessity for private subscriptions.

The Teachers.—The training of teachers is as peculiar as the other features of the English system. Lancaster and Bell introduced the monitorial system, by which one teacher could take charge of a large school, the older pupils teaching the younger ones. This idea has been perpetuated in the "pupil teacher" scheme. Children fifteen years old are apprenticed to a school to assist in the work, and in return receive instruction and a small stipend. At eighteen or nineteen they enter the teachers' college for a two years' course. They may instead at this time take an examination for the teachers' certificate, and if successful, they are known as "assistant teachers." That the "pupil teacher" idea has lost its force is shown by the following facts: From 1876 to 1893 the increase of graduate teachers was 114 per cent, the increase of "assistant teachers" 691 per cent, while there was a decrease of 15 per cent in the number of "pupil teachers." This would seem to indicate that England is demanding better prepared teachers. The 131 teachers' colleges graduate about 1900 students each year, which is about two thirds of the number of teachers needed.

Teachers' positions are practically permanent, and the salaries are good, being in 1901 an average for certificate teachers of $644 a year for men and $432 for women.

Each teacher is entitled to a pension at the age of 65. This amounts to at least $330 for men who have been in the service from their twenty-first year, and $225 for women. If obliged to retire earlier on account of break-down, the amount of pension will be proportionate to the length of service. Men teachers contribute three pounds annually and women two pounds to this fund, while the State appropriates the balance needed.

When one considers the traditions that have controlled English education for centuries, and recalls the conservatism that rules English life, one can only marvel at the tremendous stridès taken by England during the last third of a century. Victor Hugo says: "The English patrician order is patrician in the absolute sense of the word. No feudal system was ever more illustrious, more terrible, and more tenacious of life." England has had to overcome her patrician ideas in regard to education, and her growth in the last thirty years has been more rapid and more effectual than for a thousand years before. Although she still has many problems to solve, her recent educational enterprise places her in the front rank among the nations of the world in school matters. The law of 1903 consisted of many compromises which satisfy neither party. It will doubtless be followed by still further changes in the near future.

CHAPTER XLV

THE SCHOOL SYSTEM OF THE UNITED STATES

Literature. — *Boone*, Education in the United States; *Williams*, History of Modern Education; *Barnard*, *American Journal of Education*; *Horace Mann*, Annual Reports; United States Commissioner's Reports, especially the more recent ones.

EACH state in the United States has its own independent system of education; there is no national system. In 1867 Congress established a National Bureau of Education, the function of which is "to collect statistics and facts showing the condition and progress of education in the several states and territories, and diffuse such information respecting the organization and management of schools and school systems and methods of teaching as shall aid the people of the United States in the establishment and maintenance of efficient school systems, and otherwise promote the cause of education throughout the country." The bureau issues an annual report, which is replete with information concerning the educational interests of our own and other lands.

The United States government has given vast tracts of the public domain, as well as large sums of money, to the various states, out of which have been created, in some cases, large school funds which yield a permanent income.[1]

[1] In 1836 there was a large surplus in the national treasury, which, by act of Congress, was ordered "to be deposited with the several states, in proportion to their representation in Congress." The amount so distributed equaled about $30,000,000. Most of the states receiving this deposit set it aside as a permanent school fund. See Boone, "History of Education in the United States," p. 91.

Up to 1876 the United States had granted nearly eighty million acres of land for educational purposes.

The Bureau of Education is obliged to rely on such statistics as its correspondents are willing to give, yet its work has been so valuable, its information so extensive and accurate, and its educational purpose so high, that cordial coöperation is generally given. This annual report is the finest issued by any nation in the world.[1]

THE STATE SYSTEMS

Administration. — At the head of each state school system, there is an executive officer usually called the State Superintendent of Public Instruction. He is chosen for from two to five years, sometimes by popular vote, sometimes by the joint houses of the Legislature, sometimes by the State Board of Education, and in some cases is appointed by the governor. His duties are to make reports, to examine teachers, to inspect schools, to distribute school moneys, to hear appeals in school matters, and to have general oversight of the educational interests of the state. In some states there is a State Board of Education that coöperates with the State Superintendent. The interests of education seem to be best conserved when there is a non-partisan State Board of Education, which appoints the executive officers and has general charge of the schools.

The second administrative unit is the county, over which is placed a Superintendent of Schools. He is chosen by popular vote or is appointed by the State Board of Education, and holds office generally about three years. He

[1] See an article by M. Stevens on "The National Bureau of Education," in the *New York School Journal*, Vol. LVI, p. 743, for a full description of this bureau and its work.

must visit the schools, examine teachers, hold institutes, distribute school moneys, and oversee the educational work. The number of schools under the inspection of the county superintendent is often so great, and the territory so large, that his work cannot be well done. In many cases the compensation is so small that he is obliged to devote a part of his time to some other occupation. The work is of sufficient importance to demand the full time of a competent man; and the salary ought to be proportionate to such needs.

The next division is that of the township, though in most states the school district is the next unit. The so-called "township system" has been adopted in several states, and recommended in others. This system has a board of education which appoints teachers, purchases supplies, and manages the schools of the whole township. The district system has outlived its usefulness. It maintains more schools than are warranted by the small number of pupils. Many of these could be abandoned in favor of better schools in neighboring districts, to which the children could be sent. It often secures for its trustee a man of limited education and narrow views, who conducts the school on the cheapest plan possible, while the larger territory of the township furnishes better material from which to choose; it limits its educational plan to the most elementary course, whereas the "township system" contemplates a central high school open to all children of the township. The "township system" also admits of the employment of a special school inspector or superintendent if desired. In some instances, two or more townships unite in the employment of such a superintendent.

School Attendance. — The school age commences at from four to six and extends to from eighteen to twenty-one, varying greatly in the different states. The United States Commissioner's Report now covers the period of from five to eighteen. On this basis he reports that 71.54 per cent of the children who are of school age are enrolled in the schools, while the average attendance is about 69 per cent of the enrollment. This is a very low percentage as compared with that in Germany, France, and England. The longer period covered by us (five to eighteen) thus acts unfavorably. The natural period of the child's life to be devoted to education is from six to fourteen.

School attendance in the United States is by no means so regular as it should be, even during the period (six to fourteen). To remedy this, compulsory education laws have been passed in most states. They cover periods varying from eight consecutive weeks and a total of twenty weeks during the year, to the full school year. These laws are generally a dead letter, partly because of their own weakness, and partly because of the indifference of the people. Compulsory attendance to be effective must cover the whole school year, and must carry a sufficient penalty for non-enforcement.

The Schools. — The schools of the United States may be classified as follows: 1, the *elementary school* having an eight years' course which should be completed at fourteen; 2, the *secondary school* with a four years' course that fits for college or its equivalent training; 3, the *undergraduate school* or college with its four years' course; and the *graduate school* or university. The elementary school is generally separated into primary and grammar grades, and is sometimes preceded by the kindergarten. The secondary school usually offers commercial or other practical courses to those who do not wish to prepare for college. Colleges differ greatly in the scope of their work and in their courses of instruction. Most universities open their doors to those who are not graduates of colleges. In all states the elementary and the high schools are free, while in some, particularly the western states, the entire expense of the child's education from kindergarten to university is defrayed at public expense.

Support of the Schools.—The annual cost of the schools of the country is about two hundred and fifty million dollars. About two thirds of this is raised by local tax, about one fifth by state tax, and the balance is derived chiefly from permanent funds, etc. The preponderance of the local tax shows that to each community is intrusted the important matter of deciding as to the quality of school it will maintain. The American people have always been liberal toward education, and no money is voted so freely by legislative bodies as that necessary for the education of the young.

The Teachers.—There are over 440,000 teachers in the United States, of whom about 28 per cent are men and 72 per cent women. Only about 10 per cent of these have had a professional training. The average term of service is five years, and about 100,000 new teachers are needed every year. To supply this number the normal schools and other institutions for training teachers are utterly inadequate, and will remain so until the average term of service is lengthened.

The principal institutions for training teachers are the normal school, the city training school, the pedagogical departments of universities, and teachers' training classes. To these may be added the teachers' institute and the summer school, which while they stimulate and instruct the teachers, cannot be said to give them a professional training.

The course of the normal school usually covers three years, and embraces both the theory of education and practice in teaching children. Within the last few years, many colleges have established chairs of pedagogy, but the work remains inadequate for a professional training so long as practice in teaching is not added to the requirements.

Teachers are appointed by local boards generally for one year, though they often remain undisturbed year after year. The average monthly salary of men in 1902 was $49.05, and of women $39.77.

So long as professional training of the teacher guarantees neither permanence of position nor adequate remuneration, many men and women with ability to teach will be tempted to devote their energies to other work, leaving the nation's most sacred trust, the education of its children, to those who will not or cannot properly prepare themselves for that great responsibility.

But there is in present tendencies no need for discouragement. Everywhere brave men and women are preparing themselves in earnest for the high calling of teacher, hopeful that the future will bring them the recognition they deserve.

With free schools, abler teachers, consecrated to their calling, and better courses of instruction; with a people generous in expenditures for educational purposes, a co-operation of parents and teachers, and a willingness to learn from other nations; with the many educational periodicals, the pedagogical books, and teachers' institutes to broaden and stimulate the teacher, — the friends of education in America may labor on, assured that the present century will give abundant fruitage to the work which has so marvelously prospered in the past.

BIBLIOGRAPHY

The following works have a bearing upon some phase of the many topics considered in this book. Most of them have been mentioned in abbreviated form either in the literature at the beginning of each chapter or in the footnotes. They are here given with their full titles.

A

ADAMS, FRANCIS. The Free School System of the United States.

ALLEN, W. F. A Short History of the Roman People.

ALLIES. The Monastic Life.

The Formation of Christendom.

ANDREWS, E. B. Brief Institutes of General History.

ARCHER, T. A., and KINGSFORD, C. L. Crusaders.

ARNOLD, EDWIN. The Light of Asia.

ARNOLD, MATTHEW. Essays in Criticism.

ARNSTÄDT, F. A. Rabelais und sein Traité d'Education.

Fénelon.

ASCHAM, ROGER. The Scholemaster (edited by E. Arber).

AZARIAS, BROTHER. Essays Educational.

Essays Philosophical.

Philosophy of Literature.

B

BALFOUR, GRAHAM. Educational Systems of Great Britain and Ireland.

BALLANTINE, H. Midnight Marches through Persia.

BALLOU, M. M. Due West; or, Round the World in Ten Months.

Footprints of Travel.

BARDEEN, C. W. The Orbis Pictus of John Comenius.

BARNARD, HENRY. English Pedagogy.

Pestalozzi and Pestalozzianism.

American Journal of Education.

BARNES, EARL. Studies in Education.

BARROWS, JOHN HENRY. World's Parliament of Religions.
BEECHER, H. W. Life of Jesus the Christ.
BEEGER UND LEUTBECHER. Comenius Ausgewählte Schriften.
BENJAMIN, S. G. W. The Story of Persia.
Persia and the Persians.
BESANT, WALTER. Rabelais.
BOONE, RICHARD G. Education in the United States: Its History from the Earliest Settlements.
BORMANN, K. Pädagogik für Volksschullehrer.
BOWEN, H. COURTHOPE. Froebel and Education by Self-Activity.
BROOKS, PHILLIPS. Letters of Travel.
BROWNING, OSCAR. Milton's Tractate on Education.
BRUGSCH-BEY, H. History of Egypt under the Pharaohs.
BRYCE, JAMES. The Holy Roman Empire.
A Short History of the Roman Empire.
BULFINCH, T. Legends of Charlemagne.
BULKLEY, REV. C. H. A. Plato's Best Thoughts.
BURY, J. B. A History of the Later Roman Empire from Arcadius to Irene.
BUTLER, N. M. The Place of Comenius in the History of Education.
BUTLER, W. Land of the Veda.

C

CAPES, W. W. Roman Empire of the Second Century: Age of Antonines.
CARLISLE, JAMES H. Two Great Teachers — Ascham and Arnold.
CARLYLE, THOMAS. French Revolution.
CHAMBERLAIN. Education in India.
CHÂTEAUBRIAND. The Genius of Christianity.
CHURCH, ALFRED J. Pictures from Roman Life and Story.
Pictures from Greek Life and Story.
CHURCH, R. W. The Beginnings of Middle Ages.
Bacon.
CLARK, HENRY. The State and Education.
CLARKE, JAMES FREEMAN. Ten Great Religions.
COLLINS, W. LUCAS. Montaigne.
COMBE, GEORGE. Education: Its Principles and Practice.
COMENIUS. The Orbis Pictus.
Grosse Unterrichtslehre (see Zoubek).

COMPAYRÉ, GABRIEL. The History of Pedagogy (trans. by W. H. Payne).
COURTNEY, W. L. John Locke.
COX, SIR G. W. The Crusades.
CRAIK, H. The State in Relation to Education.
CURTIS, G. W. Nile Notes of a Howadji.
CURTIUS, ERNST. History of Greece (5 vols.).

D

D'AUBIGNÉ, J. H. MERLE. History of the Reformation of the Sixteenth Century.
DAVIDSON, THOMAS. Rousseau and Education according to Nature.
The Education of the Greek People and its Influence on Civilization.
Aristotle and the Ancient Educational Ideals.
History of Education.
DE GARMO, CHARLES. Herbart and the Herbartians.
DE GUIMPS, R. Pestalozzi, his Life and Works (trans. by J. Russell).
DE QUINCEY, T. Plato's Republic.
DITTES, F. Geschichte der Erziehung und des Unterrichts.
DOOLITTLE, REV. J. Social Life of the Chinese.
DRAPER, JOHN W. Conflict between Religion and Science.
History of the Intellectual Development of Europe.
DURRELL, FLETCHER. A New Life in Education.
DURUY, VICTOR. History of France (trans. by Mrs. Carey).
A History of the Middle Ages.
History of Modern Times, from the Fall of Constantinople to the French Revolution.
DYER, T. H. History of Modern Europe (3 vols.).

E

EBERS, GEORG. Uarda.
An Egyptian Princess.
EDUCATIONAL REVIEW.
EDWARDS, AMELIA B. A Thousand Miles up the Nile.
EMERSON, RALPH WALDO. Representative Men.
EMERTON, E. An Introduction to the Study of the Middle Ages.
Mediaeval Europe.
ENCYCLOPAEDIA BRITANNICA.
ENCYKLOPÄDISCHES HANDBUCH DER PÄDAGOGIK.

F

FELKIN, HENRY M. and EMMIE. Herbart's Science of Education.

FELTON, C. C. Greece, Ancient and Modern.

FÉNELON, F. Treatise on the Education of Girls.

FERGUSSON, JAMES. History of Architecture in all Countries.

FERRIS, G. T. Great Leaders.

FISHER, G. P. History of the Reformation.
The Beginnings of Christianity.

FORSYTH, W. Life of Cicero.

FOWLER, THOMAS. Locke.
Bacon.

FRAZER, ROBERT W. British India.

FREEMAN, EDWARD A. Historical Essays.

FROEBEL, F. The Education of Man (trans. by W. N. Hailmann).

FROUDE, JAMES ANTHONY. Short Studies on Great Subjects.
Life and Letters of Erasmus.

G

GASQUET. Henry VIII and the English Monasteries.

GEIKIE, C. Life of Christ.

GIBBON, EDWARD. History of the Decline and Fall of the Roman Empire.

GILL, JOHN. Systems of Education.

GILMAN, A. Story of Rome from the Earliest Times to the End of the Republic.

GRAHAM, H. G. Rousseau.

GREEN, J. R. History of the English People (4 vols.).

GROTE, GEORGE. History of Greece (12 vols.).

GUHL and KONER. The Life of Greeks and Romans. From Antique Monuments.

GUIZOT. History of Civilization (4 vols.).

H

HAILMANN, W. N. History of Pedagogy.

HALLAM, HENRY. View of the State of Europe during the Middle Ages (3 vols.).
Literary History of Europe.

HANNA, WILLIAM. Life of Christ.

HANUS, PAUL H. The Permanent Influence of Comenius (Ed. Review, N.Y., Vol. III, 226).
HARPER'S Book of Facts (compiled by J. H. Willsey).
HARRISON, J. H. Story of Greece.
HEGEL, G. W. F. The Philosophy of History.
HERBART, J. F. The Science of Education. (See Felkin.)
HERFORD, WILLIAM H. The Student's Froebel.
HINSDALE, B. A. Horace Mann.
HORTON, R. F. A History of the Romans.
HOSMER, J. K. Story of the Jews.
HOUGHTON, R. C. Women of the Orient.
HUGHES, THOMAS. Loyola and the Educational System of the Jesuits.
HURST, JOHN F. A Short History of the Reformation.
Life and Literature in the Fatherland.

I

IRVING, WASHINGTON. Mahomet and His Successors.

J

JAMESON, MRS. ANNA. Legends of the Monastic Orders.
JOHONNOT, JAMES. Geographical Reader.
JOSEPHUS, F. The Works of.
JOWETT, B. The Republic of Plato.

K

KEMP. History of Education.
KIDDLE and SCHEM. Cyclopaedia of Education.
KINGSFORD, C. L. (See Archer.)
KITCHIN, G. W. History of France.
KLEMM, L. R. European Schools.
KNOX, THOMAS W. The Boy Travelers in the Far East.
In Egypt and the Holy Land.
KÖNIGBAUER, J. Geschichte der Pädagogik und Methodik.
KRIEGE, MATILDA H. Friedrich Froebel.
KÜRSI, H. Life, Work, and Influence of Pestalozzi.

L

LABBERTON, R. H. New Historical Atlas and General History.
LANE, EDWARD W. Account of the Manners and Customs of Modern Egyptians.

LANE-POOLE, S. The Story of the Moors in Spain.
LANG, OSSIAN H. Rousseau: His Life, Work, and Educational Ideas.
Basedow: His Life and Educational Work.
Horace Mann.
LANGE, WICHARD. Gesammelte Pädagogische Schriften von F. Froebel.
LANGHORNE, J. and W. Life of Plutarch.
LARNED, J. N. History for Ready Reference (5 vols.).
LAURIE, S. S. Rise and Early Constitution of Universities.
Comenius: His Life and Educational Works.
LAVISSE, ERNST. General View of the Political History of Europe (trans. by Charles Gross).
LECKY, W. E. H. History of European Morals (2 vols.).
LE CLERC. Life of Erasmus.
LEITCH, J. MUIR. Practical Educationists and their Systems of Teaching.
LEROY-BEAULIEU. The Awakening of the East.
LESSING, G. E. Nathan der Weise.
LEWIS, CHARLES T. History of Germany.
LIDDELL, H. G. Student's History of Rome.
LORD, JOHN. Beacon Lights of History.

M

MACAULAY, T. B. Essays.
History of England.
MAHAFFY, J. P. Social Life in Greece.
Old Greek Education.
The Greek World under Roman Sway.
MAITLAND. The Dark Ages.
MANN, MARY, and GEORGE COMBE MANN. The Life and Works of Horace Mann.
Educational Writings of Horace Mann.
MARDEN, ORISON SWETT. Pushing to the Front.
MARENHOLTZ-BÜLOW, BERTHA VON. Reminiscences of Friedrich Froebel (trans. by Mary Mann).
MARSHMAN, J. C. History of India.
MARTIN, G. H. Evolution of the Massachusetts Public School System.
MARTIN, W. A. P. The Chinese: Their Education, Philosophy, and Letters.

MASPERO, G. Egyptian Archaeology (trans. by Amelia B. Edwards.)
MERIVALE, C. History of the Romans (7 vols.).
MICHAUD, J. F. History of the Crusades (trans. by W. Robson).
MILTON, J. Tractate on Education. (See Oscar Browning.)
MOMBERT, J. I. Great Lives.
History of Charles the Great (Charlemagne).
MOMMSEN, TH. History of Rome.
MONROE, PAUL. Source Book of the History of Education.
MONTAGU, BASIL. Life of Francis Bacon.
MORLEY, JOHN. Life of Rousseau.
MORRIS, CHARLES. Historical Tales (Greek-Roman).
MORRIS, WILLIAM O'CONNOR. The French Revolution and First Empire.
MORRISON, W. DOUGLAS. The Jews under Roman Rule.
MUNROE, JAMES P. The Educational Ideal.
MYERS, P. V. N. Mediaeval and Modern History.
Ancient History.

N

NIEDERGESÄSS. Geschichte der Pädagogik.
North American Review, Vol. 171.

O

OLIPHANT, MRS. Montaigne. (See W. Lucas Collins.) Dante.

P

PAINTER, F. V. N. A History of Education.
PARKMAN, FRANCIS. The Jesuits in North America in the Seventeenth Century.
PARSONS, J. RUSSELL. Prussian Schools through American Eyes.
French Schools through American Eyes.
PASTOR, LUDWIG. History of the Popes.
PATTISON, MARK. Milton.
PAULSEN, FRIEDRICH. The German Universities: Their Character and Historical Development (trans. by E. D. Perry).
Geschichte des Gelehrten Unterrichts, auf den deutschen Schulen und Universitäten.
PETERS. Justice to the Jew.
PLOETZ. Epitome of Ancient, Mediaeval, and Modern History.
PRINCE, JOHN T. Methods of Instruction, and Organization of Schools in Germany.

Q

QUICK, ROBERT H. Educational Reformers.

QUINTILIAN. Institutes of Oratory; or, Education of an Orator. (See Watson.)

R

RAGOZIN, Z. A. The Story of Chaldea: from Earliest Time to Rise of Assyria.

The Story of Media, Babylon, and Persia.

RAGOZIN, MRS. J. A. The Story of Vedic India.

RAUMER, KARL VON. Geschichte der Pädagogik.

Life and System of Pestalozzi (trans. by Tilleard).

RAWLINSON, G. Five Great Monarchies.

Ancient Egypt.

Seventh Great Oriental Monarchy.

REEVE, HENRY. Petrarch.

REIMER, KARL. Michel de Montaigne.

Emil, oder Ueber die Erziehung.

REIN, W. Am Ende der Schulreform?

Encyklopädisches Handbuch der Pädagogik.

REPORTS of the United States Commissioner of Education.

RICHARD, ERNST. The School System of France.

RICHTER, KARL. Pestalozzi.

A. H. Francke.

RIDPATH, J. C. Library of Universal History.

ROUSSEAU. Émile.

ROUTLEDGE. The Modern Seven Wonders of the World.

RUSSELL, JAMES E. German Higher Schools.

S

SANKEY, C. The Spartan and Theban Supremacies.

SCHILLER, FRIEDRICH. History of the Thirty Years' War (trans. by Morrison).

SCHMID, K. A. Encyklopädie des gesammten Erziehungs und Unterrichtswesens (11 vols.).

SCHMIDT, KARL. Geschichte der Pädagogik (4 vols.) (edited by Wichard Lange).

SCHNEIDER, E., und E. VON BREMEN. Das Volksschulwesen im preussischen Staate (3 vols.).

SCHROEDER, CHR. Das Volksschulwesen in Frankreich.
SCHWEGLER, A. A History of Philosophy (trans. by Julius H. Seelye).
SEEBOHM, F. Era of the Protestant Revolution.
SEELEY, L. Common School System of Germany.
SEIDEL, F. Froebel's Pädagogische Schriften (3 vols.).
SHARPLESS, ISAAC. English Education in Elementary and Secondary Schools.
SHEPPARD, J. Y. The Fall of Rome and the Rise of New Nationalities.
SHOUP, WILLIAM J. The History and Science of Education.
SHUMWAY, E. S. A Day in Ancient Rome.
SINE, JAMES. History of Germany.
SKINNER, H. M. The Schoolmaster in Literature.
The Schoolmaster in Comedy and Satire.
SMITH, WILLIAM. History of Greece.
History of Rome.
SONNENSCHEIN & CO. Cyclopaedia of Education.
SPOFFORD, A. R. Library of Historical Characters (10 vols.).
STEEG, M. JULES. Émile; or, Concerning Education (trans. by Eleanor Worthington).
STILLÉ, C. J. Studies in Mediaeval History.
STODDARD, JOHN L. Lectures on Travel.
STRACK, K. Geschichte des deutschen Volksschulwesens.
SYMONDS, JOHN ADDINGTON. The Renaissance in Italy.

T

TAUNTON. The English Black Monks of St. Benedict.
TAYLOR, BAYARD. History of Germany.
THALHEIMER, M. E. Mediaeval and Modern History.
TIMAYENIS, T. T. History of Greece (2 vols.).

U

UFER, C. Introduction to the Pedagogy of Herbart.
UNITED STATES COMMISSIONER OF EDUCATION REPORTS.

V

VAN LIEW, C. C. Life of Herbart and Development of his Pedagogical Doctrines.
VOGEL, AUGUST. Geschichte der Pädagogik als Wissenschaft.

W

Walker, John Brisben. The Building of an Empire. ("Cosmopolitan," Feb.–Sept., 1899.)

Warner, Charles Dudley. Library of the World's Best Literature.

Watson, J. S. Quintilian's Institutes of Oratory; or, Education of an Orator.

Weigert, Max. Die Volksschule in Frankreich.

Weir, Samuel. Key to Rousseau's Émile.

Wells, C. L. The Age of Charlemagne.

West, Andrew F. Alcuin and the Rise of the Christian Schools.

White, Rev. James. The Eighteen Christian Centuries.

Wilkins, A. S. National Education in Greece in the Fourth Century B.C.

Wilkinson, Sir J. G. Manners and Customs of the Ancient Egyptians (3 vols.).

Williams, Samuel G. The History of Modern Education.

Willmann, Otto. Herbart's Pädagogische Schriften (2 vols.).

Winship, Albert E. Horace Mann, Educator.

Y

Yonge, C. D. Three Centuries of Modern History.

Z

Zoubek, Fr. E. A. Comenius. Grosse Unterrichtslehre.

INDEX

For Teachers and School Officers

KING'S SCHOOL INTERESTS AND DUTIES

Developed from "Page's Mutual Duties of Parents and Teachers," from various Public Records and Documents, and from the Bulletins of the National Bureau of Education. By ROBERT M. KING.

Cloth, 12mo, 336 pages $1.00

This new work, original in its scope and plan, presents in one volume interesting and valuable expositions of the modern demands, best methods, and most important interests of our Public School Systems. Its central idea is to show the importance and value of co-operation in school work and the mutual duties of teachers, school officers, and parents. It also embodies synopses of the discussions on leading educational topics from the various fugitive reports and manuals issued, from time to time, by school officials and State Departments of Education. It will be found an invaluable manual and guide for school superintendents, officers, and patrons, and, indeed, for every one interested in educational work.

MANN'S SCHOOL RECREATIONS AND AMUSEMENTS

By CHARLES W. MANN, A.M., Dean of the Chicago Academy.

Cloth, 12mo, 352 pages $1.00

This volume not only opens up a new field of much needed information and direction in the matter of physical training of pupils, but also furnishes suggestions for intellectual recreations which will greatly add to the interest and value of school work and lend a charm to school life in all its phases. Some of the subjects treated in this work are: Morning Exercises, Care and Equipment of Schoolrooms, Singing Games and Songs, Indoor Exercises and Outdoor Games, Experiments in Physics and Chemistry, Recreations in Latin, Outline for Reading Circles, etc.

Copies of the above books will be sent, prepaid, to any address on receipt of the price by the Publishers:

American Book Company

New York • Cincinnati • Chicago

(204)